Betty Crocker's *Indian*

HOME COOKING

Betty Crocker's *Indian*

HOME COOKING

Recipes and Written by
RAGHAVAN IYER

HUNGRY MINDS, INC.
New York, NY ❖ Cleveland, OH ❖ Indianapolis, IN ❖ Foster City, CA

Published by
HUNGRY MINDS, INC.
909 Third Avenue
New York, NY 10022
www.hungryminds.com

For general information on Hungry Minds'
products and services please contact our
Customer Care Department within the U.S.
at 800-762-2974, outside the U.S. at
317-572-3993 or fax 317-572-4002.

For sales inquiries and reseller information,
including discounts, premium and bulk quantity
sales, and foreign-language translations, please
contact our Customer Care Department at
800-434-3422, fax 317-572-4002, or write to
Hungry Minds, Inc., Attn: Customer Care
Department, 10475 Crosspoint Boulevard,
Indianapolis, IN 46256.

Contact the Library of Congress for complete
Cataloging-in-Publication Data

ISBN: 0-7645-6315-7

GENERAL MILLS, INC.
Betty Crocker Kitchens
MANAGER, PUBLISHING: **Lois Tlusty**
EDITOR: **Lori Fox**
AUTHOR: **Raghavan Iyer**
FOOD STYLISTS: **Cindy Lund, Mary Johnson,
Carol Grones**

Photographic Services
PHOTOGRAPHER: **Valerie J. Bourassa**
COVER AUTHOR PHOTOS: **Sandy May
(left, right), Tom Rose (center)**

We would like to thank Richard Bresnahan
for generously loaning us his pottery:
pages 26, 51, 57, 77, 109, 114, 129, 133, 141,
145, 147, 161, 165, 175, 199, 201, 215, 217,
227, 237, 253, 281, 307, 317

Photography by Dan Lipow appears on:
pages 6–7, 8–9, 13, 18, 207, 220, 247

Page 2 photograph © PhotoDisc

JACKET AND BOOK DESIGN: **Edwin Kuo**
PHOTOGRAPHY ART DIRECTOR: **Pam Kurtz**
MAP DESIGN: **Edwin Kuo, original map
supplied by Frommer's®**
ARTWORK PRODUCTION: **Brian Hahn,
Kristi Hart, Holly Wittenberg**

Manufactured in the United States of America

10 9 8 7 6 5 4 3 2 1

Cover photo: Marinated Shrimp Poached in
Mint Sauce (page 88), Whole Wheat
Unleavened Breads (page 236)

About the Potter

RICHARD BRESNAHAN, potter, environmentalist and artist-in-residence at Saint John's University, Collegeville, Minnesota, has had a profound influence on ceramics in America. Bresnahan founded the Saint John's Pottery in 1979 on three premises: to be a generational program, to use only local resources in creating the ceramics and to be environmentally sustainable. The Saint John's Pottery is home of the largest wood-fired kiln in North America. Bresnahan has been the subject of two documentaries and the Emmy Award–winning PBS film *Clay, Wood, Fire, Spirit: The Pottery of Richard Bresnahan*. In 1996 he received the Earth Day Award from the Upper Midwest Network of Businesses for Social Responsibility.

Bresnahan is noted for artistic collaborations that cross creative and cultural boundaries. He believes the collaboration on this book can help change the way people look at ethnic cuisine. Says Bresnahan:

> *Cooks often believe that ethnic cuisine must be done exactly the way it would be done in the country of origin, or it's not authentic. I say stop worrying. In this cookbook, Raghavan gives us Indian recipes that can be made with ingredients found in many supermarkets and specialty grocery stores. Much of the food is shown on pottery made in Minnesota by an artist who studied in Japan. Is it authentic Indian cuisine? Yes. It is also something entirely new, made possible by creative collaboration and our cultural diversity.*

Contact the Saint John's Pottery by phone at 320-363-2930 or e-mail at pottery@csbsju.edu

For more great ideas visit **www.bettycrocker.com**

Dear friends,

Namaste! Vannakkam! Welcome! It's not an easy task for me to welcome you into my home in all of the fourteen languages that are widely spoken in India, a country that defies description merely in words. So I invite you, dear reader, to remove your shoes or slippers and enter my kitchen to savor the aromas, textures, colors and, above all, the flavors that are pure India.

I have lived in India, my birthplace, for over twenty years in addition to having spent almost half my life in the United States. When I arrived in this country, I came with only my memories of the various flavors of India and had to learn to recreate them with what was available at that time. Therein lies the beauty of Indian cooking. Once you become familiar with the basic elements of this cuisine—the herbs, spices and legumes—simply using them in the creative ways that I will show you will immerse you in the foods and tastes of the Indian kitchen.

These recipes that I share with you embrace true and tested flavors from all the regions of my vast homeland. True to Betty Crocker, the mystical cuisine of this exotic country, with its myriad spices, legumes, fruits and vegetables is unraveled in well-tested, easy-to-follow recipes. Enjoy my cooking advice peppered with cultural insights—you will find it accompanying most of the recipes under the heading "*Raghavan Ki Baaten,*" which means "Raghavan's Small Talk." So gather your family and friends and come to my home that is India in all its glory! Please e-mail me at raghavan@mm.com if you wish to share your cooking experiences with me.

Shukriya and thank you for your visit to my home kitchen—it belongs to you now!

Table of Contents

Flavors of India

Bridge over the lake, Udaipur.

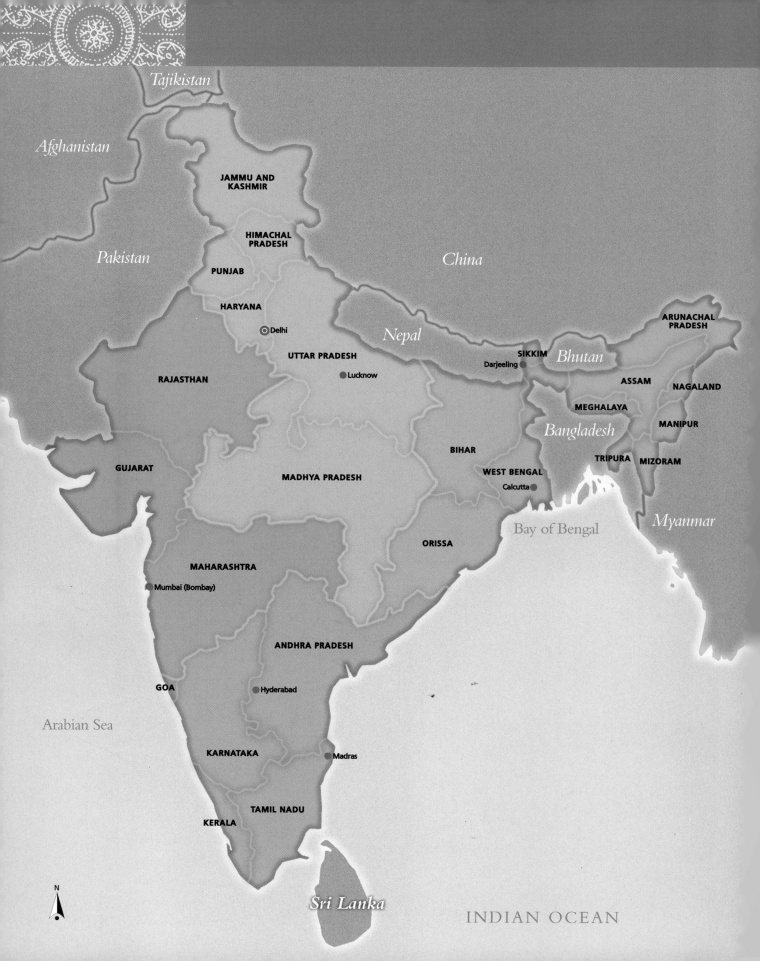

Flavors of India

I ndia exemplifies diversity, from religion to people to landscape and, above all, to food. In the world's largest democracy, its inhabitants' fourteen official languages have given birth to almost one thousand dialects—a mind-boggling number. Yet even that number pales in comparison to the varieties of herbs, spices, legumes and even mangoes used in this country's cuisine.

With its long history of vulnerability to foreign invasion, India has experienced numerous cultural, political and social influences over the centuries. From the armies of Alexander the Great to the British who governed prior to independence in 1947, this land has assimilated Spanish traders, Middle Eastern merchants and monarchs, Portuguese Jesuits, Tibetan refugees and Persian settlers among others. The cultural, dietary, religious and culinary heritages of many groups, combined with India's resources, have evolved into an exciting epicurean experience—what is now considered Indian regional cooking.

India, home to twenty-five states, plus seven union territories, houses the world's second largest population within boundaries that measure roughly one-third the area of North America. This tropical country, blessed with three large bodies of water—the Arabian Sea, Indian Ocean and Bay of Bengal, which respectively hug its western, southern and eastern coasts—nurtures coastal residents with a bountiful supply of fresh fish and other seafood. The gargantuan Himalaya Mountains adorn the northern landscape, providing cool comfort and the much-prized basmati rice. From teeming urban centers to solitary desert, from tropical jungles lush with vegetation to windswept mountain plateaus, from rich aquatic life off the coast to fertile soil in the fields, India's landscape presents a kaleidoscope of possibilities.

Four Regions of Flavor

Indian cooking can be divided into four distinct regional styles: North, South, West and East. Each region has its own intricacies, and within each region, individual cooks may also add their own personal touches to traditional recipes. No one recipe, then, may be exactly the same from kitchen to kitchen, even within a given region.

One thing all Indian dishes do have in common, however, is the masterful blending of spices and seasonings. Indian cuisine ranges from simple to complex, its cooks weaving subtleties into every dish they create. The cook often toys with your taste buds, providing you hot, bitter, sweet, tart, astringent and nutty flavors in one single bite

Foods of the North

Cinnamon, cloves, cardamom, fenugreek leaves, mango powder and bay leaves are some of the herbs and spices used in the northern region to concoct delicately flavored, refined preparations. These spices are considered to have "warm" tones and are ideal for the cooler climate. Poultry and meat are more commonly included in the northern diet than elsewhere in India. Goat is a commonly eaten meat throughout India, but in the cooler northern regions its close kin, the sheep or lamb, is the more traditional choice. (The term *mutton* refers to the meat of both goat and lamb in India. This can cause some confusion to visitors because only mature lamb is known as mutton in many other countries.) For non-meat eaters, legumes such as kidney beans, garbanzo beans and whole black lentils provide essential nutrients.

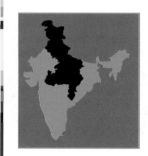

The Moghul emperors made significant architectural and cultural contributions in the North and introduced ingredients such as nuts, raisins and dates. One of the most famous monarchs, Emperor Shah Jahan, built the Taj Mahal for his beloved wife, Mumtaz, as a symbol of love, passion and romance. The regal (*moghalai*) foods the Moghuls introduced still linger in the flavors of creamy spinach sauce that drenches tender morsels of lamb, in aromatic basmati rice perfumed with saffron, whole spices and raisins, in potatoes cooked in an almond–poppy seed sauce and in the smoky kabobs cooked over open flames.

Northern flavors are familiar to many Americans because they are glorified in the abundant Indian restaurants in the United States that feature tandoori cooking. A clay-lined, bell-shaped oven, the tandoor gives food a unique earthy aroma as well as a distinctive bright reddish orange color that distinguishes it from any other foods. From this oven comes delicacies such as tender and crispy breads (*naan*), moist chicken (*tandoori murghi*) and even spicy grilled eggplant pâté (*baingan bhurta*).

Foods of the South

The architectural edifices, history, cultural regalia and foods of the South are vastly different from those of the North. The South is studded with carved-stone temples that pay tribute to Brahma (the Creator), Vishnu (the Preserver) and Shiva (the Destroyer), the deities of Hinduism, a major religion of the South, as it is throughout India. Pristine beaches, lush greenery and a multitude of rice fields grace its landscape. Southerners are descendants of native Indians called Dravidians, whose roots may be traceable to Africa. Southerners even look different than northerners. The women drape their sarees in a different manner while the men often wear *dhotis/véshtis*, a white cloth tied around their waist that drops to their ankles, very much like a long skirt.

The foods of the South are generally simple with a strong emphasis on vegetarianism. Strict priestly (Brahmin) teachings dictate for many what can and cannot be consumed. Legumes play a prominent role in the everyday diet and rice is present in almost every dish in many forms. Bold herbs and spices rule the thin stews, hot vegetables, fluffy dumplings and buttery-soft rice noodles. South Indians have a knack for extracting multiple flavors from the same ingredient. A single spice, such as mustard seed, adds different flavors to a dish whether it is used whole, dry roasted and ground or fried in hot oil. Coconut, a rich treasure from the coastal regions, is another

Rice fields, Uttar Pradesh.

example of the disparate tastes that can be contained within a single hard shell, from its firm white flesh to the milky liquid that is made by pureeing the flesh with water.

The spice blends of the South are very complex, often incorporating legumes as seasonings, a practice unheard of in the other regions of India. Chilies, roasted mustard seed and fresh karhi leaves are other native flavors of the South. When combined with sweet split and hulled pigeon peas, they unveil a fresh, crisp flavor that is unparalleled elsewhere in the world. Fish and seafood are bountiful staples in many nonvegetarian South Indian households. They share the banana leaf (a nature-friendly, disposable plate) along with *dosas* (lacy rice-lentil crepes stuffed with potatoes and red onions) and rice. Long-grain rice is widely cultivated in the South and is a prominent player in everything from appetizers to desserts.

Foods of the West

The jewel of the West coast is Mumbai (Bombay), considered the business capital of modern India. The foods here are a harmonious

blend of northern and southern flavors. Locally grown peanuts, tapioca pearls, Bishop's weed and cashews add to the mix, creating enhanced layers of tastes and textures.

The western states have experienced India's largest migratory influences, and the food of the area reflects the combined dietary laws, food habits and ingredients of Persian, Portuguese, Buddhist and Jewish settlers, among others. Some groups have very strict dietary rules. Jains, for example, from the northwestern state of

Gujarat follow the principle of equality for all forms of life and are vegetarians. They don't consume underground roots or vegetables such as onions and garlic, which are considered "passion-inducing" and a deterrent to attaining *moksha*—enlightenment and spiritual release from the endless cycle of reincarnation. Young leaves, tubers and grains are also off-limits, although mature ones can be eaten.

Dairy products such as milk, buttermilk and yogurt are staples in these parts, providing economic support to the cooperative dairy farmers. Sweet and hot flavors take center stage in the West. Farther south toward Goa, where many Portuguese settled, the European influence is apparent in the use of vinegar, as well as local treasures such as cashews and coconut milk. The Parsees, many of whom live in Mumbai (Bombay), consume fish, eggs and chicken. The Bohri Muslims, who converted from Hinduism, mainly hold onto their southern vegetarian heritage, but their diet may also include mutton, wild game and beef. Pork is taboo in communities of Islamic faith, but may be eaten in other religious households that are allowed to eat meat.

Foods of the East

During India's British regime, the East coast state of West Bengal, home of the most populous city in India, Calcutta, was staked out

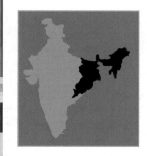

as India's political capital. This central location was accessible to the resort communities of Assam and Darjeeling for cool escapes from the oppressive summer heat. In the famous rolling tea plantations of the area, the soil, drenched by the seasonal rains, combined with the cool climate, provides the ideal home for cultivating the finest teas.

The river Ganges flows into the Bay of Bengal, where their waters offer hundreds of varieties of fish and shellfish. Along the coast, banana flowers flourish along with exotic vegetables and fruits such as drumstick and jackfruit. Eastern flavors are among the most complex, often relying on fenugreek seed, mustard oil, dried red chilies, poppy seed and fennel seed to create a bittersweet balance. In this fertile area, where both population and vegetation continue to grow at an increasing pace, rice is an everyday commodity. With its hot and humid climate, this region alone is known to have cultivated over fifty varieties of rice.

The East was home to both the literary giant Rabindranath Tagore and humble, saintlike Mother Teresa, who lived there most of her life. But it is also where India's best confectionery and sweetmeat merchants reside. *Rasmali* (homemade cheese soaked in rose-scented syrup and doused in saffron cream sauce) is ample proof of their talents.

Vegetarianism in Indian Culture

There are many reasons why an Indian follows a partial or complete vegetarian diet—religious beliefs and economic necessity are two of the main ones. Hinduism, a prominent religion throughout India, promotes abstinence from meats, fish and poultry. Instead, the emphasis is placed on fresh fruits, vegetables, legumes and dairy products. Beef is taboo and the cow remains sacred. Milk, yogurt and butter (*ghee*), considered gifts, are consumed heavily.

Among the households that do eat fish, meats and poultry, usually these are consumed in small quantities on special occasions, at family gatherings and for important affairs. Meat can cost up to five times more than vegetables, so budget constraints are a strong driving force behind the adoption of a vegetarian diet on a daily basis.

Fresh herbs and spices that form the backbone of Indian cuisine provide ample flavor to enhance India's basic diet of legumes, rice,

COCONUT GRATER
(THÉNGA THURUVAL)

STEAMER FOR
CAKES AND DUMPLINGS
(IDLI PANNAI)

NOODLE PRESS
(SEV CHAKRI)

MORTAR AND
PESTLE
(KALORAL)

GRIDDLE BREAD
ROLLING STAND AND
ROLLING PIN
(POLPAT AUR BÉLAN)

(KADHAI/VANALI)

HOPPER PAN
(APPAM KARAI)

COOKING SPOONS
(CHAMCHA/KARANDI)

COFFEE FILTER
(DIGAKSHIP FILTER)

(CHIMTA)

LADLE
(DOW)

SKILLET
(TAVA)

METAL SPATULAS
(SHATTUVAM)

POT GRABBERS
(PAKKAD)

vegetables and fruits. Flavors from herbs and spices provide the same kind of satisfaction as eating meat, but without the added fat.

Indian Kitchen Equipment

The equipment used in an Indian kitchen is quite specialized and varies regionally. However, the equipment in any American kitchen is perfectly suited to Indian cooking—you do not need to purchase any of these items to make any of the recipes in this book.

Coconut grater (*thénga thuruval*): This grater is a must in kitchens along the three coasts of India and makes the task of grating fresh coconut an easy one. It consists of a wooden stool, for squatting, with a serrated round blade at one end of the stool.

Coffee filter (*digakshin filter*): This tiny coffee filter is made from either brass or stainless steel. A large amount of ground coffee is placed in the upper container, and hot water is drizzled over it. Drops of concentrated coffee, known as *digakshin*, drip into the bottom container. A cup of steamed milk is mixed with a few drops of *digakshin* to yield southern India's favorite beverage.

Cooking spoons (*chamcha/karandi*): Often made from stainless steel, spoons come in various shapes and sizes.

Floor cleaver/knife (*armamanai*): Similar in appearance to the coconut grater, the blade is sometimes curved outward, with the round blunt surface to the floor. The sharp edge is the curve's inside. The user holds the vegetable or herb with both hands and presses it against the blade swiftly and carefully. (Not pictured.)

Griddle bread rolling stand and rolling pin (*polpat aur bélan*): Similar to a pastry board, this stand for rolling griddle breads is made from either wood, stainless steel or marble. The rolling pin is slim with stationary handles that provide leverage for rolling dough thinly.

Hopper pan (*appam karai*): A utensil of prominence in southern Indian kitchens, this cast-iron

pan looks like a mini-muffin pan on legs. 14The indentations are greased with clarified butter (*ghee*), then cardamom-scented, banana-flavored batter is poured in and fried over an open flame.

Kerosene or coal stove (*sighadi*): Common in the average Indian home and in village kitchens, this small, portable unit, the size of a large stockpot, is central to Indian cuisine. An increase in middle-income households, especially in larger cities, has made it possible to find the more modern gas-fired range-top unit with an oven below. (Not pictured.)

Ladle (*dow*): Ladles, made from wood, plastic or stainless steel, come in different shapes and sizes. A hollowed coconut shell half also makes for a serviceable ladle, providing yet another use for this sturdy fruit.

Metal spatulas (*shattuvam*): Stainless-steel spatulas are helpful for flipping griddle breads and rice-lentil crepes off a griddle (*tava*).

Mortar and pestle (*kaloral*): Stone or stainless-steel mortars and pestles are a must in Indian kitchens to pound optimum flavors from spices and herbs.

Noodle maker (*sevai nari*): Fresh rice noodles are a laboriously made delicacy in southern India. Steamed rice cake rounds are pushed through this hand-cranked noodle maker to yield buttery, thin strands. If the rice cake cools, chances of the noodle maker breaking are quite high. (Not pictured.)

Noodle press (*sev chakri*): This brass container, with a long handle and screw-top on one end, has small plates with differently shaped holes at the other end. A ball of stiff dough made with spiced garbanzo bean flour is pushed through the holes then fried in hot oil. The crispy noodles are often served as a snack with beverages.

Skillet (*tava*): Made of either cast iron or stainless steel, this round skillet with slightly sloping sides has a wooden handle that stays cool. It is used for cooking griddle breads.

Spice box (*masaala bucksa*): A round stainless-steel tin with a lid houses seven small containers filled with spices most commonly used in the household. The contents may vary from region to region and even from house to house.

Steamer for cakes and dumplings (*idli pannai*): A mold with many round indentations for batter and tiny holes for steam to pass through is placed above water in a deep wok. Fermented rice-lentil batter is poured into the mold, then covered and steamed.

Tongs (*pakkad aur chimta*): Thicker-edged tongs (*pakkad*) come in handy for woks and cooking pans in India that have metal handles that become too hot to touch. Tongs with flatter edges (*chimta*) are ideal for lifting griddle breads and lentil wafers off an open flame.

Wok (*kadhai/vanali*): The Indian wok is similar in shape to the Chinese wok and is made of cast iron or stainless steel or stainless steel with a copper bottom. Woks come in various sizes and are used for cooking curries, stir-frying and deep-frying.

Mealtime—The Essence of Family Life

Nothing is more important in Indian culture than the family unit. Life revolves around it, and food is woven throughout the entire fabric of family life.

Women prepare most of the meals in India, taking great pride in having mastered a vast repertoire of recipes. Scratch cooking predominates, and only a minimum of products are available that could be considered convenience items. The many convenience foods available in the United States—such as tamarind concentrate, coconut milk, rose essence, many forms of dried coconut and various types of fresh noodles—offers a sharp contrast to India, where most make their own from scratch.

The rangetop/oven combination that is standard in nearly every home in the United States is not often found in Indian homes,

except in larger cities. Instead, propane gas burners, kerosene stoves and portable coal-burning stoves, called *sighadis*, fuel the fires that cook the food. Almost all cooking is done on top of the stove and almost nothing is baked in an oven except in some parts of the North where tandoors (clay-lined ovens) are used.

Eating in the Indian Home

Serving several courses during a meal is not common in traditional Indian homes. Typically, everything is served at the same time, including dessert, on a large, rimmed stainless-steel platter, called a *thali,* or in the center of the table and everyone helps him- or herself. Family and communal meals in southern India are often served on large banana leaves. Most people eat at a low table or sit cross-legged on a thin bamboo mat (*chattai*) placed on the floor.

A rich main dish of legumes or meat is placed on the *thali* along with the vegetable dishes, surrounding the staple rice or bread that is placed in the center. Rice is generally served with soupier dishes and breads with thicker dishes. Soup and dessert, if part of the meal, are served in small bowls that are placed next to the main dishes. Relishes and pickles are placed in one corner and if an appetizer is included, it is placed next to the relishes. Although all the food is placed on the table at the beginning of the meal, it is nonetheless eaten in "courses." The appetizer with relish is eaten first, next the main dish with the rice or bread along with the vegetable and the dessert at the end.

Most Indians eat with their fingers, believing that food doesn't taste as good when eaten with a spoon or fork. Pancakes and breads are used as eating utensils to scoop up or wrap around delicious morsels of food; saucy dishes soak into mounds of basmati rice, making it easier to eat. Only the right hand is used for eating. The left hand, considered "unclean," is reserved for handling a glass or spooning foods onto the plate. Although offering a taste of food to your adult dinner companion may be

quite common in the United States, doing so in India is considered an act of extreme intimacy.

Breakfast—Is There Time?

Skipping breakfast, an American habit, has become the practice of harried workers in India as well. When there is time for breakfast, toast and jam are the steadfast favorites. Often, fresh fruit such as a banana or a guava becomes easy prey when time is of the essence. Occasionally, piping-hot griddle breads, made fresh in the morning for the lunch box, double as delicious breakfast fare. Weekend mornings offer more time for elaborate rice-lentil crepes or spiced hot wheat cereal with cashews. When mangoes are at their peak during the monsoon season, often a bowl of freshly pureed fruit and puffy whole wheat breads offer nourishment for the body and soul before a hard day's work. South Indians require strong coffee, usually made with lots of steamed milk, to start the day.

Lunch—The Midday Break

For the busy worker leaving early in the morning, preparing a lunch to take to work is such an unappealing chore that a restaurant lunch may be a justifiable solution. Workers who do bring brown bag lunches include nonperishable items such as griddle breads, vegetable curries or stir-fries and pickles. Southern Indians cherish their rice and often enjoy a hot lunch of rice-lentil crepes, pancakes, steamed dumplings and cakes. Street vendors' enticing offerings, with their marvelous aromas, provide yet another lunch option.

In the bustling metropolis of Mumbai (Bombay) the harried worker is rescued by *dabbawallahs*, servicemen who bring a worker's own meal, prepared by the woman of the house, from home to work. The *dabbawallah* stops by the worker's home around 9:00 A.M. to pick up the lunch, packed in several round stainless-steel containers that stack perfectly one on top of the other. A long handle fits snugly alongside the container sides and snaps into place on top, sealing in the hot or cold food. Through a complex system of relay deliveries—in trains, buses or hand-pushed carts—the lunch magically appears at the worker's desk just in time for the noon break. Once lunch is consumed, the process reverses and the empty container returns to the front doorstep. Interestingly enough, rarely has any lunch been delivered to the wrong person!

Tea Time

Tea is served in the late afternoon. Originating in the era when England ruled India, this beloved daily ritual remains steadfast in Indian culture. Indians eat dinner relatively late, so an afternoon break of Darjeeling tea leaves brewed with cooling spices in whole milk, enjoyed with a savory snack or two, offers comfort against hunger pains. Samosas (flaky pastry shells that enclose spiced potatoes and peas) purchased from a roadside vendor make an excellent snack with sweet-sour tamrind chutney, as do batter-dipped red onion slices fried just right and served with fresh mint-cilantro chutney.

Dinner—The Important Meal

Just as in the United States, the reality of the daily grind prevents families from sharing every meal. But in Indian homes each night, the family comes together for dinner, the largest and most important meal of the day. It is served late, usually 8:00 P.M. or later.

A variety of flavors, colors and textures abounds in the four to six foods usually served at dinner. Lentil-based dishes, rice or bread, vegetables, pickles and chutneys are favored choices. Water is usually served to quench the thirst; soft drinks, wine, beer, tea or coffee do not often show up at mealtime. Desserts are not typically consumed after dinner either. Fresh fruit takes care of the sweet tooth, as more labor-intensive desserts are reserved for special occasions.

Indian Snack Foods

Like Americans, Indians love their snacks. Roasted peanuts, a large variety of deep-fried vegetable- and legume-based creations and puffed rice treats satisfy those between-meal hunger cravings. Street foods appeal to the "want-it-now" crowd. In the appetizer section of this book you'll find recipes for snacks that are substantial, wholesome and delicious!

Shopping at the Bazaar

Indian shoppers rely on almost daily trips to open-air markets called bazaars. Not everyone owns a refrigerator and pantry storage space is limited, so frequent shopping trips are a necessity. Larger cities do, of course, have grocery stores, but they are what Americans might consider a small neighborhood store.

At the bazaar, many small vendors offer different fresh foods and staples, so a shopper's meandering path passes by all the favorites. A cloth bag is necessary to hold the ripest tomato, the deepest purple eggplant, fiery green and red chilies or a large, leafy head of cabbage. Along the way, the shopper may take an extra moment to haggle over the cost of rice before joining the line that has formed at the flour mill to await freshly ground wheat.

Whether you introduce your family to Indian food with just one dish or prepare a traditional Indian meal with several courses, all the exotic flavors of India are fascinating to explore. Your culinary adventures into the tastes and aromas of India are about to begin. Enjoy!

A Note on Recipe Names

We have included both Indian and English recipe titles. The Indian title is in the language of the region where the recipe originated. Hindi, Marathi, Gujarati, Tamil and Bengali are some of the languages that have made their way into the titles. Hindi, the national language, is widely spoken in the northern regions, so the names of the dishes from that region are mostly in Hindi. Tamil is a prominent language in southern India, so most of the recipe titles from the south are in Tamil.

The Indian Pantry: Getting Started

You'll be able to replicate many of the recipes in this book in your home kitchen with basic ingredients commonly available in your supermarket or natural-food store. Spices and grains have a relatively long shelf life, so they'll be conveniently handy once purchased. Buying packaged spice blends, including *garam masaala*, speeds up your Indian meal preparation. (Check out our "Getting Started" menu on page 320 for recipes using the ingredients below.)

Spices and Flavorings (Masaala)

Black or yellow mustard seed *(rai)*

Black peppercorns *(kala mir)*

Cardamom pods, green or white *(elaichi)*

Cinnamon stick *(dal chini)*

Coriander seed *(dhania)*

Cumin seed *(zeera)*

Dried bay leaves *(tez patta)*

Ground red pepper (cayenne) *(lal mirchi)*

Ground turmeric *(haldi)*

Whole cloves *(lavang)*

Whole dried red chilies *(sabud lal mirchi)*

Lentils, Beans and Peas (Legumes/Pulses/Dal)

Black-eyed peas *(lobhia)*

Garbanzo beans *(kabuli channa)*

Red kidney beans *(rajmah)*

Red lentils *(masoor dal)*

Yellow split peas *(chana dal)*

Fresh Herbs, Vegetables and Fruits (Subzi aur Phul)

Asian or regular eggplant *(baingan/katarikai)*

Bananas *(kéla)*

Cabbage *(bund gobhi)*

Carrots *(gajar)*

Cauliflower *(phool gobhi)*

Cilantro *(taaza dhania)*

Coconut *(nariyal/thénga)*

Cucumber *(kakadi)*

Fresh or frozen green peas *(mutter)*

Fresh Thai, serrano or cayenne chilies *(hara mirchi)*

Garlic *(lasoon)*

Gingerroot *(adrak)*

Green beans *(kotorangai)*

Green bell peppers *(simla mirch)*

Limes/lemons *(limbu/nimbu)*

Mint *(pudhina)*

Onions, red and yellow *(pyaaz)*

Potatoes *(aloo)*

Spinach *(paalak ka saag)*

Tomatoes *(tamatar)*

Rice and Related Grains (Chaawal)

All-purpose flour *(maida)*

Basmati rice *(basmati chaawal)*

Groceries

Blanched almonds *(baadaam)*

Canola or vegetable oil *(tél/yennai)*

Golden raisins *(kismis)*

Peanuts *(sengdana)*

Raw cashews *(kaaju)*

Sweetened condensed milk

Unsweetened coconut milk *(thenga paal)*

Dairy (Doodh aur Dahi)

Buttermilk *(chaas/more)*

Eggs *(undaa)*

Milk *(doodh)*

Regular or fat-free plain yogurt *(dahi)*

Unsalted butter *(maakhan)*

Whipping (heavy) cream *(malai)*

Buying Ingredients for Indian Cooking

Most of the ingredients in this book can be found at the supermarket in the ethnic food aisles or at natural-food stores. Some items may require a trip to an ethnic or specialty food store. Many ingredients used in Indian cooking are also used in other cuisines. So in addition to looking in Indian grocery stores, try Mediterranean, Middle Eastern, Asian and Latino markets as well. Look under grocer-retail, spices or herbs in the phone book to find any stores in your area.

Although Betty Crocker does not endorse or sponsor any particular food retailer, here are some sources that you might find helpful for ordering by mail or on-line:

KALUSTYAN'S

123 Lexington Avenue
New York, NY 10016
(212) 685-3451 TEL; (212) 683-8458 FAX
www.kalustyans.com
For a complete selection of spices, spice blends and Indian groceries.

The Complete Indian Pantry

With the following ingredients, in addition to the ingredients listed in the "Getting Started" pantry, you will be able to recreate all of the regional recipes in this book. To stock up on some of the ingredients listed below, you may need to visit your local Indian, Middle Eastern or Asian grocery store. There are also mail-order sources and on-line Web sites that specialize in Indian spices, grains, legumes and other products.

Spices and Flavorings (Masaala)

Asafetida (hing)

Bishop's weed (ajwain)

Dried fenugreek leaves (kasoori méthi)

Dried mangosteen slices (kokum)

Dried pomegranate seed (anardana)

Fennel seed (saunf)

Fenugreek seed (méthi)

Mace pieces (javintri saliya)

Mango powder (amchur)

Nigella (kalonji)

Rose essence (gulab jal)

Saffron threads (zaffran)

Tamarind (imli)

White poppy seed (safed khus khus)

White sesame seed (safed til)

Whole nutmeg (javintri)

Lentils, Beans and Peas (Legumes/Pulses/Dal)

Split and hulled black lentils (urad dal)

Split and hulled green lentils (mung/moong dal)

Split and hulled pigeon peas (toovar dal)

White or green lima beans (vaal nu dal)

Whole black lentils (sabud urad)

Whole green lentils (sabud mung/moong)

Fresh Herbs, Vegetables and Fruits (Subzi aur Phul)

Fresh mangoes (aaphoos/tayyar aam)

Fresh okra (bhindi)

Green mangoes (maangai/kuchee aam)

Karhi leaves (karhi patta)

Mustard greens (sarson ka saag)

Plantain (vazhaipazham)

Red Bananas (lal kéla)

Sweet potatoes or yams (ratalu)

Rice and Related Grains (Chaawal)

Chappati flour (roti ka atta)

Cream of wheat (rava)

Fresh or dried rice noodles (sevai)

Garbanzo bean flour (bésan/channa atta)

Rice flour (chaawal ka atta)

Sorghum flour (jowar ka atta)

Tapioca pearls (sabudana)

Groceries

Jaggery (gur)

Mustard oil (sarson ka tél)

Peanut oil (sengdana tél)

Sesame oil, light colored (nalla yennai)

Unsalted pistachio nuts (pista)

Dairy (Doodh aur Dahi)

Clarified butter (ghee)

PENZEY'S SPICES

Multiple locations
(800) 741-7787 TEL, (262) 679-7878 FAX
www.penzeys.com
For spices and spice blends.

FRIEDA'S

P.O. Box 58488
Los Angeles, CA 90058
(714) 826-6100 or (800) 421-9477
www.friedas.com
For exotic and specialty produce.

ETHNIC GROCER

Web site only
www.ethnicgrocer.com
For spices and many Indian groceries.

Betty Crocker is not affiliated with any of these businesses.

Chapter One

Spices, Blends and Basics

Clockwise from left: Spicy Garam Masala (page 34), Spicy Panchphoran (page 39), Clarified Butter (*Ghee*) (page 40), Sambhar Powder (page 35), Panchphoran (page 38)

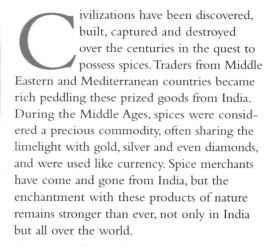

India's World of spices

Civilizations have been discovered, built, captured and destroyed over the centuries in the quest to possess spices. Traders from Middle Eastern and Mediterranean countries became rich peddling these prized goods from India. During the Middle Ages, spices were considered a precious commodity, often sharing the limelight with gold, silver and even diamonds, and were used like currency. Spice merchants have come and gone from India, but the enchantment with these products of nature remains stronger than ever, not only in India but all over the world.

Spices in India have been used not only for flavoring but also for medicinal and religious purposes. Ayurveda, a branch of medicine that is considered an alternative or complementary therapy in the United States, is widely practiced in India's villages, towns and all its major metropolitan cities. Herbs and spices are the basis of this ancient medicine, used to treat all kinds of human ailments. Spices such as sandalwood and turmeric *(haldi)* and herbs such as holy basil *(tulsi)*, in addition to availing humans, appease the hundreds of gods that rule many an Indian household during religious services.

Buying and Storing Spices

Spices are obtained from the bark, stem, buds, roots and seeds of plants, and herbs are usually their leaves. Purchase spices in their original state as much as possible, such as cumin seed as opposed to ground cumin, black peppercorns as opposed to ground black pepper and so on. Spices get their flavor from essential oils. The more a spice has been processed, the faster the oils will evaporate, and the spice will lose its flavor. The advantage of whole spices is that, if properly stored, they almost never spoil. If kept whole and ground just before use, they can provide optimum flavors for many years to come.

There are certain ingredients that are considered spices in Indian cuisine that are difficult to find in this country in whole form, such as dried whole turmeric root and dried unripe mango. They can be found at some Indian grocery stores or through mail-order or on-line Web site sources (see pages 20–21).

Buy ground spices in small quantities and replenish them often to ensure the most flavor. Mark the date of purchase on containers to help you keep track. Most ground spices can be purchased at supermarkets, but if not, Indian grocery stores, natural-food stores and mail-order are good sources.

Store spices in tightly sealed dry containers (glass or plastic), and keep them in a cool, dry cupboard or pantry. Never refrigerate or freeze spices because the moisture will affect their flavors and textures. Discard all ground spices (especially when the factory-sealed vacuum packing has been broken) that have resided in your cupboards and pantry for six months or more. Follow the first-in/first-out method for using spices.

Grinding Spices

Once spices are ground, the oils they contain will start to diminish, and they will begin to lose flavor and potency. To help prevent this, just grind the amount called for in the recipe. You will be amazed how strong the aroma and flavors will be when you follow this simple rule.

There are many ways to grind whole spices, but here are two that I use:

* A sturdy mortar and pestle. This works best for a small amount of spices. They are available in ethnic grocery stores, kitchen equipment stores and some natural-food stores.

* An electric coffee grinder. This works well for both smaller and larger amounts of spices. Reserve it for grinding spices only, or your coffee will taste spicy. They are widely available in supermarkets, kitchen equipment stores and gourmet coffeehouses. Spice grinders or mills are also available in gourmet stores.

Washing the grinder each time a spice is ground is not necessary. Wiping it clean with a paper towel will suffice. For a quick cleaning, you can grind and discard 1 tablespoon granulated sugar or a piece of fresh white bread between spices. *Note:* If whole spices aren't available, then substitute the equivalent quantity of ground spice: 1 teaspoon whole spice = 1 teaspoon ground spice. However, if you are preparing a dessert that calls for ground spices, do wipe out the grinder or mortar before use to prevent any savory spices from flavoring your dish.

A Few Words About Curry

What Indians know as curry and what Americans know as curry are two different things. Curry powders, generic blends found in abundance in the United States, are non-existent in classic Indian cooking. In the United States, one adds spice blend curry to many dishes to create an Indian flavor. In India, curry is never added—it just is!

Curries are always sauce-based preparations with just one or as many as twenty spices and herbs in various proportions. The word *curry* is considered to have its roots in the Tamil word *karhi*, meaning "sauce." A good Indian cook is always judged by how varied his or her curries are. Once you familiarize yourself with some of the basic spices and herbs and the techniques for using them, rest assured you will be able to formulate hundreds of curries that are far apart in flavor, texture, aroma and color.

The Secret of Six Flavors from One Spice

The beauty of a spice is its unique ability to provide up to six distinct flavors— if you know the secret! For example, take cumin seed, treat it six different ways and discover six different flavors. When you apply these techniques to the wide array of spices used in the Indian kitchen, you will experience a truly amazing new world of flavors.

Flavor 1   **Whole cumin seed**

Flavor 2   **Ground cumin seed**

Flavor 3   **Whole cumin seed dry-roasted until reddish brown**

Flavor 4   **Whole cumin seed dry-roasted until reddish brown and then ground**

Flavor 5   **Whole cumin seed fried in hot oil or Clarified Butter (*Ghee*), (page 40), 10 to 20 seconds until reddish brown and has a nutty aroma.**

Flavor 6   **Whole cumin seed fried in hot oil or Clarified Butter (*Ghee*), (page 40), 10 to 20 seconds until seed is reddish brown and has a nutty aroma, then removed from oil and ground.**

And that's the secret!

CORIANDER SEED
(*DHANIA*)

BLACK MUSTARD SEED
(*RAI*)

CUMIN SEED
(*ZEERA*)

SALT (*NAMAK*)

FENUGREEK SEED
(*METHI*)

TURMERIC, GROUND
(*HALDI*)

GROUND RED PEPPER
(*SUKHA LAL MIRCHI*)

DRIED MANGOSTEEN SLICES
(*KOKUM*)

DRIED FENUGREEK LEAVES
(*KASOORI METHI*)

SAFFRON
(*ZARDA/ZAFFRAN*)

TAMARIND
(*IMLI*)

DRIED POMEGRANATE SEEDS
(*ANARDANA*)

WHITE POPPY SEED
(*KHUS KHUS*)

MANGO POWDER
(*AMCHUR*)

BISHOP'S WEED
(*AJWAIN*)

ASAFETIDA
(*HING*)

MACE
(*JAVINTRI SALIYA*)

JAGGERY
(*GUR*)

NIGELLA
(*CHARNUSHKA/KALONJI*)

Substitutions for Spices and Herbs

Since every spice and herb used in Indian cooking is unique, true substitutes are often not available. Sometimes the role of a spice, like asafetida (*hing*), for instance, is to provide a subtle bitter flavor that adds to the complexity of the dish. There may not be another spice that provides just that characteristic flavor, so it is better just to leave it out. In other recipes, although there is no perfect substitute for asafetida, garlic powder has been recommended as an alternative. The beauty of Indian cooking is that it is forgiving. The absence of a flavoring ingredient does not compromise the authenticity of the recipe, but can create another spectacular rendition of the classic.

Spices, Herbs and Seasonings

Asafetida *(hing)*: The hardened sap of a gargantuan fennel-like plant, asafetida has a strong flavor and aroma. It is available either in blocks (a purer form) that must be grated, preferably with a nutmeg grater, or more commonly in powder form, which may have some turmeric added to it for color. Don't be alarmed by its strong, rather offensive odor. When cooked, the odor fades, leaving a pleasant onion-like flavor. Store asafetida in its own airtight container, as its aroma has the ability to overpower any area it's stored in.

Bay leaves *(tez patta)*: Dried bay leaves are found in any supermarket, and fresh leaves are sometimes available in specialty produce markets. The dried leaves can be used whole or dry-roasted and ground with other spices. Dried leaves are very sharp and should be removed from the dish before serving.

Bishop's weed *(ajwain)*: This seed from a weed that grows wild in southern and western India is related to the cumin and caraway family. The flavor is quite different from its relatives, with a bitter edge resembling dried thyme. It is considered to aid digestion and is usually added to lentils, beans and peas. If unavailable, there are two substitution choices: Use dried thyme leaves, or combine 1 teaspoon dried oregano leaves, 1 teaspoon celery seed and 1/4 teaspoon coarsely ground black pepper and use the same amount of this mixture as called for in the recipe.

Black peppercorns *(kala mir)*: The variety of peppercorn that is cultivated in southern India is considered one of the best in the world. They are round and black, with an intense, hot flavor masking an underlying sweetness. Always buy peppercorns whole so the piquant flavors can be released just before use.

Black salt *(kala namak)*: The name appears to be a misnomer because the salt is deep purple in color. However, in its original lump form it is brownish black, and therefore referred to as black salt. It has a strong sulfuric odor reminiscent of hard-cooked eggs. Do not be put off by the smell—the smoky taste is in no way similar to the aroma. It is widely available in Indian grocery stores. If unavailable, use regular salt. (Pictured on page 183.)

Cardamom *(elaichi)*: There are two varieties of cardamom pods: black or brown, and green or white. The black (or dark brown) pods are large and wide with more of a bitter flavor. This variety is primarily used in northern India for flavoring rice pilafs, meats and vegetable stews. The green variety is smaller, less plump and has highly aromatic seeds that smell like menthol. It is more commonly used in all regions of India, especially in desserts. White pods are simply green ones that have been sun-bleached. Pods are used to flavor oils but are never eaten. The seeds are either crushed or left whole. You can buy cardamom whole (in pods), shelled (labels often say decorticated) and ground. The seeds are at times eaten raw after a heavy meal to cleanse the breath and to help aid digestion.

Chili peppers, fresh and dried *(hara aur lal mirchi)*: There are many varieties of chilies all over the world, but the two most popular in India are cayenne and Thai chilies (also known as bird's eye chilies because of their resemblance to the shapely slits of a bird's eye). Chilies are members of the capsicum family that includes the bell pepper. The thickness of a chili pepper is one indicator of its heat level: Thinner chilies are potent, and thicker ones are sweeter and less hot. The vein that runs through the center and its seeds house the intense compound called capsaicin, which is responsible for the chili's heat. Discard the vein and seeds if your tolerance is fairly low. Indians never remove them because they provide essential flavor to many of their dishes. Use as many chilies as you are comfortable with. Ground red pepper (cayenne) is derived from the long, curvaceous red cayenne chilies after they have been sun-dried. (Pictured on page 114.)

Cilantro *(taaza dhania/kotamalli)*: Also known as Chinese parsley or coriander, this highly aromatic member of the parsley family is the herb of choice all across India. (For some people, a naturally occurring chemical in cilantro reacts with an enzyme in their saliva, leaving an unpleasant soapy taste. When cilantro is heated, the chemical is deactivated to a certain extent, which makes the herb more palatable.) Both the leaves and tender stems can be used. Store cilantro like a bouquet of flowers in a vase, with stems only in a jar of water. Cover the tops loosely with a plastic bag and refrigerate up to two weeks. Clip stem ends regularly for longer-lasting leaves. Or store cilantro in a loosely closed plastic bag for up to five days in the refrigerator. Rinse cilantro just before using. Once the leaves are wet, they will become limp and will spoil quickly. (Pictured on page 114.)

Cinnamon *(dal chini)*: Cinnamon trees are native to Sri Lanka, an island nation just south of India. Their curled, paper-thin bark is a lot mellower than the Chinese cassia bark, which is more commonly available in the United States. Sticks of cinnamon are used to flavor rice pilafs in northern India. They are never removed before serving so they continue to perfume the pilaf at the table. (Sticks are only used for flavoring, of course, and are not eaten.) Cinnamon sticks from either Sri Lanka or China can be used in Indian cooking.

Cloves *(lavang/laung)*: This tiny, nail-shaped spice is the unopened bud of the highly aromatic evergreen clove tree. Clove oil is considered an anesthetic, often used by dentists in India to numb toothaches. In northern Indian recipes, whole cloves are added to hot oil or are ground.

Coriander seed *(dhania)*: These seeds are from the cilantro (coriander) plant, a member of the parsley family, but are in no way similar to the flavor of fresh cilantro. The small, yellowish brown round seeds have an almost citrus aroma and flavor.

Cumin seed *(zeera)*: Two varieties of cumin are used in Indian cooking: the regular grayish brown seed *(safed zeera)* with a shape similar to caraway, found in supermarkets, and black cumin, a darker blackish brown seed *(kala zeera* or *shahi zeera)*, with a more peppery than nutty flavor and a flatter appearance, that can be found in Indian grocery stores. The two varieties are never used interchangeably because their flavors vary slightly.

Fennel seed *(saunf)*: This seed is highly prized as a digestive aid and is often chewed raw after a heavy meal. Its licorice-like flavor is a delicious component of many preparations from eastern India. Fresh fennel bulb and leaves are never used in Indian kitchens.

Fenugreek seed and leaves *(méthi* and *kasoori méthi)*: The leaves of this plant are highly aromatic with a perfumed bitterness. The fresh leaves have a remarkable resemblance to watercress but have a far more complex flavor. The seed is aromatically bitter and used extensively in South and East Indian kitchens. The seed is often available in natural-food stores, and the leaves are found dried in Indian grocery stores. In season, Indian stores may stock the fresh leaves as well.

Gingerroot *(adrak)*: This rhizome (a bulbous root) is widely used in Indian cooking. Choose gingerroot that is firm and smooth skinned, and snap off as much as you need. The skin is thin, and if it is clean and mold-free, you do not need to peel it. Ginger has a spicy, crisp flavor and is considered highly valuable for its medicinal qualities. Gingerroot can be stored unpeeled in a plastic bag in the crisper section of the refrigerator for up to ten days. Discard any part of the root that has dried out or has blue-green mold on the skin. Freezing whole gingerroot is not recommended because it becomes soft and more watery. Frozen whole or grated, it can be kept up to two months. Ground ginger is rarely used.

Jaggery *(gur)*: Unrefined cane sugar, made from cooking down fresh sugar cane juice, jaggery is intensely sweet. It is available in blocks in Indian grocery stores, and a recipe may call for chopping it so it melts faster. This sweetening agent is used in desserts and beverages throughout India and is a favorite in the kitchens of the northwestern state of Gujarat for savory dishes as well.

Karhi leaves *(karhi patta/neem)*: A distant relative of the citrus family, this tree is widely found in southern India. These leaves are sometimes referred to as "fresh curry leaves" because *karhi* is pronounced "curry." The leaves resemble fresh bay leaves but are smaller and less sharp. They have a mellow flavor and incredible aroma when used fresh. Avoid buying the dried leaves because they are quite dull in flavor and aroma. Fresh leaves are available through mail-order resources and in the refrigerator section of Indian grocery stores. Fresh leaves will keep refrigerated in a resealable plastic bag for up to two weeks. If you cannot use them within two weeks, dry the leaves by spreading them on paper towels in a warm, sunny spot. *Karhi* leaves dried at home have much more flavor than those available at the store. Or seal them in a freezer bag, freeze for up to two months and use without

thawing. The leaves can be eaten, but Indians will move them aside when they find them in a curry or stir-fry. (Pictured on page 114.)

Mace *(javintri saliya)*: When the red, weblike covering of the nutmeg seed is carefully removed and dried, it becomes yellow and brittle mace. The whole dried piece is commercially known as a mace blade. Mace has a spicier flavor than nutmeg and they should not be used interchangeably. Dried mace pieces can be found in Indian grocery stores.

Mango powder *(amchur)*: The sun-dried pulp from a certain variety of unripe mango yields mango powder, which is a sharp, tart souring agent used in northern Indian dishes. It is widely available in Indian grocery stores as dried pulp pieces and powder.

Mangosteen slices *(kokum)*: Though it may sound like a close relative, mangosteen bears no relation to the mango. The fresh tropical fruits are rarely imported into the United States. They have a juicy, cream-colored interior and a dark, blackish purple hard exterior. The flavor is similar to that of a tart tangerine. Dried mangosteen slices, which resemble dry shiitake mushrooms slices, are available in Indian grocery stores.

Mint *(pudhina)*: Because it is an essential herb in North Indian cooking, mint is cultivated year-round. Its refreshing flavor and aroma enhances chutneys, cold appetizers and pilafs. Store fresh mint in a plastic bag in the refrigerator for up to four weeks. (Pictured on page 114.)

Mustard seed *(rai)*: These small round seeds vary in color from yellow to brown to black. The yellow seed is more commonly used in Europe and other Western nations, but the more pungent black seed is a necessity in Indian kitchens. When mustard seed is "popped" in hot oil, it becomes sweet and nutty, far different than the usual pungent, bitter flavor often associated with it. Be careful when popping seed because they can jump right out of the skillet.

Nigella *(charnushka/kalonji)*: A tiny, tear-shaped black seed, nigella is available in Indian and other ethnic-food stores. It is sometimes referred to as black onion seed, which it resembles, although it is unrelated to the onion. Its slightly bitter, peppery flavor is valued in Bengali-speaking households of eastern India.

Nutmeg *(javintri)*: Nutmeg grows on a tall, tropical evergreen tree. When the fruit is ripe, it splits open to expose the hard, light brown, oval-shaped seed inside. Nutmeg has a slightly sweet taste and is not as spicy as mace. Nutmeg can be purchased whole and grated using a small grater designed for that purpose.

Dried pomegranate seeds *(anardana)*: Another souring agent of choice in northern India, these are seeds from the fresh pomegranate fruit that have been sun-dried to accentuate their tartness. They are readily available in Indian grocery stores in this form. The dried seeds are ground and added to curries, stir-fries and even breads.

Poppy seed *(khus khus)*: A product of the opium poppy plant, this seed has none of the plant's narcotic properties. Black poppy seed is more often used in the United States, but the nutty, sweet, white variety is the seed of choice in Indian cooking. White poppy seed is available in Indian grocery stores.

Saffron *(zarda/zaffran)*: The most expensive spice in the world, saffron threads are stamens of the violet-blossomed crocus plant. They are handpicked from the flowers that bloom for a very short time in autumn. The threads are very potent, and all you need are a few strands to permeate an entire dish. Refrain from buying powdered saffron because it may be mixed with other ingredients.

Salt *(namak)*: Although it is a mineral, salt is considered a spice in Indian cooking. It is the most important of all spices and flavorings and is the catalyst that brings out the subtleties of all spices in any recipe. India gained its independence by boldly making sea salt, a basic commodity that was heavily taxed by the British, who forbade Indians from manufacturing it! Coarse sea salt is widely used in India, but table salt is equally popular.

Sesame seed *(til)*: Creamy-white sesame seed is native to India and is used in a wide range of dishes from appetizers to desserts. It is also made into an unrefined oil that is widely used in southern Indian cooking. Unrefined sesame oil is clear to slightly yellow in color and has a mild sesame flavor. It is quite different from dark reddish brown Asian sesame oil made with toasted sesame seed, which has a much stronger flavor. The two types of oil are not interchangeable in Indian cooking. Sesame seed is available in every supermarket, but the unrefined oil is more commonly found in Indian grocery stores and natural-food stores.

Tamarind *(imli)*: India's tropical weather offers the ideal environment for some very exotic fruits and vegetables, one of which is the tamarind. The fruits of this thickly shaded tree are long pods with tough, dark greenish brown skins. When peeled, they reveal a chocolate brown, sweet-sour pulp and brown seeds. The pulp is soaked in hot water for a few minutes and discarded. The tart liquid left behind is used to flavor curries, chutneys and beverages. Tamarind is available in various forms: blocks of dried pulp with or without seeds, fresh pods, dried pods, jars of tamarind concentrate paste and individually wrapped bags of sweetened tamarind paste. Refrain from buying the sweetened variety, as most of the recipes in Indian cooking use tamarind in its purely sour form. Look for tamarind in Indian and other ethnic-food stores.

Turmeric *(haldi)*: Fresh turmeric is a rhizome, like gingerroot, with a yellowish brown skin. When cut open, it reveals a beautiful deep orange-yellow interior. In the United States, it is most commonly available in its dried and ground form. Ground turmeric has a very vibrant, vivid yellow color and bitter flavor. An overabundance of turmeric gives commercial curry powder its characteristic yellow color. The dried root is often used for religious functions, and pastes made from the spice are considered an antiseptic when applied to wounds. It is also a moisturizer, applied to a bride's skin for a yellow-orange hue as background to her display of gold jewelry. (Fresh tumeric pictured on page 114.)

Spice Blends and Basics for Indian Cooking

Reading the entire recipe is an important first step. You'll find that some ingredients must be prepared before you can add them to a recipe— and you'll want to leave yourself ample time. More importantly, you will have a chance to review the techniques—some of which may be new to you. Before starting to cook, it is essential to prepare and measure out all the ingredients first. Indian cooking emphasizes the importance of timing the addition of ingredients to the hot wok or skillet. A sizzling spice left too long in the hot cooking oil while the next ingredient is measured can ruin the flavor of the dish.

In this chapter you'll find several spice blends, "ingredient recipes" and basic techniques for ingredients that are used in other recipes throughout this book. Spice blends are as varied as India's population, with personalities as diverse as the regions they represent. In addition to whole spices, commercially prepared spice blends can also be found in Indian stores, although they may be made with slightly different ingredients or proportions than the recipes here. Homemade is always best, but these preparations are helpful to have around when you're in a pinch for time. Better yet, you may want to prepare some of these spice blends in advance to have them on hand for quick recipes. Most of them can be stored in an airtight jar at room temperature for up to one month, and others for longer. Once you become knowledgeable about spice blends, you may even want to create your own variations.

Preparing Whole Spices

Dry-Roasting Cumin Seed

Heat a heavy 6-inch skillet over medium heat about 2 minutes. (Hold hand, palm down, about 4 inches above bottom of skillet. It should feel warm.) Add seed to skillet and cook 1 to 2 minutes, stirring constantly, until seed turns reddish brown and has a strong, nutty aroma. Remove seed from skillet. If grinding seed, let cool 1 to 2 minutes, then grind in a spice grinder or in a mortar with a pestle.

Dry-Roasting Fenugreek Seed

Heat heavy 6-inch skillet over medium heat about 2 minutes. (Hold hand, palm down, about 4 inches above bottom of skillet. It should feel warm.) Add seed to skillet and cook 30 to 60 seconds, stirring constantly, until seed turns reddish brown and has an almost nutty, slightly bitter aroma. Remove seed from skillet. If grinding seed, let cool 1 to 2 minutes, then grind in a spice grinder or in a mortar with a pestle.

Crushing Cardamom Seeds

If using cardamom pods, first remove seeds from pod. Place cardamom seeds in a mortar and crush with a pestle until coarse. If mortar and pestle are unavailable, place seeds in resealable plastic bag on cutting board and crush them with a heavy rolling pin or meat mallet.

The word garam in this blend (masaala) *means "warm" or "hot," an internal feeling usually felt while enjoying dishes originating from the northern states of India that include these spices.*

Garam Masaala

1/4 CUP SPICE BLEND

1 tablespoon cumin seed

1 teaspoon cardamom seeds (removed from pods)

1/2 teaspoon whole cloves

1/2 teaspoon black peppercorns

2 dried bay leaves

2 three-inch sticks cinnamon, broken

1. Heat 6-inch skillet over medium-high heat. Place all spices in skillet, and roast 2 to 3 minutes, stirring constantly, until seeds crackle, spices turn one shade darker and the mixture has a nutty, sweet aroma. Transfer to a bowl, and cool 3 to 5 minutes.

2. Place roasted spice blend in spice grinder. Grind until mixture looks like the texture of finely ground pepper. Store in an airtight jar at room temperature for up to 1 month; beyond that, it will start to lose its full flavor.

Garam Masaala

Raghavan Ki Baaten

☀ Each household in North India has its own version of garam masaala. It can be used whole, ground raw or dry-roasted and then ground. Whatever its state, the resulting aroma puts a smile on your face and a lilt in your northern-based recipes.

☀ This version of garam masaala uses some of the basic spices often found in the kitchens of Delhi, the political capital of India.

This version of garam masaala is often found in the northwestern states of Gujarat and Maharashtra. Spices such as nutmeg and mace round out the blend, and dried red chilies add a slight kick. The flavors of the North are mingled with the robust flavors of chilies and coriander from the South, creating a marriage of bliss.

Spicy Garam Masaala

teekha Garam masaala

1/3 CUP SPICE BLEND

1 tablespoon sesame seed	1/2 teaspoon finely grated nutmeg
1 tablespoon coriander seed	4 dried bay leaves
1 tablespoon cumin seed	4 three-inch sticks cinnamon, broken
1 teaspoon cardamom seeds (removed from pods)	3 to 5 dried red Thai, serrano or cayenne chilies
1/2 teaspoon whole cloves	2 pieces whole or 1/2 teaspoon ground mace

1. Heat 6-inch skillet over medium-high heat. Place all ingredients in skillet, and roast 1 to 2 minutes, stirring constantly, until seeds crackle, spices turn one shade darker and the mixture has a nutty, sweet aroma. Transfer to a bowl, and cool 3 to 5 minutes.

2. Place roasted spice blend in spice grinder. Grind until mixture looks like the texture of finely ground pepper. Store in an airtight jar at room temperature for up to 1 month; beyond that, it will start to lose its full flavor.

Spicy Garam Masaala is pictured on page 23.

Raghavan Ki Baaten

☀ **Mace is the weblike covering of nutmeg, and it is often available in pieces at natural-food stores and Indian grocery stores.**

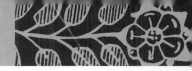

Sambhar powder combinations are as numerous as there are kitchens in South India. A combination of roasted spices and lentils, sambhar powder is typically used to flavor a stew-like dish called Pigeon Pea Stew (page 188), often considered South India's signature dish. In this region, the unusual technique of using lentils as spices is central to the cuisine. Either dry-roasted or stir-fried in oil and then ground, the lentils provide not only flavor but also texture to some of the sauces. This blend can also be added to everyday stir-fries and stews.

Sambhar Powder

Sambhar Masala

ABOUT 2/3 CUP SPICE BLEND

1/2 cup dried red Thai, serrano or cayenne chilies

2 tablespoons dried yellow split peas (chana dal), sorted

2 tablespoons dried split and hulled black lentils (urad dal) or yellow split peas, sorted

1 tablespoon coriander seed

1 teaspoon black peppercorns

1 teaspoon fenugreek seed

1 teaspoon vegetable oil

Note: Because of the large quantity of chilies, make sure you use proper ventilation, such as the exhaust hood over your range top or an open window, when roasting this blend.

Sambhar Powder is pictured on page 23.

1. Mix all ingredients in small bowl.

2. Heat 6-inch skillet over medium-high heat. Place mixture in skillet, and roast 1 to 2 minutes, stirring constantly, until seeds crackle, spices turn one shade darker and the mixture has a nutty yet pungent aroma. Transfer to a bowl, and cool 8 to 10 minutes.

3. Place 3 tablespoons roasted spice blend in spice grinder. Grind until mixture looks like the texture of finely ground pepper. Repeat with remaining blend. Mix well, and store in an airtight jar at room temperature for up to 1 month; beyond that, it will lose its full flavor.

Raghavan Ki Baaten

☀ Split and hulled black lentils (*urad dal*) are crucial to this blend's flavors and a trip to an Indian or Middle Eastern grocery store is worth the effort. However, if unable to do so, increase the yellow split peas to 1/4 cup instead.

☀ Fenugreek seed is commonly available at any natural-food store. If none is at hand, eliminate from the recipe.

Tangy Sambhar Powder

Chutputee Sambhar Masala

ABOUT 1 CUP SPICE BLEND

1/2 cup dried red Thai, serrano or cayenne chilies

1/4 cup dried yellow split peas (chana dal), sorted

2 tablespoons sesame seed

1 tablespoon tamarind pulp or grated lime or lemon peel

1 tablespoon coriander seed

1 teaspoon cumin seed

1 teaspoon black peppercorns

1. Mix all ingredients in small bowl.

2. Heat 6-inch skillet over medium-high heat. Place mixture in skillet, and roast 1 to 2 minutes, stirring constantly, until seeds crackle, spices turn one shade darker and the mixture has a nutty yet pungent aroma. Transfer to a bowl, and cool 8 to 10 minutes.

3. Place 3 tablespoons roasted spice blend in spice grinder. Grind until mixture looks like the texture of finely ground pepper. Repeat with remaining blend. Mix well, and store in an airtight jar at room temperature for up to 1 month; beyond that, it will start to lose its full flavor.

Tangy Sambhar Powder

Raghavan Ki Baaten

☀ Tamarind (page 30) pulp is available in block form in Indian and Asian grocery stores and may be in the ethnic-food section of large supermarkets. Remove and discard any seeds before use. Do not soak the pulp before using in this recipe.

In West Bengal, home state of the city of Calcutta, whole spices from the northern and southern states are combined to create unique pungent, bitter, sweet and astringent flavors. The resulting blend, left whole or ground into a paste, is a taste sensation as complex as Calcutta's millions.

Panchphoran

Panchphoran

1/4 CUP SPICE BLEND

1 tablespoon
cumin seed

1 teaspoon
fennel seed

1 teaspoon yellow
mustard seed

1 teaspoon nigella
(kalonji)

1/2 teaspoon
fenugreek seed
or yellow
mustard seed

1. Mix all ingredients in small bowl.

2. Store in an airtight jar at room temperature up to 6 months.

Panchphoran is pictured on page 23.

This combination of panchphoran packs a more potent punch in the recipes it flavors.
The chilies and mace offer a pleasing harmony, perfectly balancing hot and sweet.

Spicy Panchphoran

Teekha Panchphoran

1/4 CUP SPICE BLEND

4 or 5 dried red Thai, serrano or cayenne chilies, pounded

1 tablespoon fennel seed

1 teaspoon fenugreek seed or yellow mustard seed

1 teaspoon cumin seed

3 pieces whole mace, crumbled or 3/4 teaspoon ground mace

1. Place chilies in resealable plastic bag; seal tightly. Pound them with a rolling pin or meat mallet just enough to release some of the seeds, but leave the skin partially intact. Mix all ingredients in small bowl.

2. Store in an airtight jar at room temperature up to 6 months.

Spicy Panchphoran is pictured on page 23.

Raghavan Ki Baaten

☀ A mortar and pestle can also be used to pound the chilies. Pound them enough to release some of the seeds, but leave the skins partially intact. Wash the mortar and pestle thoroughly in hot, soapy water so the heat and flavor of the chilies doesn't transfer to the next item you use it for.

Ghee, which is clarified butter, has often been called the nectar of the gods and a gift from Mother Cow, the sacred mammal often depicted with images of Lord Krishna who was raised in a family of cowherds. Stories of youthful Krishna abound, weaving together his passions for life, beauty, frolic and the freshly churned butter that was often turned into ghee for purity and posterity.

Clarified Butter
Ghee

3/4 CUP CLARIFIED BUTTER

1 pound unsalted butter

Ghee is pictured on page 23.

1. Melt butter in heavy 1-quart saucepan over low heat. Continue simmering over low heat 15 to 20 minutes, occasionally skimming off milk solids that surface, until butter is clear and deep yellow in color. Do not stir (some of the milk solids will turn brown and sink to the bottom of pan).

2. Remove saucepan from heat. Cool 5 to 10 minutes. Do not stir.

3. Gently pour clarified butter into an airtight container, leaving the milk solids in the saucepan. Cover and store in refrigerator up to 4 weeks.

Raghavan Ki Baaten

☀ **Removing the milk solids and evaporating the water in butter to make** *ghee* increases its smoking point, extends its storage life and also gives it a nutty flavor. *Ghee* will not burn at high temperatures, so it can be used for sautéing, stir-frying, general cooking and even deep-fat frying. The French use a similar process to yield clarified butter called *buerre noisette*, a term that refers to its nuttiness.

☀ Pay extra attention when making *ghee*, as it has to be done over low heat. If the temperature is too hot, the milk solids will burn before they can be separated from the butter.

Commercially made mustard oil is available in Indian grocery stores and in some natural-food stores. There is no true substitute for the oil, but this milder version can be made at home and used if you can't purchase it.

Mustard Oil

Sarson Ka tel

1/4 CUP OIL

1/4 cup vegetable oil

2 tablespoons Dijon mustard

1. Stir together oil and mustard (mixture will not be smooth and will remain separated). Let stand at room temperature for up to 4 hours but no longer than 24 hours.

2. Strain mustard from oil, using a fine-mesh strainer. Store oil in a tightly covered container in the refrigerator up to 1 month.

This cheese from northern India is similar to farmers cheese or fresh mozzarella. Paneer is often made with either whole milk from the cow or buffalo. Reduced-fat milk is not recommended for making paneer because it won't set up very well. Because of paneer's mild flavor, this cheese lends itself to multiple uses in many recipes.

Homemade Cheese

Paneer

4 CUPS 1/2-INCH CUBES CHEESE

1 gallon (16 cups) whole milk

1/4 cup white vinegar

Vegetable oil for deep-frying

1. Heat milk to boiling in 6-quart Dutch oven or stockpot over medium-high heat, stirring frequently to prevent scorching.

2. Stir in vinegar; remove from heat. The milk will immediately separate into curds (solids) and whey (liquid).

3. Line large colander with cheesecloth or muslin; place in sink. Pour curds and whey mixture into lined colander. Lift edges of cloth; swirl in sink once or twice to remove excess liquid. Completely wrap curds in cloth; return to colander. Place a large jar, Dutch oven or stockpot filled with water or similar weight directly on curds. Leave undisturbed in sink 5 to 6 hours to drain.

4. Remove weight and remove cheese to cutting board; discard cheesecloth. Cut cheese into 1/2-inch cubes. Cover and refrigerate at least 2 hours or up to 12 hours.

5. Heat oil (2 to 3 inches deep) in wok or Dutch oven over medium-high heat until thermometer inserted in oil reads 300°.

6. Add about half the cheese cubes to hot oil. Fry 4 to 5 minutes, turning occasionally, until light golden brown. Remove with slotted spoon; drain on paper towels. Repeat with remaining cheese cubes.

7. Tightly cover and refrigerate cheese up to 3 days or freeze up to 2 months.

Homemade Cheese

Raghavan Ki Baaten

☀ I have noticed in certain Indian home kitchens that the cook uses lemon
juice instead of vinegar when making *paneer*. I prefer to use vinegar
because it leaves less of an acidic aftertaste. Also, it requires more lemon
juice to get the same results.

Commercially made garbanzo bean flour (bésan/gram flour) is available in Indian grocery stores, natural-food stores and in the ethnic-food section of some supermarkets. There is no substitute for this flour, but it can be easily made in your own kitchen.

Garbanzo Bean Flour

1/2 CUP FLOUR

1/4 cup dried garbanzo beans

Garbanzo Bean Flour is pictured on page 165.

1. Place beans in your spice or coffee grinder; grind until it looks like coarsely ground black pepper. Sift it through a fine-mesh strainer or flour sifter.

2. The larger grains left in the strainer can be reground. Do not use a blender or food processor because it will not grind the beans into a fine texture.

Fresh coconuts are available in the produce section of supermarkets. Choose a coconut that is dark brown and heavy for its size and that sounds full of liquid when shaken. The liquid keeps the coconut fresh and moist. Avoid those with damp "eyes" (the two or three indentations on the top of the coconut where it was attached to the palm tree).

Shredded Fresh Coconut

Nariyal

2 TO 3 CUPS SHREDDED COCONUT

1 medium coconut

1. Rinse coconut thoroughly to remove any dust or dirt from the shell; pat dry.

2. Pierce the eyes with an ice pick or sturdy skewer. Drain the liquid into a container. The liquid is delicious to drink and can be stored in the refrigerator in a covered container for up to 24 hours.

3. Tap the coconut firmly all over with a hammer or heavy meat mallet. It usually splits open lengthwise.

4. Work the blade of a blunt or round-ended knife between the white meat and the hard shell. Push the knife into the shell away from you and, with a twist of the wrist, the meat should pop out.

5. Peel the thin, dark brown skin from the white coconut meat, using a paring knife or vegetable peeler.

6. Shred the coconut meat in a food processor or on the large holes of a four-sided grater.

Raghavan Ki Baaten

☼ The short, blunt-bladed knife designed for opening oyster shells works well for this job. Some people like to make crisscross cuts through the white meat down to the shell before they begin prying the meat from the shell. If you use this method, the pieces will come out in the size of your slices.

☼ Frozen unsweetened, freshly shredded coconut is available in Indian and some Asian grocery stores.

☼ When I demonstrate how to use my favorite grater (pictured on page 15), the students in my cooking classes always have a good laugh!

Chapter Two

Appetizers

Top, clockwise: Sweet-and-Sour Tamarind-Date Chutney (page 288), Vegetable Fritters (page 49), Tapioca Pearl Fritters (page 55), Red Onion Chutney (page 277); bottom, clockwise: Creamy Grilled Chicken on Skewers (page 67), Mint-Cilantro Chutney (page 284), Garlic-Potato Croquettes (page 58), Plantain Chips (page 63)

These vadaas are native to the southeastern region of India. They are often made during religious events as an offering to Lord Shiva, the destroyer of evil.

Pigeon Pea Fritters

Aamai Vadaas

ABOUT 18 FRITTERS (6 SERVINGS)

1 cup dried split and hulled pigeon peas (toovar dal) or yellow split peas (chana dal), sorted and rinsed

1 tablespoon dried yellow split peas (chana dal), sorted and rinsed

3 cups warm water

2 or 3 dried red Thai, serrano or cayenne chilies

2 or 3 fresh Thai, serrano or cayenne chilies

1 tablespoon coarsely chopped gingerroot

10 to 12 fresh karhi leaves, coarsely chopped (2 tablespoons), or 2 tablespoons chopped fresh cilantro

1 teaspoon salt

1/2 teaspoon asafetida (hing) or garlic powder

Vegetable oil for deep-frying

1. Place pigeon peas, yellow split peas, water, dried and fresh chilies in medium bowl. Soak at room temperature at least 2 hours or overnight.

2. Drain peas and chilies. Place peas, chilies and gingerroot in food processor. Cover and process until smooth and soft dough. Place pea mixture in medium bowl; stir in karhi leaves, salt and asafetida.

3. Heat oil (2 to 3 inches deep) in wok or Dutch oven over medium-high heat until thermometer inserted in oil reads 350°.

4. To shape each fritter, place measuring tablespoon of soft dough into hand. Form into 1/2-inch-thick patty. Carefully drop about 6 patties into hot oil and fry 3 to 5 minutes, turning occasionally, until golden brown. Remove with slotted spoon; drain on paper towels. Repeat with remaining patties.

5. Serve fritters as is or with Yogurt with Stewed Tomatoes (page 270).

Raghavan Ki Baaten

☀ **Split and hulled pigeon peas are found in any store that sells Indian groceries. They impart sweetness that balances the harshness of chilies.**

☀ **Asafetida is often used with lentils in this region, and not only for flavor—it helps reduce flatulence!**

3 Fritters: Calories 175 (Calories from Fat 125); Fat 14g (Saturated 2g); Cholesterol 0mg; Sodium 410mg; Carbohydrate 12g (Dietary Fiber 4g); Protein 4g **% Daily Value:** Vitamin A 44%; Vitamin C 24%; Calcium 0%; Iron 6% **Diet Exchanges:** 3 Vegetable, 2 Fat

Pakoras made with Garbanzo Bean Flour (Bésan) are found in every region in India. They are often served at teatime or with cocktails. The combination of spices used in this recipe is typical of blends found in North Indian homes. The baking soda lightens the batter.

Vegetable Fritters

Subzi Pakoras

ABOUT 48 FRITTERS (6 SERVINGS)

2 cups Garbanzo Bean Flour (Bésan), (page 44)

1 tablespoon mango powder (amchur) or juice of 1 medium lime (2 tablespoons)

1 teaspoon cumin seed, ground

1 teaspoon salt

1 teaspoon ground red pepper (cayenne)

1/4 teaspoon baking soda

1/4 teaspoon ground turmeric

3 medium red potatoes (1 pound), peeled and cut into 1/4-inch cubes

1 medium onion, finely chopped (1/2 cup)

1/2 medium green bell pepper, chopped (1/2 cup)

3/4 cup warm water

Vegetable oil for deep-frying

Vegetable Fritters are pictured on page 47.

1. Sift flour into medium bowl. Stir in mango powder, cumin, salt, ground red pepper, baking soda and turmeric.

2. Stir in potatoes, onion and bell pepper. Stir in water.

3. Heat oil (2 to 3 inches deep) in wok or Dutch oven over medium-high heat until thermometer inserted in oil reads 350°.

4. Drop batter by teaspoonfuls into hot oil and fry 3 to 5 minutes, turning occasionally, until golden brown. Remove with slotted spoon; drain on paper towels.

5. Serve fritters with a chutney of your choice (pages 277–89).

Raghavan Ki Baaten

☀ The nutty, slightly tart flavor of garbanzo bean flour is crucial to this recipe's success. If you have none in your pantry, check page 44 to make your own using dried garbanzo beans.

8 Fritters: Calories 195 (Calories from Fat 99); Fat 11g (Saturated 2g); Cholesterol 0mg; Sodium 340mg; Carbohydrate 23g (Dietary Fiber 4g); Protein 5g **% Daily Value:** Vitamin A 2%; Vitamin C 10%; Calcium 2%; Iron 8% **Diet Exchanges:** 1 1/2 Starch, 2 Fat

Weddings and similar auspicious celebrations in southern Indian households are savored over two or three days of music, dance, gossip, matchmaking and, of course, food! A full stomach is essential to start the day just right. The eager gatherers savor these delicious croquettes served on small banana leaves with Coconut Chutney (page 285).

Lime–Flavored Potato Croquettes

ABOUT 18 CROQUETTES (6 SERVINGS)

Potato Filling:

4 medium red potatoes (1 1/3 pounds), peeled and cooked

1 tablespoon vegetable oil

1 teaspoon black or yellow mustard seed

2 tablespoons dried split and hulled black lentils (urad dal) or yellow split peas (chana dal), sorted

1 teaspoon salt

1/4 teaspoon ground turmeric

Juice of 1 medium lime (2 tablespoons)

10 to 12 fresh karhi leaves, coarsely chopped (2 tablespoons), if desired

2 tablespoons finely chopped fresh cilantro

2 or 3 fresh Thai, serrano or cayenne chilies, finely chopped

Batter:

1 cup Garbanzo Bean Flour (Bésan), (page 44)

1/2 teaspoon salt

1/4 teaspoon baking soda

1/4 teaspoon ground turmeric

1/2 cup warm water

Vegetable oil for deep-frying

Coconut Chutney (page 285), if desired

MAKE POTATO FILLING:

1. Mash potatoes in medium bowl; set aside.

2. Heat oil and mustard seed in 6-inch skillet over medium-high heat. Once seed begins to pop, cover skillet and wait until popping stops. Add black lentils; stir-fry about 30 seconds or until golden brown. Remove from heat.

3. Stir in remaining filling ingredients. Add to potatoes; mix well. Shape into eighteen 1 1/2-inch balls; set aside.

MAKE BATTER:

1. Sift flour, salt, baking soda and turmeric into medium bowl. Beat in 1/2 cup water, using wire whisk, to make a smooth, pancake-like batter (add additional water if necessary).

MAKE CROQUETTES:

1. Heat oil (2 to 3 inches deep) in wok or Dutch oven over medium-high heat until thermometer inserted in oil reads 350°.

2. Dip up to 8 potato balls into batter to coat; carefully place in hot oil. Fry 5 to 7 minutes, turning occasionally, until golden brown. Remove with slotted spoon; drain on paper towels. Repeat with remaining potato balls.

3. Serve croquettes as is or with chutney.

3 Croquettes: Calories 130 (Calories from Fat 25); Fat 3g (Saturated 0g); Cholesterol 0mg; Sodium 650mg; Carbohydrate 27g (Dietary Fiber 5g); Protein 5g **% Daily Value:** Vitamin A 0%; Vitamin C 6%; Calcium 2%; Iron 8% **Diet Exchanges:** 1 Starch, 2 Vegetable

Lime-Flavored Potato Croquettes with Coconut Chutney (page 285)

Raghaven Ki Baaten

☀ Pay extra attention when popping mustard seed in hot oil because its flavor will be determined by its doneness. This seed is often called the "Dr. Jekyll and Mr. Hyde" of spices. When it is popped in hot oil (not unlike popcorn), it turns nutty and sweet, a technique essential to cooking the South Indian way. When the seeds are done popping, the skillet is either removed from the heat or additional ingredients are added to the hot oil to lower its temperature and retain the sweetness of the seeds. If the seed continues to cook at high temperatures, it becomes bitter and pungent, a flavor highly prized in eastern Indian kitchens.

Families in southeastern India pay tribute to Hanuman (the monkey god) by stringing a garland made of these fritters with the assistance of eager children. The fritters are shaped in the form of doughnuts, making them easier to string. These vadaas are also a staple in South Indian restaurants, often served with Pigeon Pea Stew (page 188), a savory stew of vegetables, lentils and chilies.

"Doughnut" Fritters

medu Vadaas

ABOUT 8 FRITTERS (4 SERVINGS)

1 cup dried split and hulled black lentils (urad dal), sorted, rinsed and drained

3 cups warm water

3 or 4 fresh Thai, serrano or cayenne chilies

1/2 teaspoon black peppercorns

1 tablespoon chopped gingerroot

1 teaspoon salt

10 to 12 fresh karhi leaves, coarsely chopped (2 tablespoons), or 2 tablespoons chopped fresh cilantro

Vegetable oil for deep-frying

Coconut Chutney (page 285), if desired

1. Place lentils, water and chilies in medium bowl. Soak at room temperature at least 2 hours or overnight.

2. Drain lentils and chilies. Place lentils, chilies, peppercorns and gingerroot in food processor or blender. (If using blender, add small amount of water so mixture is soft and moist.) Cover and process until smooth. Place lentil mixture in medium bowl; beat with spoon 3 to 5 minutes or until light and fluffy. Stir in salt and karhi leaves.

3. Heat oil (2 to 3 inches deep) in wok or Dutch oven over medium-high heat until thermometer inserted in oil reads 350°.

4. Grease palms of hands with additional oil. Place 2 tablespoons lentil mixture in hand; shape into 1/2-inch-thick patties. With finger, poke a hole through the center of patties, making a doughnut-like shape. Carefully drop into hot oil and fry 3 to 5 minutes, turning occasionally, until golden brown. Remove with slotted spoon; drain on paper towels. Repeat with remaining lentil mixture.

5. Serve fritters as is or with chutney.

Shaping Friters

Shape lentil mixture into patty on greased hand.

With finger, poke hole through center to make a doughnut shape.

2 Fritters: Calories 250 (Calories from Fat 125); Fat 14g (Saturated 2g); Cholesterol 0mg; Sodium 590mg; Carbohydrate 29g (Dietary Fiber 11g); Protein 12g **% Daily Value:** Vitamin A 22%; Vitamin C 38%; Calcium 2%; Iron 26% **Diet Exchanges:** 2 Starch, 1 Very Lean Meat, 1 1/2 Fat

"Doughnut" Fritters, Coconut Chutney (page 285), Spiced Buttermilk (page 319)

Raghavan Ki Baaten

☼ The earthy, sourdough-like flavor of split and hulled black lentils is crucial to this recipe's success, so substituting another lentil will not give you the same results.

☼ Batter can be tightly covered and refrigerated up to 2 days. Freezing is not recommended because it increases the batter's water content when thawed, making it very difficult to handle.

In households in Gujarat and Mumbai (Bombay), this special appetizer is a particular favorite.

Split Green Lentil Fritters

Mung Dal Bhujiyas

ABOUT 42 FRITTERS (7 SERVINGS)

1 cup dried split and hulled green lentils (mung dal) or red lentils (masoor dal), sorted, rinsed and drained

3 cups warm water

1 tablespoon chopped gingerroot

2 or 3 fresh Thai, serrano or cayenne chilies

2 tablespoons chopped fresh cilantro

3/4 teaspoon salt

1/2 teaspoon Bishop's weed (ajwain)

1/4 teaspoon baking soda

Vegetable oil for deep-frying

Sweet-and-Hot Mango Pickle (page 273), if desired

1. Place lentils and water in medium bowl. Soak at room temperature 20 to 30 minutes.

2. Drain lentils. Place lentils, gingerroot and chilies in food processor. Cover and process until smooth. Place lentil mixture in medium bowl; stir in remaining ingredients except oil.

3. Heat oil (2 to 3 inches deep) in wok or Dutch oven over medium-high heat until thermometer inserted in oil reads 350°.

4. Drop lentil mixture by teaspoonfuls into hot oil and fry 2 to 3 minutes, turning occasionally, until golden brown. Remove with slotted spoon; drain on paper towels.

5. Serve fritters as is or with pickle.

Raghavan Ki Baaten

☀ **Bishop's weed**, also known as *ajwain*, is commonly available in stores that stock Indian groceries. In a pinch, you have two substitution choices: Use dried thyme leaves; or combine 1 teaspoon dried oregano leaves, 1 teaspoon celery seed and 1/4 teaspoon coarsely ground black pepper, and use the same amount of this mixture as the amount of Bishop's weed called for in the recipe.

6 Fritters: Calories 205 (Calories from Fat 125); Fat 14g (Saturated 2g); Cholesterol mg; Sodium 350mg; Carbohydrate 19g (Dietary Fiber 7g); Protein 8g **% Daily Value:** Vitamin A 14%; Vitamin C 24%; Calcium 4%; Iron 2% **Diet Exchanges:** 1 Starch, 1 Vegetable, 2 1/2 Fat

In the state of Maharashtra, home of Mumbai (Bombay), cooks serve an extensive repertoire of dishes made with tapioca pearls—not just dessert. In fact, tapioca pearls are much appreciated for their characteristic of blending well with many diverse flavors and textures.

Tapioca Pearl Fritters

Sabudana Chi Vadaas

ABOUT 30 FRITTERS (10 SERVINGS)

1 cup uncooked tapioca pearls (sabudana)

1/4 cup hot water

1/2 cup chopped fresh cilantro

4 to 6 fresh Thai, serrano or cayenne chilies

3 thin slices gingerroot

4 medium red potatoes (1 1/3 pounds), peeled, cooked and mashed

1/4 cup dry-roasted unsalted peanuts, coarsely chopped

1 teaspoon salt

1 teaspoon Spicy Garam Masaala (page 34)

Vegetable oil for deep-frying

Roasted-Garlic Chutney (page 286), if desired

Tapioca Pearl Fritters are pictured on page 47.

1. Place tapioca in large bowl; add enough cold water to cover. Rub tapioca gently between fingers; drain. Repeat 4 or 5 times until water is clear; drain. Add 1/4 cup hot water; soak about 30 minutes or until pearls swell up and soften. Set aside.

2. Place cilantro, chilies and gingerroot in food processor. Cover and process until finely ground. Stir into tapioca.

3. Stir in remaining ingredients except oil. Divide dough into 30 pieces. Shape each piece into a 1 1/2-inch ball; set aside.

4. Heat oil (2 to 3 inches deep) in wok or Dutch oven over medium-high heat until thermometer inserted in oil reads 350°.

5. Carefully drop about 10 balls into hot oil and fry 2 to 3 minutes, gently turning occasionally, until golden brown. Do not overcook or fritters will burst open. Remove with slotted spoon; drain on paper towels.

6. Serve fritters as is or with chutney.

Raghavan Ki Baaten

☀ Tapioca (sago), a starch, is processed from the root of the cassava plant. Pushing the sturdy mixture through molds yields its pearl-like shape. The Indian tapioca pearl is often larger in size than its Southeast Asian counterpart. Either one will work for this recipe. In the United States, tapioca pearls are widely available in natural-food stores, supermarkets and Asian grocery stores. For a beautiful and colorful fritter, try one of the pastel-colored pearls available in Asian stores.

3 Fritters: Calories 200 (Calories from Fat 90); Fat 10g (Saturated 1g); Cholesterol 0mg; Sodium 240mg; Carbohydrate 26g (Dietary Fiber 2g); Protein 2g **% Daily Value:** Vitamin A 18%; Vitamin C 32%; Calcium 2%; Iron 4% **Diet Exchanges:** 1 Starch, 1/2 Fruit, 2 Fat

Banana Fritters

Vazhaipazham Pakoras (handwritten)

ABOUT 12 FRITTERS (4 SERVINGS)

1 cup Garbanzo Bean Flour (Bésan), (page 44)

2 tablespoons chopped fresh cilantro

1/2 teaspoon salt

1/2 teaspoon ground red pepper (cayenne)

1/4 teaspoon ground turmeric

1/2 cup water

3 large firm bananas (1 1/2 pounds), peeled and cut into 2-inch pieces

Vegetable oil for deep-frying

Ridged-Squash Chutney (page 282), if desired

1. Sift flour into medium bowl. Stir in cilantro, salt, ground red pepper and turmeric. Stir in water until smooth.

2. Heat oil (2 to 3 inches deep) in wok or Dutch oven over medium-high heat until thermometer inserted in oil reads 350°.

3. Dip banana pieces in batter to coat. Carefully drop 4 to 5 battered banana pieces into hot oil and fry 3 to 5 minutes, turning occasionally, until golden brown. Remove with slotted spoon; drain on paper towels. Repeat with remaining banana pieces.

4. Serve fritters with chutney.

3 Fritters: Calories 275 (Calories from Fat 135); Fat 15g (Saturated 2g); Cholesterol 0mg; Sodium 300mg; Carbohydrate 36g (Dietary Fiber 6g); Protein 5g **% Daily Value:** Vitamin A 2%; Vitamin C 8%; Calcium 2%; Iron 8% **Diet Exchanges:** 1/2 Starch, 2 Fruit, 2 1/2 Fat

Banana Fritters, Ridged-Squash Chutney (page 282)

Raghavan Ki Baaten

☀ Firm bananas, those that have a slightly green tinge to the peel, will turn
soft and sweet when cooked. The spicy garbanzo bean flour batter adds
to the sweetness of the bananas. For the more adventurous palate, double
the ground red pepper, and watch the sparks fly!

There is a community of people called Sindhis who live in the northwestern region of India. They are extremely hospitable and often welcome guests with one of their signature appetizers, garlic-potato croquettes.

Garlic-Potato Croquettes

Aloo Ki Tikkis

ABOUT 18 CROQUETTES (6 SERVINGS)

3 medium red potatoes (1 pound), peeled and cooked

10 slices firm white bread (about 1/2 inch thick)

4 cups warm water

1 cup chopped fresh cilantro

4 to 6 fresh Thai, serrano or cayenne chilies

3 large cloves garlic

1 teaspoon salt

1 teaspoon Garam Masaala (page 32)

Vegetable oil for deep-frying

Mint-Cilantro Chutney (page 284), if desired

1. Mash potatoes in medium bowl; set aside.

2. Dip bread slices into warm water just until moist. Immediately remove slices and press between palms of hands, squeezing the water out completely. Add bread to potatoes.

3. Place cilantro, chilies and garlic in food processor. Cover and process until finely ground. Add to potato-bread mixture. Add salt and Garam Masaala; mix well.

4. Knead potato-bread mixture in bowl 3 to 5 minutes to form a compact, slightly sticky dough.

5. Heat oil (2 to 3 inches deep) in wok or Dutch oven over medium-high heat until thermometer inserted in oil reads 350°.

6. Grease palms of hands with additional oil. Divide dough into 18 pieces. Shape each piece into a ball; flatten ball into 1/2-inch patty. Set aside.

7. Carefully drop about half of the patties into hot oil and fry 3 to 5 minutes, turning occasionally, until golden brown. Remove with slotted spoon; drain on paper towels.

8. Serve croquettes as is or with chutney.

Raghavan Ki Baaten

☀ **An interesting technique to note is making dough with slices of moistened bread. Do not use flavored breads, as they will interfere with the robust flavors of the herbs and spices. Plain, firm white bread is ideal for this recipe; however, I do not recommend using very soft white bread because the croquettes will become gummy.**

3 Croquettes: Calories 365 (Calories from Fat 145); Fat 16g (Saturated 3g); Cholesterol 0mg; Sodium 780mg; Carbohydrate 50g (Dietary Fiber 3g); Protein 8g **% Daily Value:** Vitamin A 30%; Vitamin C 52%; Calcium 10%; Iron 16% **Diet Exchanges:** 3 Starch, 3 Fat

Indians believe in never wasting food and creatively use every leftover morsel. Gujaratis, from the northwestern state of Gujarat, are well known for their imaginative approach to vegetarian cooking, as is evidenced by this transformation of yesterday's steamed rice. Peanuts are native to Gujarat and take a prominent place in many of its recipes, providing a vital source of protein in addition to tasty crunch.

Griddle Rice Croquettes
Chawal Nu Theplas

ABOUT 18 CROQUETTES (6 SERVINGS)

1 cup cold cooked white rice

1 cup finely chopped red onion

1/2 cup dry-roasted unsalted peanuts, coarsely chopped

1/2 cup chopped fresh cilantro

1 tablespoon coarsely chopped gingerroot

4 to 6 fresh Thai, serrano or cayenne chilies

1 teaspoon salt

8 slices firm white bread (about 1/2 inch thick)

4 cups warm water

Vegetable oil for deep-frying

Chutney of your choice (pages 277–89)

1. Mix rice, onion and peanuts in large bowl.

2. Place cilantro, gingerroot and chilies in food processor. Cover and process until finely ground. Add cilantro mixture and salt to rice mixture; mix well.

3. Dip bread slices into warm water just until moist. Immediately remove slices and press between palms of hands, squeezing the water out completely. Add bread to rice mixture, mixing well to form a compact, slightly sticky dough.

4. Grease palms of hands with oil. Divide dough into 18 pieces. Shape each piece into a 1/2-inch-thick patty; set aside.

5. Heat 2 tablespoons oil in 10-inch skillet over medium-high heat. Place patties in skillet without overcrowding. Cook 10 to 14 minutes, turning once, until golden. Remove from skillet; drain on paper towels. Repeat with remaining patties, adding oil as needed.

6. Serve croquettes as is or with a chutney.

3 Croquettes: Calories 335 (Calories from Fat 190); Fat 21g (Saturated 3g); Cholesterol 0mg; Sodium 700mg; Carbohydrate 43g (Dietary Fiber 3g); Protein 9g **% Daily Value:** Vitamin A 28%; Vitamin C 50%; Calcium 8%; Iron 14% **Diet Exchanges:** 3 Starch, 3 Fat

Stuffed Vegetable Cutlets

Raghavan Ki Baaten

☀ These cutlets can be assembled up to 2 days ahead and fried just before serving. While you are making the second batch, keep the first batch warm in a 250° oven.

The evidence of India's colonial years under Britain's regime still lingers, and teatime snacks are an obvious product of this English influence. One of the most common teatime snacks is a delicious medley of spiced vegetables, stuffed into breaded potato shells, rolled in bread crumbs and cooked until golden brown. In the elegant dining cars of trains, waiters with elbow-length lily-white gloves often serve these cutlets accompanied by tomato ketchup.

Stuffed Vegetable Cutlets
Angrezi Kabobs

8 CUTLETS (8 SERVINGS)

Potato Shells:
3 medium red potatoes (1 pound), peeled and cooked

12 to 15 slices firm white bread (about 1/2 inch thick)

4 cups warm water

1 teaspoon salt

1 teaspoon vegetable oil

Filling:
1 tablespoon vegetable oil

1 teaspoon cumin seed

1/2 cup finely chopped red onion

1 tablespoon chopped gingerroot

2 medium cloves garlic, finely chopped

2 medium red potatoes (2/3 pound), peeled and cut into 1/4-inch cubes

1 medium carrot, finely chopped (1/2 cup)

1/2 cup frozen green peas

1/4 cup chopped fresh cilantro

2 tablespoons mango powder (amchur) or 1 tablespoon lime or lemon juice

1 teaspoon salt

1 teaspoon cumin seed, ground

1 teaspoon ground red pepper (cayenne)

1/4 cup water

Coating:
1 egg, slightly beaten

1 cup plain dry bread crumbs

Vegetable oil for brushing

Ketchup, if desired

MAKE POTATO SHELLS:

1. Mash potatoes in large bowl; set aside.

2. Dip bread slices into warm water just until moist. Immediately remove slices and press between palms of hands, squeezing the water out completely. Add bread and salt to potatoes. Knead potato-bread mixture in bowl 2 to 3 minutes to make smooth dough. (If dough is too sticky, add 2 to 3 **dry** bread slices, torn into small pieces.) Brush dough with 1 teaspoon oil; cover and set aside.

MAKE FILLING:

1. Heat 1 tablespoon oil in wok or deep 12-inch skillet over medium-high heat. Add whole cumin seed; sizzle 30 seconds.

2. Add onion, gingerroot and garlic; stir-fry 2 to 3 minutes or until onion is golden brown.

3. Stir in remaining filling ingredients except water; stir-fry 1 to 2 minutes. Stir in water; reduce heat. Cover and simmer 10 to 15 minutes or until potatoes are tender. If there is water in bottom of wok, remove lid and simmer 1 to 2 minutes longer or until water evaporates completely; remove from heat. Cool 20 minutes.

continues

1 Cutlet: Calories 320 (Calories from Fat 55); Fat 6g (Saturated 1g); Cholesterol 25mg; Sodium 1,070mg; Carbohydrate 60g (Dietary Fiber 4g); Protein 10g **% Daily Value:** Vitamin A 14%; Vitamin C 6%; Calcium 12%; Iron 18% **Diet Exchanges:** 3 Starch, 3 Vegetable, 1/2 Fat

Statue of a goddess

continued

ASSEMBLE CUTLETS:

1. Divide dough into 8 pieces. Press or roll each piece into 6-inch circle on a lightly floured surface. Spoon about 1/4 cup filling onto center of each circle. Carefully fold dough over filling to make a half-circle; pinch edges or press with fork to seal securely.

2. Brush vegetable oil in 12-inch skillet and heat over medium heat. Coat cutlets with beaten egg; coat with bread crumbs. Place 4 cutlets in skillet without overcrowding. Cook 16 to 20 minutes, turning once, until shells are golden brown and filling is warm. Remove from skillet. Brush skillet with additional vegetable oil; repeat with remaining 4 cutlets.

3. Serve cutlets with ketchup.

Often served by street vendors in Mumbai (Bombay) and Chennai (Madras), these plantain chips are hard to stop eating once you sample them.

Plantain Chips

Vazhaipazham Varuval

ABOUT 2 CUPS (4 SERVINGS)

Vegetable oil for
deep-frying

2 large green
plantains, peeled and
cut into 1/4-inch slices
(4 cups)

1/2 teaspoon salt

1/2 teaspoon
black peppercorns,
crushed

Juice of 1 medium
lime (2 tablespoons)

1. Heat oil (2 to 3 inches deep) in wok or Dutch oven over medium-high heat until thermometer inserted in oil reads 350°.

2. Carefully place about half of the plantain slices in hot oil and fry 4 to 5 minutes, turning occasionally, until golden brown. Remove with slotted spoon; drain on paper towels. Repeat with remaining plantains.

3. Place fried chips in medium bowl. Add salt and pepper; toss gently. Drizzle with lime juice; toss gently.

Raghavan Ki Baaten

☀ Plantains are those large bananas that are now available in most supermarkets. When the peel is green to yellow, the flesh is bland in flavor and starchy like a potato. That is why they are perfect for crisp fried chips.

☀ A plantain may look like a banana, but it can't be peeled like one. The best way is to wash the plantain first. Then, cut it crosswise into several pieces. For each piece, cut through the peel lengthwise, then remove the peel from around the flesh.

1/2 Cup: Calories 190 (Calories from Fat 35); Fat 4g (Saturated 1g); Cholesterol 0mg; Sodium 300mg; Carbohydrate 40g (Dietary Fiber 3g); Protein 1g **% Daily Value:** Vitamin A 12%; Vitamin C 12%; Calcium 0%; Iron 4% **Diet Exchanges:** 2 1/2 Fruit, 1 Fat

Grilled Ground Lamb on Skewers

seekh kabobs

12 KABOBS (6 SERVINGS)

1 pound ground lamb, turkey, chicken or beef

1/2 cup ground blanched almonds

1/2 cup finely chopped red onion

1 teaspoon salt

1 teaspoon ground cardamom

1 teaspoon ground cumin

3/4 teaspoon black peppercorns, ground

2 tablespoons chopped fresh cilantro

5 medium cloves garlic, finely chopped

12 six- or eight-inch bamboo* or metal skewers

Mint-Cilantro Chutney (page 284), if desired

When using bamboo skewers, soak in water at least 30 minutes before using to prevent burning.

1. Heat coals or gas grill for direct heat. Mix all ingredients except skewers in large bowl.

2. Divide lamb mixture into 12 equal parts. Shape each part around a skewer, pressing the mixture with your hands to cover half the length of the skewer.

3. Cover and grill kabobs 4 to 5 inches from medium heat 13 to 15 minutes, turning skewers occasionally to ensure even browning, until lamb is no longer pink in center.

4. Serve kabobs as is or with chutney.

To Broil: Set oven control to broil. Place kabobs on rack in broiler pan. Broil with tops 2 to 3 inches from heat 13 to 15 minutes, turning skewers occasionally to ensure even browning, until lamb is no longer pink in center.

2 Kabobs: Calories 205 (Calories from Fat 135); Fat 15g (Saturated 5g); Cholesterol 45mg; Sodium 430mg; Carbohydrate 4g (Dietary Fiber 1g); Protein 14g **% Daily Value:** Vitamin A 0%; Vitamin C 0%; Calcium 4%; Iron 8% **Diet Exchanges:** 2 Medium-Fat Meat, 1 Vegetable, 1 Fat

Grilled Ground Lamb on Skewers, Mint-Cilantro Chutney (page 284)

Raghavan Ki Baaten

☀ This popular street food is often served with Mint-Cilantro Chutney
(page 284), and for a little extra money, a simple salad of raw red onion,
chilies and cilantro with wedges of lime. If you like, add these simple
accompaniments when serving kabobs.

Grilled Tandoori-Style Lamb Kabobs

Mutton Kabobs

8 KABOBS (8 SERVINGS)

1 pound lamb, beef or pork boneless loin, cut into 2-inch cubes

1/2 cup plain yogurt (regular or fat-free)

1/4 cup chopped fresh cilantro

1 tablespoon coriander seed, ground

5 medium cloves garlic, finely chopped

1 teaspoon salt

1 teaspoon ground red pepper (cayenne)

1 teaspoon cumin seed, ground

1 teaspoon Garam Masaala (page 32)

8 six- or eight-inch bamboo* or metal skewers

Mint-Cilantro Chutney (page 284), if desired

When using bamboo skewers, soak in water at least 30 minutes before using to prevent burning.

1. Mix all ingredients except skewers in mixing bowl. Cover and refrigerate at least 2 hours but no longer than 24 hours.

2. Heat coals or gas grill for direct heat. Thread lamb pieces on skewers, leaving space between each piece.

3. Cover and grill kabobs 4 to 5 inches from medium heat 7 to 8 minutes, turning skewers occasionally to ensure even browning, until lamb is slightly pink in center.

4. Serve kabobs as is or with chutney.

To Broil: Set oven control to broil. Place kabobs on rack in broiler pan. Broil with tops 2 to 3 inches from heat 7 to 8 minutes, turning skewers occasionally to ensure even browning, until lamb is slightly pink in center.

Raghavan Ki Baaten

☼ **Mutton in India can be meat from a mature goat or lamb, and is often tough, requiring a marinating period to tenderize its tough tendons. Tender baby or spring lamb is often a better and more readily available substitute.**

1 Kabob: Calories 95 (Calories from Fat 35); Fat 4g (Saturated 2g); Cholesterol 40mg; Sodium 340mg; Carbohydrate 2g (Dietary Fiber 0g); Protein 13g **% Daily Value:** Vitamin A 0%; Vitamin C 0%; Calcium 4%; Iron 6% **Diet Exchanges:** 2 Very Lean Meat, 1/2 Fat

These creamy kabobs are traditionally cooked in a tandoor, a bell-shaped, clay-lined oven, in rural villages in northern India and in restaurants that specialize in foods from this region. But grilling or broiling will also give great results.

Creamy Grilled Chicken on Skewers

Malai Kabobs

16 KABOBS (8 SERVINGS)

1 pound boneless, skinless chicken breasts or turkey breast, cut into 4 × 1-inch strips

1/4 cup half-and-half

1 tablespoon coriander seed, ground

1 tablespoon finely chopped gingerroot

1 tablespoon chopped fresh cilantro

1 teaspoon cumin seed, ground

2 medium cloves garlic, finely chopped

1/2 teaspoon salt

1/2 teaspoon ground red pepper (cayenne)

1/2 teaspoon Garam Masaala (page 32)

16 six- or eight-inch bamboo* or metal skewers

Mint-Cilantro Chutney (page 284), if desired

*When using bamboo skewers, soak in water at least 30 minutes before using to prevent burning.

1. Mix all ingredients except skewers in medium bowl. Cover and refrigerate at least 2 hours but no longer than 24 hours.

2. Heat coals or gas grill for direct heat. Thread each chicken strip lengthwise, accordion-style, on skewer.

3. Cover and grill kabobs 4 to 5 inches from medium heat 5 to 7 minutes, turning skewers occasionally to ensure even browning, until chicken is no longer pink in center.

4. Serve kabobs as is or with chutney.

To Broil: Set oven control to broil. Place kabobs on rack in broiler pan. Broil with tops 2 to 3 inches from heat 5 to 7 minutes, turning skewers occasionally to ensure even browning, until chicken is no longer pink in center.

2 Kabobs: Calories 85 (Calories from Fat 25); Fat 3g (Saturated 1g); Cholesterol 35mg; Sodium 180mg; Carbohydrate 1g (Dietary Fiber 0g); Protein 13g **% Daily Value:** Vitamin A 0%; Vitamin C 0%; Calcium 2%; Iron 4% **Diet Exchanges:** 1 Very Lean Meat, 1/2 Fat

Pastry Shells with Spiced Potatoes, Mint-Cilantro Chutney (page 284), Sweet-and-Sour Tamarind-Date Chutney (page 288)

Raghavan Ki Baaten

☀ It's best to work on one round of dough at a time and keep the remainder in the fridge. Chilled dough will be a little stiff to roll out at first, but it's much easier to shape it into triangles.

☀ Leftover fried *samosas* can be frozen for up to a month. Thaw *samosas* overnight in refrigerator before heating. To heat, place on a cookie sheet and warm in a 300° oven for 10 to 12 minutes or until centers of *samosas* are hot.

Samosas, *a street food favorite, are a substantial snack often consumed in India between meals or for tea. Punjabi refers to this snack's origin in the northern state of Punjab, the wheat-growing capital of India. Every region of India has its own variation of samosa, made with a different outer shell. Indians in the northwestern states prefer their wrappers paperthin, similar to egg roll skins. Punjabi samosa wrappers are flaky and thicker, like pastry crusts in Europe and the United States.*

Pastry Shells with Spiced Potatoes

Punjabi samosas

20 PASTRY SHELLS (10 SERVINGS)

Pastry Dough:
2 cups all-purpose flour

1/4 teaspoon salt

1/2 cup chilled butter, cut into thin slices

1/2 cup cold water

Filling:
2 tablespoons vegetable oil

1 teaspoon cumin seed

1 medium onion, finely chopped (1/2 cup)

1 tablespoon finely chopped gingerroot

3 medium red potatoes (1 pound), peeled, cooked and cut into 1/4-inch cubes

1 cup frozen green peas, thawed

1/4 cup chopped fresh cilantro

1 tablespoon coriander seed, ground

1 tablespoon mango powder (amchur) or 1 tablespoon lime or lemon juice

2 or 3 fresh Thai, serrano or cayenne chilies, finely chopped

1 teaspoon cumin seed, ground

1 teaspoon salt

Vegetable oil for deep-frying

Mint-Cilantro Chutney (page 284) and Sweet-and-Sour Tamarind-Date Chutney (page 288), if desired

MAKE PASTRY DOUGH:

1. Mix flour and salt in medium bowl. Cut in butter, using pastry blender or rubbing mixture between palms of hands, until mixture looks like coarse bread crumbs.

2. Add water, 2 tablespoons at a time, mixing by hand or with wooden spoon. Continue adding enough water to bring dough together into a ball that is neither sticky nor dry. Knead in bowl or on lightly floured surface 2 to 3 minutes or until dough is smooth. Roll dough into 2-inch-thick log. Cover with plastic wrap and refrigerate at least 30 minutes but no longer than 2 days.

MAKE FILLING:

1. Heat 2 tablespoons oil in wok or deep 12-inch skillet over medium-high heat. Add whole cumin seed; sizzle 30 seconds.

2. Stir in onion and gingerroot. Cook 2 to 3 minutes, stirring constantly, until onion is golden brown.

3. Stir in remaining ingredients except oil; remove from heat. Cool completely, 20 to 30 minutes.

ASSEMBLE SAMOSAS:

1. Cut dough into 10 slices. Work with only one slice of dough at a time; cover and refrigerate remaining dough. Roll each slice of dough on lightly floured surface into a 6-inch circle.

2. Cut each dough circle in half. Spoon slightly less than 2 tablespoons filling onto center of each half; do not overfill or pastry will burst. Brush edges with water. Fold each half over filling to form a triangle; press edges together to seal completely. Seal dough completely, or the filling will leak out when fried.

continues

2 Samosas: Calories 325 (Calories from Fat 200); Fat 22g (Saturated 8g); Cholesterol 25mg; Sodium 370mg; Carbohydrate 31g (Dietary Fiber 3g); Protein 4g **% Daily Value:** Vitamin A 16%; Vitamin C 18%; Calcium 2%; Iron 10% **Diet Exchanges:** 2 Starch, 4 Fat

continued

Place on floured plate to prevent sticking while working with remaining dough. Repeat with remaining dough. (Samosas can be assembled up to 2 hours before frying; refrigerate uncovered on a plate or cookie sheet generously dusted with flour.)

3. Heat oil (2 to 3 inches deep) in wok or Dutch oven over medium-high heat until thermometer inserted in oil reads 350°.

4. Carefully place samosas in hot oil without overcrowding and fry 4 to 6 minutes, turning occasionally, until golden brown. Remove with slotted spoon; drain on paper towels.

5. Serve samosas as is or with chutneys.

Peanuts are called groundnuts in India, because the plants bend down toward the earth when they flower to bury their pods containing the nuts. Peanuts are grown in the northwestern region and usually abound in the markets during the monsoon season—June through September. Freshly picked peanuts are cooked in their shells in boiling salted water, cooled and eaten as a tasty snack with a tall glass of ice-cold beer, cup of hot Chai (page 316) or scotch, straight up.

Fresh-Roasted Spiced Peanuts

Mungphali masaala

ABOUT 2 1/4 CUPS (9 SERVINGS)

1 tablespoon peanut or vegetable oil

1 teaspoon cumin seed

2 cups raw blanched Spanish peanuts

1 medium onion, finely chopped (1/2 cup)

2 tablespoons finely chopped fresh cilantro

1 tablespoon sugar

1 teaspoon salt

1/2 teaspoon ground red pepper (cayenne)

1/4 teaspoon ground turmeric

1. Heat oil in wok or Dutch oven over medium heat. Add cumin seed; sizzle 10 to 15 seconds.

2. Add peanuts; stir-fry 6 to 8 minutes or until brown.

3. Stir in remaining ingredients. Stir-fry 3 to 4 minutes or until onion is golden brown. Serve warm or room temperature.

Raghavan Ki Baaten

☀ Raw blanched Spanish peanuts can be found in many supermarkets, natural food stores or food co-ops. For a variation, mix in 1/2 cup golden raisins with the roasted peanuts for a sweeter flavor. Pass wedges of fresh lime to add a tart flavor to the snack.

1/4 Cup: Calories 320 (Calories from Fat 235); Fat 26g (Saturated 4g); Cholesterol 0mg; Sodium 400mg; Carbohydrate 13g (Dietary Fiber 4g); Protein 13g **% Daily Value:** Vitamin A 0%; Vitamin C 0%; Calcium 4%; Iron 6% **Diet Exchanges:** 1 Starch, 1 1/2 High-Fat Meat, 2 Fat

The southerners call them pappadums *and the rest of the nation refers to them as papads, but these wafer-thin crackers, made with assorted lentil flours, are a must in every household in India. A great snack or a good substitute for bread, these are often flavored with cumin, garlic, black pepper, ground red pepper (cayenne) or green chilies.*

Spiced Lentil Wafers

Masala Pappadums

8 WAFERS (8 SERVINGS)

2 medium red potatoes (2/3 pound), peeled, cooked and cut into 1/2-inch cubes (2 cups)

1 medium tomato, finely chopped (3/4 cup)

1/2 cup finely chopped red onion

2 tablespoons finely chopped fresh cilantro

Juice of 1 medium lime (2 tablespoons)

1 teaspoon salt

2 fresh Thai, serrano or cayenne chilies, finely chopped

8 pappadums (any flavor), at least 4 inches in diameter

1. Mix all ingredients except pappadums in medium bowl; set aside.

2. Place 1 pappadum in the microwave. Microwave uncovered on High 30 to 45 seconds or until pappadum puffs up and is golden brown. Cool 1 to 2 minutes. Repeat with remaining pappadums. (Pappadums can also be deep-fried, following package directions.)

3. To assemble, spread 1/4 cup potato mixture on each pappadum.

1 Wafer: Calories 45 (Calories from Fat 0); Fat 0g (Saturated 0g); Cholesterol 0mg; Sodium 430mg; Carbohydrate 13g (Dietary Fiber 2g); Protein 3g **% Daily Value:** Vitamin A 12%; Vitamin C 24%; Calcium 2%; Iron 12% **Diet Exchanges:** 1/2 Starch, 1 Vegetable

Spiced Lentil Wafers

Raghavan Ki Baaten

☀ *Pappadums* are available in the ethnic-food section of supermarkets, natural-food stores and specialty stores. Indian grocery stores often carry hundreds of varieties, and half the fun is trying them all. They can be fried, baked, broiled, flame roasted (often the case in India) or cooked in a microwave.

☀ The regional influences usually dictate which lentil flour is used to prepare the papads. The South uses split and hulled black lentils *(urad dal)*, while the Gujaratis of the Northwest use split and hulled green lentils *(mung dal)*. *Papads* are also made with tapioca pearls, rice flour or even potato starch.

A delightfully spicy variation of unflavored Paneer (page 42), this cheese can be served in many ways: as is; cut into strips, dipped in batter and fried until golden brown; or brushed with oil and grilled or broiled until brown.

Spiced Homemade Cheese

Masala Paneer

8 SERVINGS

1/4 cup finely chopped red onion

1/4 cup finely chopped fresh mint leaves

1 teaspoon salt

1 teaspoon ground red pepper (cayenne)

1 teaspoon roasted cumin seed, ground (page 31)

1/2 gallon (8 cups) whole milk

3 tablespoons white vinegar

1 large lime, cut into 8 wedges

Mint-Cilantro Chutney (page 284), if desired

1. Mix all ingredients except milk, vinegar and lime in small bowl; set aside.

2. Heat milk to boiling in 3-quart saucepan over medium-high heat, stirring frequently to prevent scorching.

3. Stir in vinegar; turn off heat. The milk will immediately separate into curds and whey.

4. Line large colander with cheesecloth or muslin; place in sink. Pour curds and whey mixture into lined colander. Lift edges of cloth; swirl in sink once or twice to remove excess liquid. Add onion mixture to curds in cheesecloth; mix well. Completely wrap curds in cloth; return to colander. Place a large heavy Dutch oven, stockpot or large jar filled with water or similar weight directly on curds. Leave undisturbed in sink 5 to 6 hours to drain.

5. Remove weight and remove cheese to cutting board; discard cheesecloth. Cut cheese into 2 × 1/2-inch strips. Serve with lime wedges and chutney.

1 Serving: Calories 155 (Calories from Fat 70); Fat 8g (Saturated 5g); Cholesterol 35mg; Sodium 420mg; Carbohydrate 13g (Dietary Fiber 0g); Protein 8g **% Daily Value:** Vitamin A 6%; Vitamin C 8%; Calcium 30%; Iron 2% **Diet Exchanges:** 1 Skim Milk, 1 1/2 Fat

Raghavan Ki Baaten

☀ This tasty treat can be made ahead. Cover it tightly and refrigerate up to 1 week or freeze up to 2 months. Thaw in the refrigerator about 8 hours before using.

☀ If you are lucky to have succulent homegrown tomatoes, slice them thin and serve along with slices or cubes of *paneer* for a refreshingly light lunch or snack. Make sure you offer wedges of fresh lime to squeeze over the tomatoes and cheese for extra zip.

Chapter Three

Meat, Fish and Poultry

Clockwise from top: Butter Chicken (page 105), Basmati Rice with Green Peas (page 205), Fish Poached with Coconut Milk (page 81), Marinated Grilled Shrimp (page 85), Whole Wheat Unleavened Breads (page 236)

The next time you succumb to your fish-and-chips craving, try this fried fish instead, dipped in a delightfully spiced batter of garbanzo bean flour. Serve Plantain Chips (page 63) as an alternative to the traditional fried potato "chips."

Battered Spiced Fish

Bésan Muchee

4 SERVINGS

Vegetable oil for deep-frying

1 cup Garbanzo Bean Flour (Bésan), (page 44)

2 tablespoons chopped fresh cilantro

1 tablespoon Bishop's weed (ajwain), if desired

1 teaspoon salt

1 teaspoon ground red pepper (cayenne)

1/4 teaspoon ground turmeric

1/2 cup water

5 medium cloves garlic, finely chopped

4 pollock, halibut, monkfish or other firm fish fillets (6 ounces each), skin removed

1 lime or lemon, cut into wedges

1. Heat oil (2 to 3 inches deep) in wok or Dutch oven over medium-high heat until thermometer inserted in oil reads 350°.

2. Meanwhile, sift flour into medium bowl. Stir in cilantro, Bishop's weed, salt, ground red pepper and turmeric. Stir in water and garlic until smooth.

3. Dip fish fillets into batter. Carefully drop battered fillets into hot oil and fry 5 to 7 minutes, turning occasionally, until golden brown. Remove with slotted spoon; drain on paper towels. Serve with lime wedges.

Raghavan Ki Baaten

☀ **Vegetable oil cannot be reused once fish and meats are fried in it; the oil may become fishy tasting, and meat's high water content lowers oil's smoke point (the temperature at which oil starts to smoke).**

1 Serving: Calories 295 (Calories from Fat 145); Fat 16g (Saturated 3g); Cholesterol 80mg; Sodium 570mg; Carbohydrate 9g (Dietary Fiber 3g); Protein 32g **% Daily Value:** Vitamin A 2%; Vitamin C 0%; Calcium 4%; Iron 10% **Diet Exchanges:** 1/2 Starch, 4 Lean Meat, 1 Fat

In Calcutta, one of the most populous cities of the world, special meals often hinge on a fish called hilsa, *a silver freshwater fish that spawns in the Ganges River. Hilsa, an oily fish with a strong flavor, is not available in the United States, but salmon or other firm fish make a fine substitute.*

Fish Steamed with Mustard-Fennel Paste

Sorshe Bata Diyea Maach

4 SERVINGS

2 tablespoons Mustard Oil (page 41) or vegetable oil

1/4 cup water

1 tablespoon white or black poppy seed

1 teaspoon fennel seed, ground

1 teaspoon cumin seed, ground

1 teaspoon black or yellow mustard seed, ground

3/4 teaspoon salt

4 dried red Thai, serrano or cayenne chilies

6 large cloves garlic

4 salmon, swordfish, bluefish, buffalo fish or other firm fish fillets (6 ounces each), skin removed

1. Place all ingredients except fish fillets and oil in blender. Cover and blend on medium speed until a smooth paste forms.

2. Rub both sides of fish well with oil. Rub both sides of fish fillets with mustard-fennel paste. Cover and refrigerate at least 1 hour but no longer than 24 hours.

3. Brush grill rack with vegetable oil. Heat coals or gas grill to high for direct heat. Grill fish uncovered 5 to 6 inches from heat 1 to 2 minutes, turning once, until lightly browned.

4. Remove fish from grill; place each fillet on 18 × 12-inch piece of heavy-duty aluminum foil; wrap foil securely around fish. Cover and grill foil packets, seam sides up, 5 to 6 inches from high heat 10 to 15 minutes, turning once, until fish flakes easily with fork.

To Broil: Set oven control to broil. Brush broiler rack with vegetable oil. Place fish on rack in broiler pan. Broil with tops 2 to 3 inches from heat 1 to 2 minutes, turning occasionally to ensure even browning. Remove fish from broiler pan. Set oven control to bake; heat oven to 350°. Wrap each fillet in 18 × 12-inch piece of heavy-duty aluminum foil. Bake 8 to 10 minutes or until fish flakes easily with fork.

Raghavan Ki Baaten

☼ **If fresh or frozen banana leaves are available (in Asian or Latin American grocery stores), use them instead of foil. Or use large leaves such as Swiss chard. Collard greens, though ideal in size, impart a slight bitterness to the fish. Wrap each fillet in a leaf and secure with toothpicks.**

1 Serving: Calories 270 (Calories from Fat 145); Fat 16g (Saturated 3g); Cholesterol 85mg; Sodium 530mg; Carbohydrate 4g (Dietary Fiber 1g); Protein 29g **% Daily Value:** Vitamin A 14%; Vitamin C 2%; Calcium 6%; Iron 10% **Diet Exchanges:** 4 Lean Meat, 1 Vegetable, 1/2 Fat

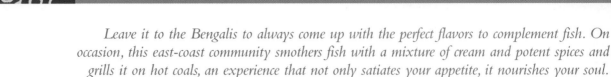

Leave it to the Bengalis to always come up with the perfect flavors to complement fish. On occasion, this east-coast community smothers fish with a mixture of cream and potent spices and grills it on hot coals, an experience that not only satiates your appetite, it nourishes your soul.

Grilled Fish with Garlic and Cream

4 SERVINGS

4 halibut, tuna or other firm fish steaks (6 ounces each), skin removed

1 tablespoon Mustard Oil (page 41) or vegetable oil

1/4 cup whipping (heavy) cream

1 tablespoon Spicy Panchphoran (page 39), ground

1 tablespoon finely chopped fresh cilantro

1/2 teaspoon salt

5 medium cloves garlic, finely chopped

1. Place fish in shallow baking dish. Rub with mustard oil; set aside.

2. Mix remaining ingredients; pour over fish. Turn to coat with marinade. Cover and refrigerate at least 30 minutes but no longer than 24 hours.

3. Brush grill rack with vegetable oil. Heat coals or gas grill to high for direct heat. Cover and grill fish 5 to 6 inches from heat 6 to 10 minutes, turning once, until fish flakes easily with fork.

To Broil: Set oven control to broil. Brush broiler pan rack with vegetable oil. Place fish on rack in broiler pan. Broil with tops 2 to 3 inches from heat 6 to 10 minutes, turning once, until fish flakes easily with fork.

1 Serving: Calories 200 (Calories from Fat 90); Fat 10g (Saturated 4g); Cholesterol 90mg; Sodium 420mg; Carbohydrate 2g (Dietary Fiber 1g); Protein 27g **% Daily Value:** Vitamin A 4%; Vitamin C 0%; Calcium 4%; Iron 4% **Diet Exchanges:** 4 Lean Meat

Keralites from Kerala, one of the most pristine, lush green states in southwestern India, use a lot of coconut in their everyday cooking. When coconut milk is combined with another bountiful resource, fish, the result is simply heavenly.

Fish Poached with Coconut Milk

Meen Curry

4 SERVINGS

1 pound cod, walleye, bass or other mild flavor fish fillets, skin removed

1 can (14 ounces) unsweetened coconut milk

8 medium cloves garlic

4 fresh Thai, serrano or cayenne chilies

1 tablespoon Garbanzo Bean Flour (*Bésan*), (page 44)

1/2 teaspoon salt

1/4 teaspoon ground turmeric

1 tablespoon vegetable oil

1 teaspoon black or yellow mustard seed

1 cup finely chopped red onion

1 medium tomato, finely chopped (3/4 cup)

12 to 15 fresh karhi leaves or 1/4 cup finely chopped fresh cilantro

Steamed Basmati Rice (pages 202 and 203), if desired

Fish Poached with Coconut Milk is pictured on page 77.

1. If fish fillets are large, cut fish into 4 serving pieces; set aside.

2. Place 1/4 cup of the coconut milk, the garlic, chilies, flour, salt and turmeric in blender. Cover and blend on medium speed until a smooth paste forms. Add remaining coconut milk. Cover and blend on medium speed until smooth; set aside.

3. Heat oil and mustard seed in 10-inch skillet over medium-high heat. Once seed begins to pop, cover skillet and wait until popping stops. Add onion; stir-fry 2 to 3 minutes or until onion is golden brown.

4. Stir coconut milk mixture, tomato and karhi leaves into onion mixture. Heat to boiling. Add fish, spooning sauce over fish; reduce heat. Cover and cook 6 to 8 minutes or until fish flakes easily with fork. Serve with rice.

1 Serving: Calories 175 (Calories from Fat 70); Fat 8g (Saturated 5g); Cholesterol 50mg; Sodium 250mg; Carbohydrate 7g (Dietary Fiber 2g); Protein 21g **% Daily Value:** Vitamin A 12%; Vitamin C 24%; Calcium 2%; Iron 4% **Diet Exchanges:** 3 Very Lean Meat, 1 Vegetable, 1 Fat

Raghavan Ki Baaten

☀ **Garbanzo bean flour plays a dual role in this recipe: It helps to slightly thicken the sauce (curry), and it prevents the coconut milk from curdling.**

The roots of the Zoroastrians, later known as Parsees, can be traced back to a group of Persians who fled Iran in order to protect their religious beliefs. Most eventually settled in Mumbai (Bombay) and Navsari (Gujarat), on the western coast. Their food habits and religious traditions are an interesting blend of their Persian ancestry and the influences of migration. This is one of their signature dishes, often served at religious events and for auspicious occasions.

Fish Steamed in Greens

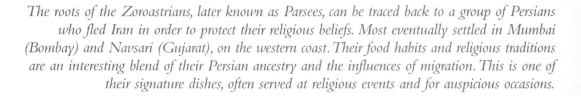

4 SERVINGS

1/2 cup Shredded Fresh Coconut (page 45) or 1/4 cup dried unsweetened shredded coconut

1/3 cup water

1/4 cup finely chopped fresh mint leaves

2 tablespoons chopped fresh cilantro

Juice of 1 medium lime (2 tablespoons)

8 medium cloves garlic

3 fresh Thai, serrano or cayenne chilies

1 1/2 teaspoons salt

1/2 teaspoon cumin seed

1 pound cod, walleye, tilapia or other mild flavor fish fillets, skin removed

4 large banana leaves, thawed if frozen, or Swiss chard

1. Place all ingredients except fish and banana leaves in blender. Cover and blend on medium speed until smooth; set aside.

2. If fish fillets are large, cut into 4 serving pieces. Rub fish with coconut mixture. Cover and refrigerate at least 1 hour but no longer than 24 hours.

3. Wrap each fish fillet completely in banana leaf; secure with 1 or 2 toothpicks.

4. Place steamer basket or bamboo steamer in 1/2 inch water in saucepan or skillet (water should not touch bottom of basket). Place fish packets in steamer basket. Cover tightly and heat to boiling; reduce heat to low. Cover and steam about 5 minutes or until fish flakes easily with fork. Remove fish from banana leaves; discard leaves.

1 Serving: Calories 130 (Calories from Fat 35); Fat 4g (Saturated 2g); Cholesterol 50mg; Sodium 680mg; Carbohydrate 5g (Dietary Fiber 1g); Protein 20g **% Daily Value:** Vitamin A 22%; Vitamin C 38%; Calcium 2%; Iron 4% **Diet Exchanges:** 3 Very Lean Meat, 1 Vegetable

Fish Steamed in Greens

Raghavan Ki Baaten

☼ Fresh banana leaves are not widely available in the United States, but Asian and Latin American stores often stock frozen leaves. If unavailable, use large leaves such as Swiss chard. Collard greens, though ideal in size, do add a slight bitterness to the fish. Or place each fish fillet on an 18 × 12-inch piece of heavy-duty aluminum foil; wrap foil securely around fish.

As you stroll along the beaches of Trivandrum in the southwestern state of Kerala, a common sight is fishermen in white loin cloths (dhotis) adroitly balancing their canoes and fishing nets filled with giant prawns against the choppy waves of the Arabian Sea. Later, kitchens in Kerala are filled with nose-tingling aromas of shrimp, chilies and coconut mingling with the salty ocean breeze wafting through the windows.

Pan-Seared Coconut Shrimp

Keralite Jhinga

4 SERVINGS

1 pound uncooked extra-jumbo shrimp (16 to 20), peeled and deveined

1/2 cup coconut milk

1 tablespoon finely chopped gingerroot

12 to 15 fresh karhi leaves, chopped (1 tablespoon), or 2 tablespoons finely chopped fresh cilantro

1 teaspoon salt

2 fresh Thai, serrano or cayenne chilies, finely chopped

1/2 teaspoon tamarind concentrate paste or juice of 1 medium lime (2 tablespoons)

2 tablespoons vegetable oil

1 teaspoon black or yellow mustard seed

8 medium shallots, thinly sliced

1. Mix all ingredients except oil, mustard seed and shallots in medium bowl. Cover and refrigerate 30 to 60 minutes to blend flavors.

2. Heat oil and mustard seed in 12-inch skillet over medium-high heat. Once seed begins to pop, cover skillet and wait until popping stops. Add shallots; stir-fry 1 to 2 minutes or until light golden brown.

3. Add shrimp mixture. Cook 5 to 7 minutes, turning frequently, until shrimp are pink and firm.

1 Serving: Calories 120 (Calories from Fat 65); Fat 7g (Saturated 3g); Cholesterol 105mg; Sodium 430mg; Carbohydrate 2g (Dietary Fiber 0g); Protein 12g **% Daily Value:** Vitamin A 4%; Vitamin C 2%; Calcium 2%; Iron 10% **Diet Exchanges:** 2 Very Lean Meat, 1 Fat

Shrimp is not a staple in the diet of the inhabitants of India's northern states because they are far removed from the coastal areas of the West (Arabian Sea), South (Indian Ocean) and East (Bay of Bengal). However, when prepared in the traditional grilling style of the North, the flavors in this marinade yield a remarkably smoky, subtle taste that allows this delicate shellfish to shine.

Marinated Grilled Shrimp

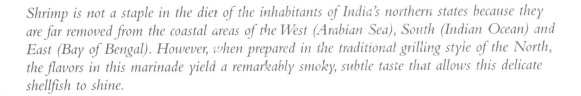

Tandoori Jhinga

4 SERVINGS

1 pound uncooked extra-jumbo shrimp (16 to 20), peeled (leaving tails on) and deveined

1/4 cup plain yogurt (regular or fat-free)

Juice of 1 medium lime (2 tablespoons)

1 tablespoon finely chopped fresh cilantro

2 medium cloves garlic, finely chopped

1 teaspoon ground cumin

1 teaspoon Bishop's weed (ajwain)

1 teaspoon Garam Masaala (page 32)

4 ten-inch bamboo* or metal skewers

*When using bamboo skewers, soak in water at least 30 minutes before using to prevent burning.

Marinated Grilled Shrimp is pictured on page 77.

1. Mix all ingredients except skewers in medium bowl. Cover and refrigerate at least 30 to 60 minutes to blend flavors but no longer than 24 hours.

2. Brush grill rack with vegetable oil. Heat coals or gas grill for direct heat. Thread 4 shrimp on each skewer, leaving space between each shrimp. Cover and grill 5 to 6 inches from high heat 3 to 5 minutes, turning once, until shrimp are pink and firm.

To Broil: Set oven control to broil. Brush broiler rack with vegetable oil. Place skewered shrimp on rack in broiler pan. Broil with tops 2 to 3 inches from heat 3 to 5 minutes, turning once, until shrimp are pink and firm.

Raghavan Ki Baaten

☼ This is a great dinner when accompanied by Basmati Rice with Mushrooms (page 205), and it also makes an elegant first course when served with Mint-Cilantro Chutney (page 284).

---

1 Serving: Calories 55 (Calories from Fat 10); Fat 1g (Saturated 0g); Cholesterol 80mg; Sodium 105mg; Carbohydrate 2g (Dietary Fiber 0g); Protein 10g **% Daily Value:** Vitamin A 2%; Vitamin C 2%; Calcium 4%; Iron 8% **Diet Exchanges:** 1 1/2 Very Lean Meat

Shrimp, considered humble fisherman's food, is widely consumed because of its abundance along India's three coastlines. Though not regional to the North, when shrimp is combined with the classic northern flavors of almonds, peppercorns and cloves, it elevates itself to kingly (moghalai) status.

Almond-Coated Shrimp

moghalai Jhinga

4 SERVINGS

1 pound uncooked extra-jumbo shrimp (16 to 20), peeled and deveined

1/2 cup slivered almonds, ground

1/4 cup half-and-half

1 teaspoon cumin seed, ground

1/2 teaspoon salt

1/2 teaspoon whole cloves, ground

1/2 teaspoon black peppercorns, ground

1/4 teaspoon cardamom seeds (removed from pods), ground

2 tablespoons finely chopped fresh cilantro

2 tablespoons vegetable oil

1/2 cup tomato sauce

1. Mix all ingredients except 1 tablespoon of the cilantro, the oil and tomato sauce in medium bowl. Cover and refrigerate 30 minutes to blend flavors.

2. Heat oil in 10-inch skillet over medium-high heat. Add shrimp mixture. Cook each side of shrimp 30 to 60 seconds or until partially pink.

3. Stir in tomato sauce. Cover and cook 3 to 4 minutes, turning shrimp occasionally, until shrimp are pink and firm. Serve sprinkled with remaining cilantro.

1 Serving: Calories 175 (Calories from Fat 115); Fat 13g (Saturated 2g); Cholesterol 85mg; Sodium 480mg; Carbohydrate 5g (Dietary Fiber 2g); Protein 12g **% Daily Value:** Vitamin A 6%; Vitamin C 4%; Calcium 6%; Iron 12% **Diet Exchanges:** 2 Lean Meat, 1 Vegetable, 1 Fat

Almond-Coated Shrimp, Basmati Rice with Saffron (page 210)

Raghavan Ki Baaten

☀ Take extra care not to overcook shrimp to a chewy rubberlike texture. When shrimp changes from a raw blue-green color to pink and firm, it is at its juiciest and best.

☀ This thick tomato-based curry is great as a first course; when served with Basmati Rice with Saffron (page 210), it makes for an impressive entrée.

A very fast and easy recipe to wow your weekday guest! You can use any seafood you may have at hand.

Marinated Shrimp Poached in Mint Sauce

4 SERVINGS

1 pound uncooked extra-jumbo shrimp (16 to 20), peeled and deveined

1 tablespoon finely chopped fresh cilantro

1 teaspoon Spicy Garam Masaala (page 34)

1 teaspoon salt

1 medium tomato, chopped (3/4 cup)

1/2 cup sliced daikon or radishes

1/2 cup finely chopped fresh mint leaves

1/4 cup water

3 medium cloves garlic

1 or 2 fresh Thai, serrano or cayenne chilies

Juice of 1 medium lime (2 tablespoons)

1 tablespoon vegetable oil

1. Mix shrimp, cilantro, Spicy Garam Masaala and 1/2 teaspoon of the salt in medium bowl. Cover and refrigerate at least 30 minutes but no longer than 24 hours.

2. Place remaining 1/2 teaspoon salt and remaining ingredients except oil in blender. Cover and blend on medium speed until smooth.

3. Heat oil in 12-inch skillet over medium-high heat. Arrange shrimp in single layer in skillet. Cook each side 30 to 60 seconds or until partially pink.

4. Stir mint sauce into shrimp. Cover and cook 2 to 4 minutes, turning shrimp once or twice, until shrimp are pink and firm.

1 Serving: Calories 90 (Calories from Fat 25); Fat 3g (Saturated 1g); Cholesterol 105mg; Sodium 570mg; Carbohydrate 5g (Dietary Fiber 1g); Protein 12g **% Daily Value:** Vitamin A 18%; Vitamin C 28%; Calcium 4%; Iron 12% **Diet Exchanges:** 2 Very Lean Meat, 1 Vegetable

Marinated Shrimp Poached in Mint Sauce

Raghavan Ki Baaten

☀ Fresh shrimp may have descriptive market names such as "extra-jumbo" or "extra-large," but the important part is the count or number per pound. When you ask for a pound of extra-jumbo raw shrimp in the shell, the yield should be 16 to 20 very large shrimp.

☀ Be careful not to overcook shrimp or they will be tough. If you use smaller shrimp than extra-jumbo-size, check for doneness after cooking 2 minutes. Shrimp are done when they are pink and firm.

Pork tenderloin is very lean and tender, but boneless chicken or turkey is also delicious in this recipe.

Pork Tenderloin with Pickles and Peppers

4 SERVINGS

1 tablespoon vegetable oil

1 tablespoon finely chopped gingerroot

5 medium cloves garlic, finely chopped

1 pound pork tenderloin, cut into 2 × 1/2-inch strips

1 medium green or red bell pepper, cut into 1/4-inch strips

1/4 cup Sweet-and-Hot Mango Pickle (page 273)

2 tablespoons finely chopped fresh cilantro

1. Heat oil in wok or Dutch oven over medium-high heat. Add gingerroot and garlic; stir-fry 30 to 60 seconds or until garlic is light golden brown.

2. Add pork; stir-fry 8 to 10 minutes or until pork is slightly pink in center.

3. Add bell pepper and Sweet-and-Hot Mango Pickle; stir-fry 2 to 4 minutes or until pepper strips are crisp-tender. Serve sprinkled with cilantro.

1 Serving: Calories 185 (Calories from Fat 65); Fat 7g (Saturated 2g); Cholesterol 65mg; Sodium 50mg; Carbohydrate 7g (Dietary Fiber 1g); Protein 25g **% Daily Value:** Vitamin A 2%; Vitamin C 24%; Calcium 2%; Iron 8% **Diet Exchanges:** 3 Lean Meat, 1 Vegetable

Pork Tenderloin with Pickles and Peppers, Basmati Rice with Mushrooms (page 204)

Raghavan Ki Baaten

☀ This recipe uses Sweet-and-Hot Mango Pickle (page 273), but try any of the other pickles for different flavors. For a very piquant alternative, Spicy Lemon Pickle (page 272) will appeal to the adventurous at your table. Your supermarket or favorite Indian grocery store offers many varieties of pickles. Use them in a pinch if you don't have time to make homemade.

While many groups in India avoid eating certain kinds of meat, the Portuguese community in Goa, a state just south of Mumbai (Bombay), includes pork in their diet. In this signature dish, pork is flavored with a paste of cashews, peppers, garlic and vinegar, a combination unique to the region. Serve this curry with rice or bread to soak up the delicious broth-like sauce.

Pork in Cashew-Pepper Curry

Sorpotel

4 SERVINGS

1/2 cup white vinegar

1/4 cup raw cashew pieces

6 medium cloves garlic

2 or 3 fresh Thai, serrano or cayenne chilies

2 tablespoons vegetable oil

1/2 cup finely chopped red onion

1 teaspoon salt

1/2 teaspoon whole cloves, ground

1/2 teaspoon ground cinnamon

1 1/2 pounds pork boneless loin chops, cut crosswise into 1/4-inch slices

1/2 cup water

1 1/2 teaspoons roasted cumin seed (page 31), ground

1/4 cup chopped fresh cilantro

1. Place vinegar, cashews, garlic and chilies in blender. Cover and blend on medium speed until smooth.

2. Heat oil in wok or Dutch oven over medium-high heat. Add onion; stir-fry 3 to 4 minutes or until golden brown. Add vinegar mixture; stir-fry 1 to 2 minutes or until oil starts to separate from paste.

3. Stir in salt, cloves, cinnamon and pork. Cook uncovered 3 to 5 minutes, stirring occasionally, until pork is partially cooked.

4. Stir in water; reduce heat. Cover and simmer 8 to 10 minutes or until pork is slightly pink in center. Stir in cumin. Serve sprinkled with cilantro.

Raghavan Ki Baaten

☀ **For this dish, a stainless-steel or dark or nonstick pan is the best choice. Although cast-iron woks are popular in Indian kitchens, the metal can react with the vinegar to produce unpleasant flavors and colors.**

1 Serving: Calories 390 (Calories from Fat 200); Fat 22g (Saturated 6g); Cholesterol 105mg; Sodium 660mg; Carbohydrate 9g (Dietary Fiber 1g); Protein 40g **% Daily Value:** Vitamin A 22%; Vitamin C 34%; Calcium 2%; Iron 12% **Diet Exchanges:** 1/2 Starch, 5 1/2 Lean Meat, 1 Fat

This is a classic curry from the Himalayan-kissed state of Kashmir, combining the flavors of almonds, cardamom and cloves in a rich tomato sauce with chunks of tender lamb morsels. The lengthy cooking time softens the connective tissues to yield tender, succulent meat that will fall apart as you eat it.

Almond–Lamb Curry

Roghan Josh

4 SERVINGS

2 tablespoons vegetable oil

1 teaspoon cumin seed

1/2 cup finely chopped red onion

2 tablespoons finely chopped gingerroot

5 medium cloves garlic, finely chopped

1/2 cup slivered almonds, ground (1/2 cup)

1 teaspoon coriander seed, ground

1/2 teaspoon salt

1/2 teaspoon ground red pepper (cayenne)

1/2 teaspoon cardamom seeds (removed from pods), ground

1/2 teaspoon whole cloves, ground

1/4 teaspoon black peppercorns, ground

1/2 cup tomato sauce

3/4 cup water

1 pound boneless leg of lamb, cut into 2-inch cubes

2 tablespoons finely chopped fresh cilantro

1/2 cup whipping (heavy) cream

1. Heat oven to 300°.

2. Heat oil in heavy 2-quart saucepan over medium-high heat. Add cumin seed; sizzle 15 to 30 seconds.

3. Add onion, gingerroot and garlic; stir-fry 3 to 5 minutes or until onion and garlic are light golden brown.

4. Add ground almonds, ground coriander, salt, ground red pepper, ground cardamom, ground cloves and ground pepper; stir-fry 1 to 2 minutes or until almonds are partially brown.

5. Stir in tomato sauce and 1/4 cup of the water; reduce heat. Partially cover and simmer 4 to 5 minutes or until thin film of oil starts to separate from sauce.

6. Stir in lamb and 1 tablespoon of the cilantro. Cover and simmer 5 to 7 minutes, stirring occasionally, until lamb is partially cooked. Stir in remaining 1/2 cup water. Spoon into ungreased 2-quart casserole.

7. Cover and bake 40 to 45 minutes. Uncover and bake about 45 minutes longer or until lamb is tender and sauce is slightly thickened.

8. Gently stir in whipping cream, using wire whisk. Serve sprinkled with remaining cilantro.

Raghavan Ki Baaten

☀ Substitute beef or pork if lamb is not readily available in your supermarket.

☀ Serve Steamed Basmati Rice (pages 202 and 203) with this or any other saucy preparation. This curry is also often served with loaves of piping-hot Tandoori Bread (page 252), sliced red onions and long, curvaceous fresh cayenne chilies.

1 Serving: Calories 380 (Calories from Fat 260); Fat 29g (Saturated 10g); Cholesterol 95mg; Sodium 540mg; Carbohydrate 9g (Dietary Fiber 2g); Protein 23g **% Daily Value:** Vitamin A 10%; Vitamin C 4%; Calcium 8%; Iron 14% **Diet Exchanges:** 3 Lean Meat, 1 Vegetable, 4 Fat

Gosht is Hindi for "red meat," but is more often used to specify goat meat. A restaurant menu favorite in the United States, lamb is more readily available.

Lamb–Spinach Curry

Saag Gosht

6 SERVINGS

2 tablespoons vegetable oil

2 tablespoons finely chopped gingerroot

5 medium cloves garlic, finely chopped

1 cup tomato sauce

1 tablespoon coriander seed, ground

1 teaspoon cumin seed, ground

1 teaspoon ground red pepper (cayenne)

1 teaspoon salt

2 packages (10 ounces each) frozen chopped spinach, thawed (do not drain)

1 pound boneless lamb, cut into 1-inch cubes

1/2 cup whipping (heavy) cream

1 teaspoon Garam Masaala (page 32)

1. Heat oil in 3-quart saucepan over medium-high heat. Add gingerroot and garlic; stir-fry 1 to 2 minutes or until garlic is golden brown.

2. Stir in tomato sauce, ground coriander, ground cumin, ground red pepper and salt; reduce heat. Partially cover and simmer 7 to 8 minutes or until thin film of oil starts to separate from sauce.

3. Stir in undrained spinach and lamb. Simmer uncovered 6 to 8 minutes, stirring occasionally, until spinach is wilted. Cover and simmer 35 to 40 minutes longer, stirring occasionally, until lamb is tender; remove from heat.

4. Gradually stir in whipping cream; stir in Garam Masaala.

1 Serving: Calories 220 (Calories from Fat 135); Fat 15g (Saturated 6g); Cholesterol 65mg; Sodium 730mg; Carbohydrate 8g (Dietary Fiber 3g); Protein 16g **% Daily Value:** Vitamin A 56%; Vitamin C 10%; Calcium 12%; Iron 14% **Diet Exchanges:** 2 Lean Meat, 2 Vegetable, 1 1/2 Fat

Lamb-Spinach Curry, Steamed Basmati Rice (pages 202 and 203), Tandoori Breads (page 252)

Raghavan Ki Baaten

☀ Adding whipping cream to a tomato-base mixture may give the dish a
curdled appearance. This will not affect the flavor but may not look very
tasty. To help prevent the curdling, I gradually add the cream while
stirring constantly with a spoon.

Mutton, which can be either mature lamb or goat in India, is a delicacy, not only in the North, but also in the south-central city of Hyderabad where many Muslims dwell alongside their Hindu neighbors. They have retained their Moghul influences, as is evidenced by the city's architectural wonders and their spices of choice: cinnamon, cloves and garlic. Along with these seasonings, they have incorporated such quintessential South Indian elements as popping mustard seed and using fresh karhi leaves to create an altogether unique culinary style.

Ground Lamb with Peas

Mutter Kheema

6 SERVINGS

1 tablespoon vegetable oil

1 teaspoon black or yellow mustard seed

2 three-inch sticks cinnamon

1 cup finely chopped red onion

5 medium cloves garlic, finely chopped

1 or 2 fresh Thai, serrano or cayenne chilies, finely chopped

10 to 12 fresh karhi leaves or 2 to 3 dried bay leaves

1 pound ground lamb

1 cup frozen green peas

1 medium tomato, finely chopped (3/4 cup)

1 teaspoon salt

1 teaspoon Spicy Garam Masaala (page 34)

1/2 cup plain yogurt (regular or fat-free)

2 tablespoons finely chopped fresh cilantro

1. Heat oil and mustard seed in wok or deep 12-inch skillet over medium-high heat. Once seed begins to pop, cover wok and wait until popping stops.

2. Add cinnamon sticks, onion, garlic, chilies and karhi leaves; stir-fry 2 to 4 minutes or until onion is brown.

3. Stir in lamb and peas. Cook 8 to 10 minutes, stirring occasionally, until lamb is brown.

4. Stir in remaining ingredients except cilantro. Cook 1 to 2 minutes, stirring occasionally, just until tomato and yogurt are warm. (If using bay leaves, remove and discard.) Sprinkle with cilantro. Serve with cinnamon sticks left in, but do not eat them.

1 Serving: Calories 205 (Calories from Fat 115); Fat 13g (Saturated 5g); Cholesterol 50mg; Sodium 460mg; Carbohydrate 9g (Dietary Fiber 2g); Protein 15g **% Daily Value:** Vitamin A 10%; Vitamin C 18%; Calcium 6%; Iron 8% **Diet Exchanges:** 2 Lean Meat, 2 Vegetable, 1 Fat

Ground Lamb with Peas

Raghavan Ki Baaten

☀ Butchers and meat departments in supermarkets grind lamb to order.
If ground lamb is unavailable, substitute ground turkey, chicken or
even beef.

Cashew trees aplenty grow in Goa, the tropical paradise by the Arabian Sea. These bushy trees with thick trunks bear fruit that resembles a small orange bell pepper with an inverted cashew nut hanging from its end. Slightly bittersweet cashew fruit is used in many a Goan recipe as a vegetable but is rarely exported because it perishes so quickly.

Grilled Chicken with Roasted Cashew Sauce

4 SERVINGS

1 cup raw
cashew pieces

1/4 cup white vinegar

8 medium cloves garlic

4 to 6 fresh Thai,
serrano or cayenne
chilies

2 cups coconut milk

1 teaspoon salt

3- to 3 1/2-pound cut-up
broiler-fryer chicken,
skin removed

2 tablespoons
vegetable oil

1 teaspoon roasted
cumin seed (page 31),
ground

2 red onions, cut in
half and thinly sliced

1 medium tomato,
finely chopped
(3/4 cup)

2 tablespoons chopped
fresh cilantro

1. Place 1/2 cup of the cashews, the vinegar, garlic and chilies in blender. Cover and blend on medium speed until smooth. Add 1 cup of the coconut milk and 1/2 teaspoon of the salt. Cover and blend on medium speed until smooth.

2. Place chicken in large bowl. Pour cashew mixture over chicken; turn to coat with mixture. Cover and refrigerate at least 2 hours but no longer than 24 hours.

3. Heat 1 tablespoon of the oil in 10-inch skillet over medium-high heat. Add remaining 1/2 cup cashews; stir-fry 30 to 60 seconds or until golden brown. Place browned cashews, remaining 1 cup coconut milk, remaining 1/2 teaspoon salt and the ground cumin in blender. Cover and blend on medium speed until smooth; set aside.

4. Heat coals or gas grill to medium for indirect heat. Remove chicken from marinade; reserve marinade. Cover and grill chicken 4 to 5 inches from heat 45 to 50 minutes, turning occasionally and brushing with marinade, until juice of chicken is no longer pink when centers of thickest pieces are cut. Discard any remaining marinade.

5. Meanwhile, heat remaining 1 tablespoon oil in same skillet over medium-high heat. Add onions; stir-fry 3 to 4 minutes or until golden brown. Stir in tomato. Cook 1 to 2 minutes or until warm. Remove from heat; set aside.

6. Place chicken on serving platter. Pour cashew sauce over chicken. Top with onion mixture and cilantro.

1 Serving: Calories 630 (Calories from Fat 370); Fat 41g (Saturated 19g); Cholesterol 115mg; Sodium 610mg; Carbohydrate 24g (Dietary Fiber 5g); Protein 46g **% Daily Value:** Vitamin A 26%; Vitamin C 46%; Calcium 6%; Iron 20% **Diet Exchanges:** 1 Starch, 6 Medium-Fat Meat, 2 Vegetable, 1 1/2 Fat

Grilled Chicken with Roasted Cashew Sauce

Raghavan Ki Baaten

☀ Flavors from Goa are highlighted in this recipe that combines locally
grown cashews with Portuguese-influenced vinegar and chilies.

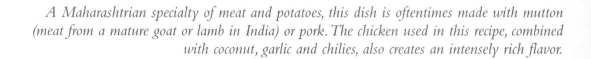

A Maharashtrian specialty of meat and potatoes, this dish is oftentimes made with mutton (meat from a mature goat or lamb in India) or pork. The chicken used in this recipe, combined with coconut, garlic and chilies, also creates an intensely rich flavor.

Chicken with Potatoes

Batata Murghi

4 SERVINGS

2 medium baking potatoes

3 tablespoons vegetable oil

5 medium cloves garlic, finely chopped

1/2 cup Shredded Fresh Coconut (page 45) or 1/4 cup dried unsweetened shredded coconut

1 tablespoon coriander seed

1 or 2 fresh Thai, serrano or cayenne chilies

1/2 cup water

1 pound boneless, skinless chicken breasts, cut crosswise into 1/2-inch strips

2 medium tomatoes, chopped (1 1/2 cups)

1 teaspoon salt

1 teaspoon Spicy Garam Masaala (page 34)

1/4 teaspoon ground turmeric

2 tablespoons finely chopped fresh cilantro

1. Scrub potatoes; cut each potato lengthwise into 8 wedges. Heat 1 inch salted water in a 10- to 12-inch skillet to boiling. Add potatoes; cover and heat to boiling. Reduce heat; simmer 15 minutes or until just tender. Drain; set aside.

2. Heat 1 tablespoon of the oil in wok or deep 12-inch skillet over medium-high heat. Add garlic; stir-fry 30 to 60 seconds or until golden brown. Stir in coconut, coriander seed and chilies. Cook 1 to 2 minutes, stirring constantly, until coconut is golden brown.

3. Place coconut mixture and water in blender. Cover and blend on medium speed until smooth; set aside.

4. Heat remaining 2 tablespoons oil in same wok or skillet over medium-high heat. Cook chicken in oil 2 to 3 minutes, stirring occasionally, until chicken is golden brown.

5. Stir potatoes, coconut mixture and remaining ingredients except cilantro into chicken; reduce heat. Simmer uncovered 10 to 12 minutes, stirring occasionally, until chicken is no longer pink in center. Serve sprinkled with cilantro.

Raghavan Ki Baaten

☀ **Frozen potatoes can be used if you want to. I have used 16 frozen potatoes wedges with skins from a 24-ounce bag. Cook them following the directions on the bag before adding them to the chicken.**

1 Serving: Calories 375 (Calories from Fat 125); Fat 14g (Saturated 5g); Cholesterol 70mg; Sodium 670mg; Carbohydrate 38g (Dietary Fiber 5g); Protein 29g **% Daily Value:** Vitamin A 14%; Vitamin C 42%; Calcium 4%; Iron 18% **Diet Exchanges:** 2 Starch, 3 Lean Meat, 2 Vegetable

Karhai is Hindi for "wok," though the Indian version is slightly different than the Chinese one. Karhais are usually made of a black stone that is quite similar to cast iron in weight and heat conduction. Meats and vegetables are usually stir-fried at high temperatures in minimal amounts of fat to maintain their juices and flavors, ensuring a quick, healthy meal even on the most harried evenings.

Stir-Fried Chicken

Karhai Murghi

4 SERVINGS

1 tablespoon vegetable oil

1 teaspoon cumin seed

1 medium onion, chopped (1/2 cup)

2 tablespoons chopped gingerroot

5 medium cloves garlic, finely chopped

1 tablespoon ground coriander

1 teaspoon salt

1 teaspoon ground cumin

1/2 teaspoon ground black pepper

1/4 teaspoon ground cloves

1/4 teaspoon ground cardamom

1 pound cut-up chicken breast for stir-fry

1 medium tomato, chopped (3/4 cup)

2 tablespoons finely chopped fresh cilantro

1. Heat oil in wok or 12-inch skillet over medium-high heat. Add cumin seed; sizzle 15 to 20 seconds.

2. Add onion, gingerroot and garlic; stir-fry 2 to 4 minutes or until onion and garlic are light golden brown.

3. Add coriander, salt, cumin, pepper, cloves and cardamom; stir-fry 2 to 3 minutes or until mixture begins to have a nutty aroma.

4. Add chicken; stir-fry 2 to 3 minutes or until chicken turns white. Reduce heat to low. Cover and cook 10 to 12 minutes, stirring occasionally, until chicken is no longer pink in center.

5. Stir in tomato. Cook 1 to 2 minutes or until just warm. Serve sprinkled with cilantro.

Raghavan Ki Baaten

☀ I sometimes use the chicken breast that is already cut up and labeled "stir-fry" to save time. But feel free to cut up boneless, skinless chicken breast, or use any other cuts of meat, such as turkey and pork.

1 Serving: Calories 190 (Calories from Fat 70); Fat 8g (Saturated 2g); Cholesterol 70mg; Sodium 65mg; Carbohydrate 5g (Dietary Fiber 1g); Protein 26g **% Daily Value:** Vitamin A 2%; Vitamin C 5%; Calcium 2%; Iron 8% **Diet Exchanges:** 3 Lean Meat, 1 Vegetable

This Indian dish is popular in restaurants across America. It combines an array of peppers, onions and spices (jalfrezie) with tender chicken chunks in a mellow tomato-based curry. Serve this with Steamed Basmati Rice (pages 202 and 203) or Whole Wheat Unleavened Breads (page 236).

Stir-Fried Chicken with Peppers and Onions

Murgh Jalfrezie

4 SERVINGS

2 tablespoons vegetable oil

1 medium yellow or white onion, finely chopped (1/2 cup)

1 tablespoon coarsely chopped gingerroot

2 medium cloves garlic, finely chopped

1/2 cup tomato sauce

1 tablespoon coriander seed, ground

1 teaspoon cumin seed, ground

1/2 teaspoon salt

1/2 teaspoon ground turmeric

1/2 teaspoon ground red pepper (cayenne)

1 pound boneless, skinless chicken breasts, cut into 1-inch pieces

1 medium green bell pepper, cut into 1/2-inch cubes (1 cup)

1 medium red onion, cut into 1/2-inch cubes

1 medium tomato, cut into 1/2-inch cubes (3/4 cup)

1/2 cup water

1/2 cup plain yogurt (regular or fat-free)

2 tablespoons finely chopped fresh cilantro

1. Heat oil in wok or deep 12-inch skillet over medium-high heat. Add yellow onion, gingerroot and garlic; stir-fry 3 to 4 minutes or until onion and garlic are deep golden brown.

2. Stir in tomato sauce, ground coriander, ground cumin, salt, turmeric and ground red pepper; reduce heat to low. Partially cover and simmer 5 to 7 minutes or until a very thin film of oil starts to separate from sauce.

3. Stir in chicken. Simmer uncovered 4 to 5 minutes, stirring occasionally, until chicken is partially cooked.

4. Stir in bell pepper, red onion, tomato and water. Cover and simmer 8 to 10 minutes or until chicken is no longer pink in center.

5. Stir in yogurt. Simmer uncovered 1 minute, stirring occasionally, just intil yogurt is warm. Serve sprinkled with cilantro.

1 Serving: Calories 245 (Calories from Fat 90); Fat 10g (Saturated 2g); Cholesterol 70mg; Sodium 570mg; Carbohydrate 14g (Dietary Fiber 3g); Protein 28g **% Daily Value:** Vitamin A 8%; Vitamin C 34%; Calcium 10%; Iron 10% **Diet Exchanges:** 3 Lean Meat, 3 Vegetable

Stir-Fried Chicken with Peppers and Onions, Whole Wheat Unleavened Breads (page 236), Steamed Basmati Rice (pages 202 and 203)

Raghavan Ki Baaten

☀ Thin slices of beef, pork, or lamb sirloin can be substituted for the chicken in this recipe. Even shrimp can be used, but the cooking time will be shorter so add them with the bell pepper.

This Portuguese-influenced chicken curry hails from Goa, a small state south of Mumbai (Bombay). Goa is known for groves of cashew trees, beautiful Arabian Sea–kissed resorts, majestic churches with stained-glass interiors and the cultural and architectural influences of the Portuguese settlers and Jesuits.

Portuguese-Style Chicken Curry

Murgh Vindaloo

4 SERVINGS

2 tablespoons vegetable oil

2 medium onions, coarsely chopped (1 1/2 cups)

1 tablespoon coarsely chopped gingerroot

5 medium cloves garlic, coarsely chopped

3/4 cup tomato sauce

1 tablespoon coriander seed, ground

1 teaspoon cumin seed, ground

1/2 teaspoon salt

1/2 teaspoon ground red pepper (cayenne)

1/4 teaspoon ground turmeric

1 pound boneless, skinless chicken breasts, cut crosswise into 1/2-inch strips

1/4 cup white vinegar

1/2 cup coconut milk

1/4 cup plain yogurt (regular or fat-free)

Steamed Basmati Rice (pages 202 and 203), if desired

1. Heat oil in wok or 10-inch skillet over medium-high heat. Add onions, gingerroot and garlic; stir-fry about 5 minutes or until onions and garlic are golden brown.

2. Stir in tomato sauce, ground coriander, ground cumin, salt, ground red pepper and turmeric; reduce heat. Partially cover and simmer about 5 minutes or until a thin film of oil starts to form on surface of sauce. (The longer sauce simmers, the more oil will form.) Remove from heat; cool 3 to 4 minutes.

3. Place sauce in blender. Cover and blend on medium speed until smooth. Return sauce to saucepan.

4. Stir chicken into sauce. Simmer uncovered 3 to 5 minutes, stirring occasionally, until chicken is partially cooked.

5. Stir in vinegar and coconut milk. Simmer uncovered 5 to 7 minutes, stirring occasionally, until chicken is no longer pink in center.

6. Beat yogurt with wire whisk until smooth; stir into chicken mixture. Cook uncovered 1 minute, stirring occasionally, just until yogurt is warm. Serve with rice.

Raghavan Ki Baaten

☀ **The term vindaloo on restaurant menus conjures up images of the after-effects of fiery hot chilies: sweat running down your forehead and the naturally euphoric state of light-headedness related to an endorphin rush. How funny, then, that vindaloo actually means "vinegary." The amount of ground red pepper that you add is a purely personal choice. If you are inclined to relive your restaurant experiences at home, use more than the recipe recommends!**

1 Serving: Calories 290 (Calories from Fat 135); Fat 14g (Saturated 6g); Cholesterol 70mg; Sodium 660mg; Carbohydrate 13g (Dietary Fiber 3g); Protein 28g **% Daily Value:** Vitamin A 4%; Vitamin C 8%; Calcium 6%; Iron 10% **Diet Exchanges:** 3 1/2 Lean Meat, 2 Vegetable, 1 Fat

This North Indian specialty is often served in restaurants and for special-occasion family meals. Restaurants will often cook the marinated chicken first in a clay-lined oven (tandoor) and then simmer it in the fenugreek-accented tomato sauce.

Butter Chicken

Murgh makhani

4 SERVINGS

1 pound boneless, skinless chicken breasts, cut crosswise into 1/2-inch strips

1/4 cup whipping (heavy) cream

2 tablespoons finely chopped gingerroot

5 medium cloves garlic, finely chopped

1 tablespoon finely chopped fresh cilantro

1 teaspoon coriander seed, ground

1/2 teaspoon cumin seed, ground

1/2 teaspoon salt

1/4 teaspoon ground red pepper (cayenne)

2 tablespoons Clarified Butter (Ghee), (page 40) or butter

1/2 cup tomato sauce

1/4 cup finely chopped fresh or 2 tablespoons crumbled dried fenugreek leaves (méthi)

1. Mix all ingredients except Clarified Butter, tomato sauce and fenugreek in medium bowl. Cover and refrigerate at least 1 hour but no longer than 24 hours.

2. Heat Clarified Butter in 10-inch skillet over medium heat. Add chicken mixture and tomato sauce. Cook about 5 minutes, stirring frequently, or until chicken is partially cooked.

3. Stir in fenugreek; reduce heat. Cover and simmer about 10 minutes or until chicken is no longer pink in center.

Butter Chicken is pictured on page 77.

Raghavan Ki Baaten

☀ This dish derives a unique flavor of perfumed harmony from the fenugreek leaves. If unavailable, substitute watercress leaves to yield a similar-looking sauce with a mellower flavor.

The Moghul era in northern India, prior to the start of British rule, was a time of wealth, good times and rich foods, as is reflected in this recipe. Homemade cheese (paneer), golden raisins (sultanas), spiced onions and leaves of tender spinach are used in the filling. Once the chicken breasts are stuffed, they simmer in a delicate tomato-cream sauce laced with fenugreek. Platters of aromatic basmati rice scented with whole spices would be a delectable accompaniment.

Chicken Breast Stuffed with Cheese and Raisins

6 SERVINGS

6 boneless, skinless chicken breast halves (about 1 1/4 pounds)

1/4 cup Clarified Butter (Ghee), (page 40), or vegetable oil

1/2 cup golden raisins

1 teaspoon cumin seed

1 cup finely chopped red onion

1 bag (10 to 12 ounces) washed fresh spinach, chopped

1 teaspoon Garam Masaala (page 32)

1 teaspoon salt

1 cup crumbled Homemade Cheese (page 42)

1 cup tomato sauce

1/4 cup finely chopped fresh or 2 tablespoons dried fenugreek leaves (méthi), crumbled

1/4 cup whipping (heavy) cream

1. Flatten each chicken breast half to 1/4-inch thickness between sheets of plastic wrap or waxed paper; set aside.

2. Heat 2 tablespoons of the Clarified Butter in wok or 12-inch skillet over medium heat. Add raisins; stir-fry about 1 minute or until raisins plump up.

3. Add cumin seed; sizzle 10 to 15 seconds. Add onion; stir-fry 2 to 3 minutes or until golden brown. Mix in spinach; toss 2 to 3 minutes or until wilted.

4. Stir in Garam Masaala and salt; cook 1 minute. Place spinach mixture in medium bowl. Stir in cheese.

5. Spread one-fourth of the spinach mixture evenly over each chicken breast half. Fold long sides of chicken over spinach mixture. Fold ends up; secure each end with toothpick.

6. Heat remaining 2 tablespoons butter in 12-inch skillet over medium heat. Cook chicken in butter 6 to 8 minutes, turning occasionally, until golden brown on all sides.

7. Add tomato sauce and fenugreek; reduce heat. Cover and simmer 12 to 15 minutes, turning chicken occasionally, until chicken is no longer pink in center.

8. Remove chicken with slotted spoon; place on serving platter.

9. Stir whipping cream into tomato sauce mixture; pour over chicken.

1 Serving: Calories 420 (Calories from Fat 200); Fat 22g (Saturated 13g); Cholesterol 120mg; Sodium 1,210mg; Carbohydrate 28g (Dietary Fiber 5g); Protein 32g **% Daily Value:** Vitamin A 92%; Vitamin C 30%; Calcium 32%; Iron 26% **Diet Exchanges:** 1 Starch, 3 Lean Meat, 1 Vegetable, 1 Skim Milk, 1 1/2 Fat

Chicken Breast Stuffed with Cheese and Raisins

Raghavan Ki Baaten

☀ If I don't have any homemade cheese on hand, I use crumbled firm tofu or feta cheese as an alternative. Because feta cheese is salty, reduce the amount of salt in the filling by 1/2 teaspoon.

☀ Watercress leaves are an alternative for fenugreek leaves in the tomato-cream sauce, to create a similar-looking sauce without the complex flavors of fenugreek leaves.

Tandoori chicken (murghi) in all its reddish pink glory has been synonymous in the western world with Indian cooking. The tandoor is a bell-shaped, clay-lined oven used primarily in northern India. Home versions are normally the size of a very large stockpot and restaurant models can weigh over a ton. The intense heat (up to 700°) and the oven's inner clay walls ensure juicy, succulent meat. The flavors of meat, bread and vegetables cooked in a tandoor can be closely replicated on a charcoal or gas grill.

Marinated Grilled Chicken

4 SERVINGS

3- to 4-pound whole roasting chicken, skin removed

1 cup plain yogurt (regular or fat-free)

1/4 cup finely chopped gingerroot

10 medium cloves garlic, finely chopped

1 tablespoon coriander seed, ground

1 tablespoon sweet paprika

1 tablespoon Garam Masaala (page 32)

2 teaspoons salt

1 teaspoon cumin seed, ground

1 teaspoon ground red pepper (cayenne)

1/4 teaspoon red food color, if desired

1 medium red onion, cut into 1/2-inch slices

1 medium green bell pepper, seeds removed and cut into 1/2-inch rings

2 tablespoons finely chopped fresh cilantro

1 large lime or lemon, cut into 4 wedges

1. Make 6 to 8 deep cuts on breast and thighs of chicken with sharp knife. Place in large bowl.

2. Mix remaining ingredients except onion, bell pepper, cilantro and lime. Rub mixture on chicken and into cuts, coating evenly. Cover and refrigerate at least 6 hours but no longer than 24 hours.

3. Brush grill rack with vegetable oil. Heat coals or gas grill to medium for indirect heat. Remove chicken from marinade; reserve marinade. Cover and grill chicken, breast side up, 4 to 5 inches from heat 1 to 1 1/2 hours, turning and brushing occasionally with marinade, until meat thermometer reads 180° and juice is no longer pink when center of thigh is cut.

4. While chicken grills for the last 5 minutes, add onion and bell pepper rings to grill, turning occasionally, until crisp-tender.

5. Place chicken, onion and pepper rings on serving platter. Sprinkle with cilantro and serve with lime wedges to squeeze over chicken.

1 Serving: Calories 450 (Calories from Fat 215); Fat 24g (Saturated 7g); Cholesterol 150mg; Sodium 760mg; Carbohydrate 10g (Dietary Fiber 2g); Protein 50g **% Daily Value:** Vitamin A 16%; Vitamin C 24%; Calcium 12%; Iron 14% **Diet Exchanges:** 7 Lean Meat, 2 Vegetable

Marinated Grilled Chicken

Raghavan Ki Baaten

☀ Skin-on chicken is rarely eaten in India. Removing the skin and cutting into the flesh of the chicken allows the wonderful flavors of the marinade to penetrate the meat.

☀ You might want to try turkey, marinated and grilled in this fashion, for a fitting centerpiece at the Thanksgiving table.

A northern Indian delicacy, this recipe combines the healthful benefits of skinless chicken and yogurt. The chicken is enlivened with a coating made tart by mango powder. Take extra care not to overheat the yogurt or it will break apart and curdle.

Cumin-Scented Chicken

4 SERVINGS

2 tablespoons all-purpose flour

2 tablespoons mango powder (amchur) or 2 tablespoons grated lemon or lime peel

1 tablespoon cumin seed

1 teaspoon salt

1 teaspoon ground red pepper (cayenne)

3- to 3 1/2-pound cut-up broiler-fryer chicken, skin removed

2 egg whites, beaten

2 tablespoons vegetable oil

1/2 cup water

1/2 cup plain yogurt (regular or fat-free)

1 teaspoon roasted cumin seed (page 31), ground

2 tablespoons finely chopped fresh cilantro

1. Mix flour, mango powder, whole cumin seed, salt and ground red pepper in medium bowl.

2. Dip chicken pieces into egg whites, then coat with flour mixture.

3. Heat oil in 12-inch skillet over medium-high heat. Fry chicken 4 to 5 minutes, turning occasionally, until golden brown; drain any excess fat from pan.

4. Add water to chicken; reduce heat to medium. Cover and simmer 10 to 12 minutes, turning occasionally, until juice of chicken is no longer pink when centers of thickest pieces are cut.

5. Mix yogurt and ground cumin. Add yogurt mixture to chicken. Cook 1 to 2 minutes, stirring occasionally, just until yogurt is warm. Serve sprinkled with cilantro.

1 Serving: Calories 330 (Calories from Fat 145); Fat 16g (Saturated 4g); Cholesterol 120mg; Sodium 600mg; Carbohydrate 5g (Dietary Fiber 0g); Protein 42g **% Daily Value:** Vitamin A 2%; Vitamin C 0%; Calcium 8%; Iron 14% **Diet Exchanges:** 6 Lean Meat

Peppers in two forms are glorified in this recipe: fresh chilies and black peppercorns. This potent combination yields astonishingly sweet flavors when combined with coconut milk and sesame oil (light colored).

Grilled Rock Cornish Hens

Kozhi

4 SERVINGS

2 Rock Cornish hens (about 1 1/2 pounds each), skin removed

1/2 cup coconut milk

1/4 cup chopped fresh cilantro

1/4 cup chopped fresh karhi leaves

2 tablespoons grated gingerroot

2 tablespoons sesame oil (light colored)

1 tablespoon Sambhar Powder (page 35)

1 teaspoon salt

2 or 3 fresh Thai, serrano or cayenne chilies, finely chopped

1. Make 6 to 8 deep cuts on breast and thighs of each hen with sharp knife. Place hens in large bowl.

2. Mix remaining ingredients. Rub mixture on hens and into cuts, coating evenly. Cover and refrigerate at least 6 hours but no longer than 24 hours.

3. Brush grill rack with vegetable oil. Heat coals or gas grill to high for direct heat. Remove chicken from marinade; reserve marinade. Cover and grill hens, breast sides up, 5 to 6 inches from heat 30 to 40 minutes, brushing occasionally with marinade, until golden brown and juice is no longer pink when center of thickest part of breast is cut.

4. Cut each hen lengthwise in half along backbone from tail to neck with kitchen scissors before serving.

Raghavan Ki Baaten

☀ **Rock Cornish hens are small, specially bred chickens (also referred to as *game hens*) that weigh 1 to 1 1/2 pounds and have only white meat. Look for these hens in the grocery freezer case. They are not as meaty as other chickens and are often served in restaurants as individual portions. The wild chickens often used in New Delhi are very similar to these hens. You can substitute a broiler-fryer chicken of similar weight or for a more authentic flavor, pheasant or grouse.**

☀ **If karhi leaves are unavailable, eliminate from recipe.**

1 Serving: Calories 190 (Calories from Fat 90); Fat 10g (Saturated 4g); Cholesterol 100mg; Sodium 360mg; Carbohydrate 2g (Dietary Fiber 0g); Protein 23g **% Daily Value:** Vitamin A 2%; Vitamin C 2%; Calcium 0%; Iron 4% **Diet Exchanges:** 3 1/2 Lean Meat

Chapter Four

Vegetables

Clockwise from top: Stuffed Bell Peppers (page 120), Gujarati Cabbage Slaw (page 122), Eggplant with Shallots (page 135), Steamed Basmati Rice (pages 202 and 203)

COCONUT
(NARIYAL)

OPA SQUASH
(DUDHI)

MUSTARD GREENS
(SARSON KA SAAG)

YARD-LONG
GREEN BEANS
(KOTORANGAI)

MANGO
(TAYYAR AAM)

GREEN MANGO
(KUCHEE AAM)

GINGERROOT
(ADRAK)

PLANTAIN
(VAZHAIPAZHAM)

FRESH TURMERIC ROOT
(HALDI)

RIDGED SQUASH
(PEERKANGAI)

KARHI LEAVES
(KARI PATTA)

OKRA (BHINDI)

ASIAN EGGPLANT
(BAINGAN)

BABY BANANAS
(CHOTA KÉLA)

SWEET POTATO OR
YAM (RATALU)

BABY CUCUMBER
(TINDLA)

RED BANANAS
(LAL KÉLA)

CILANTRO
(TAAZA DHANIA)

MINT (PUDHINA)

ENGLISH
CUCUMBER

FRESH THAI, SERRANO
OR CAYENNE CHILIES
(HARA MIRCHI)

Fresh Produce of India

With India's long history of vegetarianism, much emphasis is placed on fresh fruits and vegetables. In India, most people shop daily at the open-air markets, called bazaars, for their fresh produce. At your local grocery store, supermarket and farmers' market, a fabulous bounty of fruits and vegetables is just waiting to be picked. You'll find a year-round cornucopia of familiar favorites and exotic newcomers. Most fresh fruits and vegetables are at the best price and flavor when they're in season. Your local Indian grocery store or other ethnic food stores will also offer up some delicious choices that you may not find elsewhere.

Asian eggplant *(baingan):* A light purple, 6- to 8-inch-long vegetable found in the ethnic-produce section of large supermarkets and Asian grocery stores. It is milder in flavor and cooks faster than regular eggplant; if unavailable, use regular eggplant.

Bananas *(kéla):* There are many varieties of banana in India. Each kind has its best use. For instance, one variety of yellow banana is offered to the gods with an incense stick inserted in the center at religious functions.

Baby banana *(chota kéla):* This short, chubby banana is also called a finger or dwarf banana. It is fully ripe when the peel is completely black, but some prefer the flavor when the peel is still partly yellow. The creamy textured fruit has a flavor reminiscent of apples and pears.

Plantain *(vazhaipazham):* Also referred to as vegetable-banana or tropical potato, the taste of this large banana changes as it ripens. When the peel is green to yellow, the flesh is firm and starchy (similar to a potato) and the flavor is bland. It is cooked and used as a vegetable. As the peel turns yellow-brown to black, the flesh remains firm but the flavor becomes

sweet so it can be used for desserts. Plantains are never eaten raw. They are readily available in most supermarkets and Asian and Latin grocery stores.

Red banana *(lal kéla):* The deep red peel does not change color as the fruit ripens. It is ready to eat if it feels soft when gently pressed and the peel is streaked with black. The flesh is pale pink-orange with a sweet, slightly floral flavor. It can be enjoyed raw or cooked.

Chilies *(hara mirchi):* See **Chili peppers, fresh and dried** on page 27.

Cilantro *(taaza dhania):* See **Cilantro** on page 28.

Coconut *(nariyal):* The coconut palm grows in India and yields thousands of coconuts over a lifetime. A coconut has several layers: a smooth, tan outer layer, a hard hairy dark brown layer with three "eyes," a thin brown skin and finally the jewel of the coconut—the creamy white meat. Usually the tan outer layer is removed before shipping to the United States. Fresh coconuts are readily available in most supermarkets and ethnic grocery stores. Select a coconut that is heavy for its size and sounds full of liquid when shaken. An unopened coconut can be stored at room temperature for several months. (For instructions on how to shred fresh coconut in a food processor or using a hard grater, see page 45.)

Cucumber *(kakadi)*: Believed to have originated in India or Thailand, the cucumber has been around for thousands of years. There are many different types, shapes and sizes, but one guideline remains the same: If the seeds are mature and the skin is thick, both should be removed. Baby cucumbers, known as *tindla* in the Northwest and *kovakkai* in the Southeast of India, are tiny and crisp with tender skin that does not need to be peeled before cooking. The baby cucumbers found in India, and at Indian food stores, aren't tasty raw, so they are always cooked in recipes. English cucumbers are long and seedless and have a mild flavor. They are a good substitute if baby or tender-skinned young cucumbers are unavailable.

Daikon radish *(mooli)*: A large, long white radish of Asian origin, daikon is sometimes called Japanese radish. It ranges from 6 to 15 inches in length and has a diameter of 2 to 3 inches and sometimes more. Its flesh is crisp, juicy and white with a sweet, fresh flavor. It has a pungency level between that of a garden-variety red radish and strong horseradish. Daikon can be served raw, cooked or as a garnish. Scrub it with a brush under running water before using. Refrigerate it wrapped in plastic up to 1 week. (Not pictured.)

Drumstick *(murungakai)*: This long, green vegetable has a woody exterior and is usually about 12 inches long and 1/2 inch thick. Drumsticks are never eaten raw; when cooked, the sticks are split open, and just the interior pulp is consumed. The mellow flavor and strong aroma are similar to asparagus. Canned drumsticks can usually be found at Indian grocery stores. When in season, fresh drumsticks may be available in the refrigerated section of Indian grocery stores as well. If unavailable, use asparagus instead. (Not pictured.)

Gingerroot *(adrak)*: See **Gingerroot** on page 29.

Karhi leaves *(kari patta)*: See **Karhi leaves** on page 29.

Mango *(aam)*: There are well over 150 varieties of mangoes in India, a concept hard to grasp when in the United States one is accustomed to seeing only one or two kinds at the grocery store. The mango that stands out as "the king of fruits" in India is the Alphonso. Called *Ratnagiri mango* *(aphoos)* after a village in the western state of Maharashtra, this smooth-skinned, saffron-hued, pulpy fruit graces the streets of Mumbai (Bombay) during the onset of the monsoon in early June. The pulp is very tender and devoid of any fiber, those pesky strands that are so common in mangoes available in the United States. Although Alphonsos are never exported fresh, they are available canned, either as slices soaked in sugar syrup or as a smooth pulp. Check your Indian grocery store or ethnic-food store for availability.

Green mango *(maangai/kuchee aam)*: Also known as the raw mango, this parrot-green, oval-shaped fruit is widely available in Asian grocery stores. Green mango is very firm to the touch and can be peeled and cut much like any hard vegetable. First, the skin can be easily removed with a vegetable peeler. The fruit inside ranges in color from snow white to a mellow egg-yolk yellow. The center of the fruit houses a small seed inside a tender shell that becomes firmer as the mango ripens. Then cut the mango lengthwise as close to the seed as possible. Cut the other half of the mango from the seed. Continue to cut off any flesh that remains on the seed and discard the seed. The mango flesh can then be cut or grated on the large holes of a four-sided grater.

Mint *(pudhina)*: See **Mint** on page 29.

Mustard greens *(sarson ka saag)*: There are many varieties of this green, and the most common in the United States is emerald green with frilly, scalloped edges. Sharp and pungent, this green tastes similar to prepared mustard with a hint of radish. Green leafy vegetables, such as spinach, kale, mustard greens and collard greens, are called *saag* in Hindi, India's national language. If mustard greens are unavailable, feel free to substitute any other fresh leafy green.

Okra *(bhindi)*: Also known as ladyfingers in India, tender, bright green okra pods taste a bit like a cross between asparagus and eggplant. Okra becomes rather sticky when cooked, but its delicate flavor overcomes its appearance. Fresh okra is widely available in supermarkets.

Opa Squash *(dudhi)*: This bowling pin–shaped summer squash is found in Indian and Asian grocery stores. It has a thin, light green skin and a wonderfully delicate flavor. Opa squash should be prepared in the same way as a cucumber: Slice the squash lengthwise and discard the seeds in the center. If unavailable, zucchini can be substituted, but then the peel and seeds do not need to be removed.

Papaya *(papeeka)*: This large, oblong yellowish green fruit contains black seeds. The sweet and juicy flesh of the Hawaiian papaya is bright yellow to orange, and the flesh of the Mexican papaya is bright orange to salmon red. Store fruit at room temperature until it yields to gentle pressure, then refrigerate up to 3 days. Papaya is available year-round, but peak season for some varieties is January through June. (Not pictured.)

Ridged squash *(peerkangai)*: This olive green squash with a ridged exterior is about a foot long. The flesh is tender and the seeds inside are normally not discarded, as they are soft and edible too. But the tough, coarse skin should be removed with a vegetable peeler. The squash is usually cooked in a little water until very tender and then pureed with other spices and ingredients. Ridged squash is widely available in Asian and Indian grocery stores. If unavailable, substitute peeled yellow summer squash.

Sweet potatoes *(ratalu)*: This large, edible root is native to tropical regions, including India. There are many varieties of sweet potato, but the two that are readily available are the pale orange–skinned sweet potato and the darker skinned one that is usually called a yam (although it is not a true yam). The pale-skinned potato is not as sweet and the flesh is dry. Sweet potatoes are used in many dishes throughout India.

Turmeric root *(haldi)*: See **Turmeric** on page 30.

Yard-long green beans *(kotorangai)*: This pencil-thin legume is usually harvested when it is about 18 inches long. It is used extensively in the southeastern region of India. A member of the black-eyed pea family, it has a delicate flavor and is more tender than a string bean. Also known as Chinese long bean, asparagus bean or pea bean, it is readily available at Asian markets and some supermarkets.

There are many varieties of bananas in India. Large, firm, green bananas, known as plantains, are used as a vegetable. When thinly sliced, fried and seasoned, they are a popular crunchy snack, similar to potato chips. Here, they are cooked until tender in a fragrant curry.

Plantain Curry

Vazhaipazham Curry

6 SERVINGS

1 tablespoon vegetable oil

1 teaspoon black or yellow mustard seed

1/4 teaspoon asafetida (hing)

2 tablespoons dried split and hulled black lentils (urad dal), sorted

2 large green plantains, peeled and cut crosswise into 1/4-inch slices (4 cups)

12 fresh karhi leaves

1 teaspoon Tangy Sambhar Powder (page 36)

1 cup water

1 teaspoon salt

1 tablespoon finely chopped fresh cilantro

1. Heat oil and mustard seed in wok or deep 12-inch skillet over medium-high heat. Once seed begins to pop, cover wok and wait until popping stops.

2. Add asafetida and lentils; stir-fry about 30 seconds or until lentils are brown. Add plantain slices, karhi leaves and Tangy Sambhar Powder; stir-fry 1 to 2 minutes.

3. Stir in water and salt. Heat to boiling; reduce heat. Cover and simmer 10 to 12 minutes or until plantain slices are tender. Serve sprinkled with cilantro.

Raghavan Ki Baaten

☀ In the United States, plantains are available in the produce section of large supermarkets, and Indian or Latin American grocery stores. Choose plantains that are green and very firm; those with yellow or dark streaks may still be firm but will impart an unwanted sweetness to this dish. Ripe plantains will, however, make a delicious dessert when cooked.

☀ If asafetida or karhi leaves are unavailable, eliminate from recipe.

1 Serving: Calories 130 (Calories from Fat 20); Fat 2g (Saturated 0g); Cholesterol 0mg; Sodium 400mg; Carbohydrate 29g (Dietary Fiber 3g); Protein 2g **% Daily Value:** Vitamin A 8%; Vitamin C 8%; Calcium 0%; Iron 6% **Diet Exchanges:** 3 Vegetable, 1 Fruit

Few vegetables are eaten raw in India, but beets are one of the exceptions. This salad is often served in restaurants and on street corners as an accompaniment to Garbanzo Bean Stew with Tomatoes (page 185) and Egg-Flavored Puffy Breads (page 251).

Raw Beet Salad

Kaccha Chukandar Salade

6 SERVINGS

4 medium beets, peeled and cut into julienne strips (2 cups)

2 medium red onions, cut in half and thinly sliced

1/4 cup finely chopped fresh cilantro

1 or 2 fresh Thai, serrano or cayenne chilies, finely chopped

1 tablespoon mango powder (amchur) or juice of 1 medium lime (2 tablespoons)

1 teaspoon black salt or regular salt

1. Mix all ingredients in medium bowl.

2. Cover and refrigerate at least 1 hour to blend flavors but no longer than 24 hours.

Raghavan Ki Baaten

☀ Beets, a root vegetable, are normally sold with their tops, which are edible and nutritious. Choose beets that are very firm. Deep red beets make for a beautiful salad. Since many supermarkets now sell a variety of multicolored beets, such as yellow and light red, this salad has the potential to become even more visually stunning than ever.

1 Serving: Calories 40 (Calories from Fat 0); Fat 0g (Saturated 0g); Cholesterol 0mg; Sodium 440mg; Carbohydrate 10g (Dietary Fiber 2g); Protein 2g **% Daily Value:** Vitamin A 16%; Vitamin C 16%; Calcium 2%; Iron 2% **Diet Exchanges:** 1 1/2 Vegetable

Simla, a breathtakingly spectacular hill-station (resort) nestled close to the Himalayas on the northeastern border of India, is often considered the Switzerland of India. During colonial rule, this resort was home to many English officials and their families who sought to escape the oppressive summer heat.

Stuffed Bell Peppers

Bharee Simla Mirch

8 SERVINGS

5 medium red potatoes (1 2/3 pounds), peeled and cut into fourths

4 large bell peppers in assorted colors (2 pounds)

1/2 cup chopped fresh cilantro

8 large cloves garlic

4 to 6 fresh Thai, serrano or cayenne chilies

1 teaspoon salt

1 teaspoon Spicy Garam Masaala (page 34)

Stuffed Bell Peppers are pictured on page 113.

1. Heat 1 inch salted water to boiling; add potatoes. Cover and heat to boiling; reduce heat. Cook about 20 minutes or until tender; drain. Mash potatoes in medium bowl; set aside.

2. Cut thin slice from stem end of each bell pepper. Remove seeds and membranes; rinse peppers. Cook peppers in enough boiling water to cover about 5 minutes or until crisp-tender; drain and set aside.

3. Heat oven to 350°.

4. Place remaining ingredients in food processor. Cover and process until coarsely ground. Add to potatoes; mix well.

5. Stuff peppers with potato mixture. Stand upright in ungreased square baking dish, 8 × 8 × 2 inches. Cover with aluminum foil and bake 30 to 35 minutes. Uncover and bake about 5 minutes longer or until potatoes are hot and peppers are tender. Cut each pepper lengthwise in half.

Raghavan Ki Baaten

☀ **Giant bell peppers are synonymous with the northeastern region of Simla, and many a succulent recipe pays homage to their sweetness. This robust filling of garlicky potatoes spiked with chilies offers a deliciously different approach. Use bell peppers in assorted colors to serve as a visually appealing side dish.**

1 Serving: Calories 95 (Calories from Fat 0); Fat 0g (Saturated 0g); Cholesterol 0mg; Sodium 300mg; Carbohydrate 24g (Dietary Fiber 3g); Protein 3g **% Daily Value:** Vitamin A 26%; Vitamin C 100%; Calcium 2%; Iron 6% **Diet Exchanges:** 1/2 Starch, 3 Vegetable

Utter the words "cooked cabbage and peas," and the odds are quite high that one of your picky eaters at the dinner table will say "yuck." Rest assured that this warm coconut-based cabbage salad is a recipe that will bring accolades from one and all and will be the talk of every gathering you share it with.

Cabbage with Peas

Muttaikose Patani

6 SERVINGS

2 tablespoons vegetable oil

1 teaspoon black or yellow mustard seed

2 tablespoons dried split and hulled black lentils (urad dal) or yellow split peas (chana dal), sorted

1 medium head green cabbage (1 1/2 pounds), shredded (8 cups)

1 cup frozen green peas

1/2 cup water

1 cup Shredded Fresh Coconut (page 45) or 1/2 cup dried unsweetened shredded coconut

2 or 3 fresh Thai, serrano or cayenne chilies

1 teaspoon salt

10 to 12 fresh karhi leaves, coarsely chopped (2 tablespoons)

1/4 cup chopped fresh cilantro

1. Heat oil and mustard seed in wok or deep 12-inch skillet over medium-high heat. Once seed begins to pop, cover skillet and wait until popping stops.

2. Add lentils; stir-fry about 30 seconds or until lentils are brown. Add cabbage; stir-fry 2 to 4 minutes or until partially wilted.

3. Stir in peas and water; reduce heat. Cover and simmer 5 to 7 minutes or until cabbage is tender.

4. Meanwhile, place coconut and chilies in food processor. Cover and process until mixture is coarsely ground. Stir coconut mixture, salt and karhi leaves into cabbage mixture. Cook uncovered 1 to 2 minutes. Serve sprinkled with cilantro.

1 Serving: Calories 145 (Calories from Fat 90); Fat 10g (Saturated 5g); Cholesterol 0mg; Sodium 440mg; Carbohydrate 16g (Dietary Fiber 7g); Protein 5g **% Daily Value:** Vitamin A 4%; Vitamin C 44%; Calcium 8%; Iron 10% **Diet Exchanges:** 3 Vegetable, 1 1/2 Fat

Raghavan Ki Baaten

☀ **If you do not have karhi leaves, omit from recipe.**

The state of Gujarat, just north of Mumbai (Bombay), is well known for its extraordinary vegetarian dishes. This deliciously crispy cabbage "slaw," that so eloquently balances sweet, hot and tart, includes peanuts, an important crop from this region.

Gujarati Cabbage Slaw

Bund Gobhi Nu Shaak

6 SERVINGS

1/4 cup peanut or vegetable oil

1/4 teaspoon asafetida (hing), (page 27)

1 cup dry-roasted unsalted peanuts, coarsely chopped

1 medium head green cabbage (1 1/2 pounds), finely shredded (8 cups)

1 cup Shredded Fresh Coconut (page 45) or 1/2 cup dried unsweetened shredded coconut

1/4 cup finely chopped fresh cilantro

3 fresh Thai, serrano or cayenne chilies, finely chopped

3 tablespoons sugar

1 teaspoon salt

1/2 teaspoon ground turmeric

Juice of 1 medium lime (2 tablespoons)

1. Heat oil in wok or deep 12-inch skillet over medium-high heat. Add asafetida and peanuts; sizzle 30 seconds.

2. Add remaining ingredients except lime juice; stir-fry about 5 minutes or until cabbage is hot; remove from heat. Stir in lime juice.

Gujarati Cabbage Slaw is pictured on page 113.

Raghavan Ki Baaten

☀ **Shred cabbage with a sharp knife, as opposed to a food processor. Supermarkets often stock shredded cabbage mix for coleslaw, making your job in the kitchen much easier.**

☀ **If asafetida is not at hand, omit from recipe.**

1 Serving: Calories 310 (Calories from Fat 215); Fat 24g (Saturated 7g); Cholesterol 0mg; Sodium 430mg; Carbohydrate 21g (Dietary Fiber 6g); Protein 9g **% Daily Value:** Vitamin A 4%; Vitamin C 44%; Calcium 10%; Iron 8% **Diet Exchanges:** 4 Vegetable, 4 1/2 Fat

Poshto is Bengali for a paste of roasted white poppy seed and cashews, a combination that's creamy-rich in flavor and texture. White poppy seed is available in Indian grocery stores and natural-food stores; if you can't find it, use black poppy seed instead.

East Indian Carrots and Peas

Poshto Diye Gajar Maatar shuti

6 SERVINGS

1 package (10 ounces) frozen green peas

2 tablespoons Mustard Oil (page 41) or vegetable oil

1/2 cup raw cashew pieces

1 tablespoon white or black poppy seed

1/2 cup plain yogurt (regular or fat-free)

1 teaspoon salt

1 tablespoon Panchphoran (page 38)

2 dried red Thai, serrano or cayenne chilies

5 medium carrots, cut into 1/4-inch slices (2 1/2 cups)

1/2 cup water

2 tablespoons chopped fresh cilantro

1. Rinse frozen peas under running cold water to separate; drain. Set aside.

2. Heat 1 tablespoon of the mustard oil in 10-inch skillet over medium-high heat. Add cashews and poppy seed; stir-fry 30 to 60 seconds or until cashews and poppy seed are brown.

3. Place cashew mixture, yogurt and salt in blender. Cover and blend on medium speed until smooth; set aside.

4. Heat remaining 1 tablespoon oil and the Panchphoran in same skillet over medium heat. Once seed begins to pop, cover skillet and wait until popping stops.

5. Add chilies; stir-fry about 15 seconds or until slightly blackened. Add carrots; stir-fry 1 to 2 minutes.

6. Stir in yogurt mixture, peas and water; reduce heat. Cover and simmer 12 to 15 minutes or until carrots are tender. Serve sprinkled with cilantro.

1 Serving: Calories 160 (Calories from Fat 90); Fat 10g (Saturated 2g); Cholesterol 0mg; Sodium 460mg; Carbohydrate 16g (Dietary Fiber 4g); Protein 6g **% Daily Value:** Vitamin A 82%; Vitamin C 10%; Calcium 8%; Iron 8% **Diet Exchanges:** 3 Vegetable, 2 Fat

Raghavan Ki Baaten

☀ **Dark yellow mustard oil, often used in its pure form in Bengali households in India, is very pungent and bitter. The oil is heated at high temperatures to rid it of impurities, a technique that warrants wide-open spaces. Sniffing hot mustard oil is comparable to slicing a 10-pound bag of potent onions. Tears flow as forcefully as the Ganges empties into the Bay of Bengal. Indian stores in this country stock mustard oil blended with soybean oil, offering a less intense experience with milder flavor. If mustard oil is not at hand, you can create your own version at home (page 41).**

Mumbai (Bombay), in the western state of Maharashtra, harbors a style of cuisine that balances the northern flavors of garlic with the southern flavor and texture of freshly grated coconut.

Cauliflower with Peppers

Phool Gobhi chi Bhaji

8 SERVINGS

2 tablespoons vegetable oil

1 teaspoon cumin seed

2 tablespoons dry-roasted unsalted peanuts

10 medium cloves garlic, finely chopped

1 medium head cauliflower (2 pounds), separated into flowerets

1 medium red bell pepper, cut into 1/2-inch cubes (1 cup)

1 cup water

1 cup Shredded Fresh Coconut (page 45) or 1/2 cup dried unsweetened shredded coconut

3 fresh Thai, serrano or cayenne chilies, finely chopped

1 teaspoon salt

2 tablespoons finely chopped fresh cilantro

1. Heat oil in wok or 3-quart saucepan over medium-high heat. Add cumin seed; sizzle 30 seconds.

2. Add peanuts and garlic; stir-fry 1 to 2 minutes or until garlic is golden brown. Add cauliflower and bell pepper; stir-fry 1 to 2 minutes.

3. Stir in remaining ingredients except cilantro; reduce heat to medium. Cover and simmer 10 to 12 minutes or until vegetables are tender. Serve sprinkled with cilantro.

1 Serving: Calories 95 (Calories from Fat 65); Fat 7g (Saturated 4g); Cholesterol 0mg; Sodium 320mg; Carbohydrate 8g (Dietary Fiber 3g); Protein 3g **% Daily Value:** Vitamin A 10%; Vitamin C 52%; Calcium 2%; Iron 4% **Diet Exchanges:** 2 Vegetable, 1 Fat

Cauliflower with Peppers

Raghavan Ki Baaten

☼ Peanuts are grown locally in Maharashtra. have added some to complement
the garlic, coconut and chili flavors and provide a little crunchy texture to
this dish.

Fenugreek leaves impart a bittersweet flavor and a heavenly perfumed aroma to this dish, making it well worth the effort to venture out to the nearest Indian grocery store. If unavailable, use fresh watercress leaves for a milder-flavored alternative.

Fenugreek-Scented Cauliflower

Methi Gobhi

6 SERVINGS

1/4 cup vegetable oil

1 large onion, finely chopped (1 cup)

10 medium cloves garlic, finely chopped

1 tablespoon dried pomegranate seeds (anardana), ground

1 tablespoon mango powder (amchur)

1 teaspoon cumin seed, ground

1/2 teaspoon ground red pepper (cayenne)

1 medium head cauliflower (2 pounds), separated into flowerets

1/2 cup water

2 cups plain yogurt (regular or fat-free)

2 cups finely chopped fresh or 1 cup crumbled dried fenugreek leaves

1 teaspoon salt

1. Heat oil in wok or 3-quart saucepan over medium-high heat. Add onion and garlic; stir-fry 2 to 4 minutes or until partially brown.

2. Stir in ground pomegranate seeds, mango powder, ground cumin and ground red pepper; stir-fry 1 minute. Add cauliflower; stir-fry 1 to 2 minutes.

3. Stir in water; reduce heat to medium. Cover and simmer 10 to 12 minutes or until cauliflower is crisp-tender.

4. Beat yogurt with wire whisk until smooth. Stir yogurt and remaining ingredients into cauliflower mixture; remove from heat. Cover and let stand 2 to 4 minutes or until yogurt is warm.

Raghavan Ki Baaten

☀ **Dried pomegranate seeds and mango powder are sour-tasting ingredients used primarily in the northern and western parts of India. If unavailable, substitute lemon or lime juice, teaspoon for teaspoon.**

☀ **Instead of cauliflower, you can use other vegetables such as broccoli, potatoes or asparagus. The yogurt used here gives a creamy texture and pleasantly tart flavor to this curry.**

1 Serving: Calories 15 (Calories from Fat 80); Fat 9g (Saturated 2g); Cholesterol 5mg; Sodium 490mg; Carbohydrate 15g (Dietary Fiber 3g); Protein 7g **% Daily Value:** Vitamin A 6%; Vitamin C 44%; Calcium 20%; Iron 4% **Diet Exchanges:** 3 Vegetable, 2 Fat

It is the monsoon season in Mumbai (Bombay), the rainy period that is a much-needed respite from the long, hot days of summer. The first rainfall hits the red soil to release the enticing, almost nutty aroma of Mother Earth herself. But the damp summer breeze brings along a far more alluring perfume: roasting cobs of corn. A man forcing a rickety pushcart topped with hundreds of ears of fresh-picked corn surrounding a charcoal-fired grill bellows out, "Sighadi bhutta!" (grilled corn).

Grilled Corn with Lime

4 SERVINGS

4 ears corn

1/2 teaspoon salt

1/2 teaspoon ground red pepper (cayenne)

1 medium lime, cut into 4 wedges

1. Heat coals or gas grill to medium for direct heat.

2. Remove husks and silk from corn; rinse corn. Grill corn uncovered 4 to 5 inches from heat for 15 to 20 minutes, turning occasionally, until golden brown.

3. Mix salt and red pepper. Dip lime wedges into salt mixture. Rub evenly over ears of corn.

1 Serving: Calories 110 (Calories from Fat 10); Fat 1g (Saturated 0g); Cholesterol 0mg; Sodium 310mg; Carbohydrate 25g (Dietary Fiber 3g); Protein 3g **% Daily Value:** Vitamin A 2%; Vitamin C 6%; Calcium 0%; Iron 2% **Diet Exchanges:** 1 1/2 Starch

It's amazing how corn and green beans come alive when matched with just the right ingredients. In addition to being simple to prepare, this recipe is extremely quick and will make that picky eater at your table enjoy every last kernel.

Cumin-Scented Corn and Green Beans

8 SERVINGS

3 ears corn

1 tablespoon Clarified Butter (Ghee), (page 45) or vegetable oil

1 tablespoon cumin seed

3/4 pound green beans, cut into 1-inch pieces

1/2 cup water

1/4 cup finely chopped fresh cilantro

1 cup Shredded Fresh Coconut (page 40) or 1/2 cup dried unsweetened shredded coconut

1 teaspoon salt

2 to 3 fresh Thai, serrano or cayenne chilies, finely chopped

1 teaspoon Spicy Garam Masaala (page 34)

1. Cut enough kernels from ears corn to measure 1 1/2 cups; set aside.

2. Heat Clarified Butter in wok or deep 12-inch skillet over medium-high heat. Add cumin seed; sizzle 30 seconds.

3. Add corn and remaining ingredients except Spicy Garam Masaala; stir-fry 30 seconds. Reduce heat. Cover and simmer 8 to 10 minutes or until vegetables are tender. Stir in Spicy Garam Masaala.

1 Serving: Calories 80 (Calories from Fat 45); Fat 5g (Saturated 4g); Cholesterol 5mg; Sodium 300mg; Carbohydrate 10g (Dietary Fiber 3g); Protein 2g **% Daily Value:** Vitamin A 4%; Vitamin C 2%; Calcium 2%; Iron 6% **Diet Exchanges:** 2 Vegetable, 1/2 Fat

Cumin-Scented Corn and Green Beans

Raghavan Ki Baaten

☀ I like to use fresh corn and green beans when they are at their seasonal peak. However, I do like to enjoy this dish all year, so I use a 10-ounce box of frozen whole-kernel corn and a 9-ounce box of frozen cut green beans. You don't need to add the 1/2 cup water because the frozen vegetables will give off more water than fresh.

Stir-Fried Baby Cucumbers

Tindla Nu shaak

6 SERVINGS

1 pound baby cucumbers (tindla) or English cucumbers	2 tablespoons sugar
	1 teaspoon cumin seed, ground
1 tablespoon vegetable oil	1/2 teaspoon salt
1 teaspoon cumin seed	1/2 teaspoon ground turmeric
1 teaspoon Bishop's weed (ajwain)	1/2 teaspoon ground red pepper (cayenne)
1/4 cup dry-roasted unsalted peanuts, coarsely chopped	1 cup water
	2 tablespoons finely chopped fresh cilantro

1. Trim off 1/4 inch from each end of cucumbers. Cut each cucumber lengthwise; set aside.

2. Heat oil in wok or deep 12-inch skillet over medium-high heat. Add cumin seed, Bishop's weed and peanuts; sizzle 30 seconds.

3. Add cucumbers and remaining ingredients except water and cilantro; stir-fry 1 to 2 minutes.

4. Stir in water; reduce heat. Cover and simmer 8 to 10 minutes or until cucumbers are crisp-tender. Serve sprinkled with cilantro.

Raghavan Ki Baaten

☀ Known as *tindla* in the Northwest and *kovakkai* in the Southeast, baby cucumbers are available in Indian grocery stores. If unavailable, substitute seedless English cucumbers: Trim off 1/4 inch from each end, then cut cucumbers into 1/2-inch slices. Cut each slice into 1/2-inch sticks.

1 Serving: Calories 80 (Calories from Fat 45); Fat 5g (Saturated 1g); Cholesterol 0mg; Sodium 200mg; Carbohydrate 8g (Dietary Fiber 1g); Protein 2g **% Daily Value:** Vitamin A 2%; Vitamin C 2%; Calcium 2%; Iron 4% **Diet Exchanges:** 2 Vegetable, 1/2 Fat

Sweet-and-Sour Eggplant

Mithu-tauk Begun

4 SERVINGS

4 medium Asian eggplants or 1 medium eggplant (1 1/2 pounds)

1 tablespoon Mustard Oil (page 41) or vegetable oil

1 tablespoon Panchphoran (page 38)

2 tablespoons sugar

1 tablespoon coriander seed, ground

1 teaspoon salt

1/2 teaspoon ground red pepper (cayenne)

1/4 teaspoon ground turmeric

1/2 cup water

1 tablespoon tamarind concentrate paste or juice of 2 medium limes (1/4 cup)

2 tablespoons chopped fresh cilantro

1. Cut eggplant crosswise into 1/2-inch-thick slices. Cut slices into 1/2-inch strips; set aside.

2. Heat oil and Panchphoran in wok or 12-inch skillet over medium-high heat. Once seed begins to crackle and pop, cover wok and wait until popping stops.

3. Add eggplant; stir-fry 1 to 2 minutes. Add sugar, ground coriander, salt, ground red pepper and turmeric; stir-fry about 1 minute or until spices begin to have a nutty aroma.

4. Stir in water; reduce heat to medium. Cover and simmer 5 to 8 minutes or until eggplant is tender. (If using regular eggplant, cook 10 to 15 minutes, or until tender.) Stir in tamarind paste. Cook uncovered 1 to 2 minutes or until paste is dissolved. Serve sprinkled with cilantro.

Raghavan Ki Baaten

☀ Asian eggplant is a light purple, 6- to 8-inch-long vegetable found in the ethnic-produce section of large supermarkets and Asian grocery stores. It is milder in flavor and cooks faster than regular eggplant; if unavailable, use regular eggplant.

1 Serving: Calories 85 (Calories from Fat 25); Fat 3g (Saturated 0g); Cholesterol 0mg; Sodium 600mg; Carbohydrate 17g (Dietary Fiber 4g); Protein 1g **% Daily Value:** Vitamin A 0%; Vitamin C 4%; Calcium 2%; Iron 4% **Diet Exchanges:** 3 Vegetable, 1/2 Fat

Smoky eggplant flavor offers an excellent backdrop to the subtle aromas of cloves and cinnamon in the Garam Masaala.

Grilled Eggplant Pâté

Baingan Bhurta

6 SERVINGS

2 small eggplants (about 1 pound each)

2 teaspoons coriander seed, ground

1 teaspoon cumin seed, ground

1 teaspoon salt

1/2 teaspoon ground red pepper (cayenne)

1/4 teaspoon ground turmeric

1 large onion, finely chopped (1 cup)

1/2 cup tomato sauce

Juice of 1/2 medium lime (1 tablespoon)

1 tablespoon grated gingerroot

2 medium cloves garlic, finely chopped

1/2 cup finely chopped fresh cilantro

2 tablespoons Clarified Butter (Ghee), (page 40) or vegetable oil

1 teaspoon cumin seed

1 teaspoon Garam Masaala (page 32)

1 large lime, cut into 8 wedges

Tandoori Breads (page 252) or Puffy Whole Wheat Breads (page 248), if desired

1. Heat coals or gas grill to high for direct heat.

2. Pierce each eggplant with fork in 5 or 6 places to vent steam when grilling. Place eggplants directly on coals or if using gas grill, on rack. Grill 15 to 20 minutes, turning occasionally, until skin is completely blistered.

3. Place eggplant in large bowl; cover with plastic wrap and let stand about 30 minutes. Peel and discard eggplant skin. Mash pulp until smooth.

4. Stir ground coriander, ground cumin, salt, ground red pepper, turmeric, 1/2 cup of the onion, the tomato sauce, lime juice, gingerroot, garlic and 1/4 cup of the cilantro into eggplant.

5. Heat Clarified Butter in wok or deep 12-inch skillet over medium-high heat. Add cumin seed; sizzle 30 seconds. Add 2 tablespoons of the onion; stir-fry 2 to 3 minutes or until golden brown.

6. Add eggplant mixture; stir-fry 15 to 20 minutes or until almost all liquid has evaporated. Stir in Garam Masaala; remove from heat.

7. Served sprinkled with remaining onion and cilantro and garnish with lime wedges. Serve with bread.

To Broil: Set oven control to broil. Place eggplant on rack in broiler pan. Broil eggplant with tops 2 to 3 inches from heat 15 to 20 minutes, turning occasionally, until skin is completely blistered.

1 Serving: Calories 75 (Calories from Fat 25); Fat 3g (Saturated 2g); Cholesterol 5mg; Sodium 520mg; Carbohydrate 14g (Dietary Fiber 4g); Protein 2g **% Daily Value:** Vitamin A 6%; Vitamin C 6%; Calcium 2%; Iron 6% **Diet Exchanges:** 3 Vegetable

Grilled Eggplant Pâté, Tandoori Breads (page 252)

Raghavan Ki Baaten

☀ Traditionally, in northern Indian villages and in North Indian restaurants in
the United States, eggplant is cooked on hot coals in the bell-shaped, clay-
lined oven called a tandoor, which can generate intense heat (up to 700°).
The same technique can be duplicated on a charcoal or gas grill.

Place a mild vegetable like eggplant in the hands of a Maharashtrian from the western state of Maharashtra, then sit back and experience the spicy fireworks on your palate. This delicacy is made with the long, light purple Asian eggplant. If unavailable, use the common variety and add about 5 to 10 more minutes to the simmering time.

Spiced Eggplant with Peanuts

8 SERVINGS

4 medium Asian eggplants or 1 medium eggplant (1 1/2 pounds)

1 cup dry-roasted unsalted peanuts

3/4 cup water

2 tablespoons mango powder (amchur) or juice of 1 medium lime (2 tablespoons)

1 tablespoon coriander seed, ground

2 teaspoons cumin seed, ground

1 teaspoon salt

1 teaspoon ground red pepper (cayenne)

1 teaspoon Spicy Garam Masaala (page 34)

1/4 teaspoon ground turmeric

1/4 cup vegetable oil

2 tablespoons chopped fresh cilantro

1. Cut each eggplant lengthwise in half; set aside.

2. Place remaining ingredients except oil and cilantro in blender. Cover and blend on medium speed until a smooth paste forms. Spread peanut mixture evenly over cut sides of eggplant.

3. Heat oil in 12-inch skillet over medium heat. Carefully place eggplant in skillet; reduce heat to low. Cover and simmer 7 to 10 minutes or until eggplant is tender. (If using regular eggplant, cook 15 to 18 minutes, or until tender.)

4. Carefully remove eggplant from skillet. Serve sprinkled with cilantro.

1 Serving: Calories 180 (Calories from Fat 135); Fat 15g (Saturated 2g); Cholesterol 0mg; Sodium 300mg; Carbohydrate 9g (Dietary Fiber 3g); Protein 5g **% Daily Value:** Vitamin A 0%; Vitamin C 0%; Calcium 2%; Iron 4% **Diet Exchanges:** 2 Vegetable, 3 Fat

Goshtu is Tamil (a prominent language in southern India) for a mixture of coarsely chopped vegetables. This combination of eggplant and shallots is native to the southeastern region of India.

Eggplant with Shallots

Katarikai Goshtu

8 SERVINGS

2 tablespoons vegetable oil

1 teaspoon black or yellow mustard seed

16 medium shallots, thinly sliced

1 medium eggplant (1 1/2 pounds), cut into 1/4-inch cubes

1 teaspoon tamarind concentrate paste dissolved in 1/4 cup water, or juice of 2 medium limes (1/4 cup)

3 or 4 dried red Thai, serrano or cayenne chilies

1 tablespoon coriander seed

1 teaspoon salt

Eggplant with Shallots is pictured on page 113.

1. Heat 1 tablespoon of the oil and mustard seed in wok or deep 12-inch skillet over medium-high heat. Once seed begins to pop, cover wok and wait until popping stops.

2. Add shallots and eggplant; stir-fry 5 to 7 minutes or until eggplant is partially cooked. Stir in tamarind-water mixture; reduce heat. Cover and simmer 3 to 5 minutes.

3. Meanwhile, heat remaining 1 tablespoon oil in 6-inch skillet over medium-high heat. Add chilies; roast about 30 seconds or until slightly blackened. Remove from skillet with slotted spoon.

4. Add coriander seed to same oil; roast 5 to 10 seconds or until seed is reddish brown. Remove from skillet with slotted spoon; stir into chilies.

5. Place chili mixture in spice grinder or mortar. Grind or crush with pestle until coarsely ground. Add chili mixture and salt to eggplant mixture; mash.

Raghavan Ki Baaten

☀ Tamarind concentrate, which comes in a paste form in plastic jars, is available in Asian and Indian grocery stores. If unavailable, substitute lime juice. Serve this eggplant recipe as an accompaniment to any of the lentil-based dishes (pages 168–77), along with Steamed Basmati Rice (pages 202 and 203).

1 Serving: Calories 55 (Calories from Fat 25); Fat 3g (Saturated 0g); Cholesterol 0mg; Sodium 310mg; Carbohydrate 8g (Dietary Fiber 3g); Protein 2g **% Daily Value:** Vitamin A 2%; Vitamin C 10%; Calcium 4%; Iron 4% **Diet Exchanges:** 1 1/2 Vegetable, 1/2 Fat

When tossed with golden raisins, I find that an extremely simple stir-fry of fresh greens becomes sweetly intriguing.

Greens with Garlic and Raisins

4 SERVINGS

2 tablespoons vegetable oil

1/2 cup golden raisins

1 small to medium red onion, cut in half and thinly sliced

5 medium cloves garlic, coarsely chopped

1 bag (12 ounces) washed fresh spinach

1 teaspoon Garam Massala (page 32)

1/2 teaspoon salt

1. Heat oil in wok or deep 12-inch skillet over medium-high heat. Add raisins; stir-fry about 1 minute or until raisins plump up.

2. Add onion and garlic; stir-fry 2 to 3 minutes or until onion is golden brown.

3. Mix in spinach; toss 2 to 3 minutes or until wilted. Stir in Garam Masaala and salt. Cook 1 minute.

1 Serving: Calories 140 (Calories from Fat 55); Fat 6g (Saturated 1g); Cholesterol 0mg; Sodium 370mg; Carbohydrate 21g (Dietary Fiber 3g); Protein 4g **% Daily Value:** Vitamin A 70%; Vitamin C 22%; Calcium 10%; Iron 16% **Diet Exchanges:** 3 Vegetable, 1/2 Fruit, 1 Fat

Greens with Garlic and Raisins

Raghavan Ki Baaten

☼ Green leafy vegetables such as spinach, kale, mustard greens and collard
greens are called saag in Hindi, India's national language. You can use any
one of these greens or a combination in this recipe.

A Tamilian favorite, this chili-spiked spinach stew is a very simple and quick accompaniment to many a main-course dish. You can also enjoy it with some Steamed Basmati Rice (pages 202 and 203) or Whole Wheat Unleavened Breads (page 236).

Spinach Stewed with Lime Juice

Keerai masiyal

6 SERVINGS

1 tablespoon vegetable oil

1 teaspoon black or yellow mustard seed

1/4 teaspoon asafetida (hing) or garlic powder

1 tablespoon dried split and hulled black lentils (urad dal) or yellow split peas (chana dal), sorted

2 packages (10 ounces each) frozen chopped spinach, thawed (do not drain)

1/2 teaspoon salt

12 fresh karhi leaves or 2 or 3 fresh or dried bay leaves

2 fresh Thai, serrano or cayenne chilies, cut lengthwise in half

Juice of 1 medium lime (2 tablespoons)

1. Heat oil and mustard seed in 2-quart saucepan over medium-high heat. Once seed begins to pop, cover saucepan and wait until popping stops.

2. Add asafetida and lentils; stir-fry about 30 seconds or until lentils are golden brown.

3. Stir in undrained spinach and remaining ingredients except lime juice; reduce heat. Partially cover and simmer 10 minutes. Stir in lime juice. If using bay leaves, remove and discard.

1 Serving: Calories 50 (Calories from Fat 25); Fat 3g (Saturated 0g); Cholesterol 0mg; Sodium 250mg; Carbohydrate 5g (Dietary Fiber 2g); Protein 3g **% Daily Value:** Vitamin A 48%; Vitamin C 8%; Calcium 10%; Iron 6% **Diet Exchanges:** 1 Vegetable, 1/2 Fat

Fresh okra, known as ladyfingers in India, is widely available in supermarkets. To clean fresh okra, rinse well in a colander under running water. Pat dry on paper towels. Remove stem ends of okra. You can use okra whole, or slice it. If fresh is unavailable, substitute frozen okra.

Okra Curry

Vendakkai Bhaaji

6 SERVINGS

1 tablespoon vegetable oil

1 teaspoon black or yellow mustard seed

1 cup chopped red onion

2 medium tomatoes, chopped (1 1/2 cups)

1 can (14 ounces) coconut milk

1 teaspoon tamarind concentrate paste or juice of 1 medium lime (2 tablespoons)

8 to 10 fresh karhi leaves or 2 tablespoons finely chopped fresh cilantro

1 pound fresh okra, cut into 1-inch pieces (4 cups)

1 tablespoon dried yellow split peas (chana dal), sorted

1 teaspoon coriander seed

1/4 teaspoon fenugreek seed (méthi)

4 to 6 dried red Thai, serrano or cayenne chilies

1 teaspoon salt

1. Heat oil and mustard seed in wok or deep 12-inch skillet over medium-high heat. Once seed begins to pop, cover wok and wait until popping stops.

2. Add onion; stir-fry 3 to 5 minutes or until golden brown. Stir in tomatoes, coconut milk, tamarind paste and karhi leaves; reduce heat to medium. Cover and simmer 3 to 5 minutes or until tomatoes are softened.

3. Stir in okra. Cover and simmer 5 to 7 minutes or until okra is crisp-tender.

4. Meanwhile, heat 6-inch skillet over medium-high heat. Add split peas, coriander, fenugreek and chilies. Roast 1 to 2 minutes, stirring constantly, until slightly darkened in color. Place spice blend in a spice grinder. Grind until coarsely ground.

5. Stir ground spice blend and salt into okra mixture. Cover and simmer 10 to 12 minutes or until okra is tender.

Raghavan Ki Baaten

☀ Tamarind paste contains a lot of acid, so do not use a cast-iron wok or skillet because the acid will react with the iron, discoloring the wok and making the curry taste metallic.

☀ When frying mustard seed, make sure you keep the skillet covered because the seed will pop right out of the skillet. Once it stops popping, you can remove the lid.

☀ Fenugreek seed has a bittersweet flavor and perfumed aroma; if unavailable, use yellow mustard seed instead.

1 Serving: Calories 55 (Calories from Fat 20); Fat 2g (Saturated 0g); Cholesterol 0mg; Sodium 400mg; Carbohydrate 10g (Dietary Fiber 4g); Protein 3g **% Daily Value:** Vitamin A 8%; Vitamin C 20%; Calcium 8%; Iron 4% **Diet Exchanges:** 2 Vegetable

When okra is stir-fried over low heat and simmered in its own moisture with no additional water, the result is surprisingly dry. This phenomenon is quite the opposite from that experienced in gumbo, the Louisiana delicacy.

Fresh Okra with Peanuts

4 SERVINGS

1 tablespoon peanut or vegetable oil

1 teaspoon cumin seed

1 pound fresh okra, stem ends removed

1/4 cup dry-roasted unsalted peanuts, coarsely chopped

1/4 cup chopped fresh cilantro

1 tablespoon sugar

1 teaspoon salt

1 teaspoon cumin seed, ground

1/2 teaspoon ground red pepper (cayenne)

1/4 teaspoon ground turmeric

1. Heat oil in wok or 12-inch skillet over medium heat. Add cumin seed; sizzle 10 to 15 seconds.

2. Add remaining ingredients; stir-fry 2 to 3 minutes. Reduce heat to low. Cover and simmer 15 to 20 minutes, stirring occasionally, until okra is tender.

1 Serving: Calories 110 (Calories from Fat 65); Fat 7g (Saturated 1g); Cholesterol 0mg; Sodium 600mg; Carbohydrate 11g (Dietary Fiber 4g); Protein 5g **% Daily Value:** Vitamin A 6%; Vitamin C 10%; Calcium 12%; Iron 8% **Diet Exchanges:** 2 Vegetable, 1 1/2 Fat

Fresh Okra with Peanuts

Raghavan Ki Baaten

☀ When purchasing fresh okra, choose those that are roughly 2 to 3 inches long and about 1/2 inch thick. Longer and thicker okra can have a woody texture.

☀ Pay extra attention to maintaining the cooking temperature at a low setting, or the spices will burn and impart a bitter flavor to this dish.

French fries, Gujarati style! This recipe was simplified by using frozen potatoes—feel free to substitute any cut of frozen French fries. Here's a classic example of how seasonings from the North (ground cumin) are mixed with ingredients from the South (karhi leaves) and given a typically northwestern twist (ground red pepper and sugar) to create a flavor balance that is unique to this region.

Spicy Potato Fry

Batata Nu Shaak

4 SERVINGS

1 package (14 ounces) frozen shoestring potatoes

1 tablespoon vegetable oil

2 medium tomatoes, finely chopped (1 1/2 cups)

3 tablespoons sugar

1 tablespoon chopped fresh cilantro

1 teaspoon cumin seed, ground

1 teaspoon salt

1 teaspoon ground red pepper (cayenne)

12 to 15 fresh karhi leaves

1 cup water

1. Bake potatoes as directed on package until golden brown and crispy; set aside.

2. Heat oil in wok or deep 12-inch skillet over medium-high heat. Add remaining ingredients except water; stir-fry 2 to 4 minutes or until tomatoes are softened.

3. Stir in potatoes and water. Simmer uncovered 5 to 8 minutes or until almost all water has evaporated.

1 Serving: Calories 185 (Calories from Fat 25); Fat 3g (Saturated 0g); Cholesterol 0mg; Sodium 980mg; Carbohydrate 40g (Dietary Fiber 3g); Protein 3g **% Daily Value:** Vitamin A 4%; Vitamin C 18%; Calcium 2%; Iron 6% **Diet Exchanges:** 1 Starch, 2 Vegetable, 1 Fruit

Raghavan Ki Baaten

☀ **If karhi leaves are unavailable, omit from recipe.**

The strong Kashmiri influence of almonds and poppy seed, originating from the Moghuls, elevates the humble potato to a kingly status. Although traditionally baked on hot coals, these potatoes can also be cooked in the oven.

Chunky Potatoes in Almond–Poppy Seed Sauce

4 SERVINGS

Vegetable oil for deep-frying

1 pound new potatoes (8 small)

1 tablespoon Clarified Butter (Ghee), (page 40) or vegetable oil

1 teaspoon cumin seed

1/2 cup finely chopped red onion

5 medium cloves garlic, finely chopped

1/4 cup slivered almonds, ground

1 tablespoon white or black poppy seed

1 1/2 teaspoons salt

1/2 teaspoon black peppercorns, ground

1/2 teaspoon ground red pepper (cayenne)

1 cup plain yogurt (regular or fat-free)

1 cup water

1 teaspoon Garam Masaala (page 32)

2 tablespoons finely chopped fresh cilantro

1. Heat oil (2 to 3 inches deep) in wok or Dutch oven over medium-high heat until thermometer inserted in oil reads 350°.

2. Remove the peel from half of each potato. Pierce each potato with fork or knife in 3 or 4 places to vent steam when frying. Carefully drop potatoes into hot oil, using slotted spoon, and fry 4 to 5 minutes, turning occasionally, until golden brown. Remove with slotted spoon; drain on paper towels.

3. Heat oven to 350°. Lightly grease 2-quart casserole.

4. Heat Clarified Butter in deep 12-inch skillet over medium-high heat. Add cumin seed; sizzle 30 seconds. Add onion and garlic; stir-fry 2 to 3 minutes or until onion is golden brown.

5. Stir in ground almonds, poppy seed, salt, ground black pepper and ground red pepper. Cook 30 to 60 seconds, stirring constantly, until almonds are golden brown. Stir in yogurt. Cook 4 to 5 minutes, stirring constantly, until water in yogurt has evaporated. Stir in water, fried potatoes and Garam Masaala.

6. Place potato mixture in casserole. Cover and bake 30 to 35 minutes or until potatoes are tender. Uncover and bake 10 minutes. Stir before serving; sprinkle with cilantro.

Raghavan Ki Baaten

☀ Evaporating the water in the yogurt makes it more tart, which adds extra flavor to this recipe. Even though water is added back in the next step, the tart flavor remains.

1 Serving: Calories 250 (Calories from Fat 110); Fat 12g (Saturated 3g); Cholesterol 10mg; Sodium 940mg; Carbohydrate 32g (Dietary Fiber 4g); Protein 7g **% Daily Value:** Vitamin A 2%; Vitamin C 10%; Calcium 18%; Iron 6% **Diet Exchanges:** 1 Starch, 3 Vegetable, 2 Fat

New Potatoes with Red Onions

Aloo Do Piaza

4 SERVINGS

2 tablespoons Clarified Butter (Ghee), (page 40) or vegetable oil

4 medium red onions, cut in half and thinly sliced (2 cups)

2 medium tomatoes, finely chopped (1 1/2 cups)

3 or 4 fresh Thai, serrano or cayenne chilies, crushed

1 teaspoon roasted cumin seed (page 31), ground

1 teaspoon salt

1/2 teaspoon cardamom seeds (removed from pods), ground

1/2 teaspoon whole cloves, ground

1/2 teaspoon black peppercorns, ground

1 pound new potatoes (8 small)

1/2 cup water

2 tablespoons finely chopped fresh cilantro

1. Heat Clarified Butter in wok or deep 12-inch skillet over medium heat. Add onions; stir-fry 10 to 12 minutes or until golden brown.

2. Stir in remaining ingredients except potatoes, water and cilantro. Simmer uncovered 5 to 7 minutes or until tomatoes are softened.

3. Stir in potatoes and water. Cover and simmer 15 to 20 minutes or until potatoes are tender. Serve sprinkled with cilantro.

1 Serving: Calories 195 (Calories from Fat 55); Fat 6g (Saturated 4g); Cholesterol 15mg; Sodium 610mg; Carbohydrate 36g (Dietary Fiber 5g); Protein 4g **% Daily Value:** Vitamin A 10%; Vitamin C 28%; Calcium 4%; Iron 12% **Diet Exchanges:** 1 Starch, 1 Vegetable, 1 Fruit, 1 Fat

New Potatoes with Red Onions

Raghavan Ki Baaten

☀ North Indian restaurants usually offer a meat-based dish called Do Piaza, an extremely aromatic preparation made with a large proportion of red onions. This vegetable recipe is an adaptation made with new potatoes instead. They are abundant during the onset of the summer months.

Here is a simple potato and pea curry that makes a deliciously quick side dish for many a harried weekday dinner.

Potatoes with Peas

Aloo Mutter

6 SERVINGS

1 tablespoon
vegetable oil

1 teaspoon cumin seed

1/2 cup finely chopped
red onion

2 medium tomatoes,
cut into 1-inch pieces
(1 1/2 cups)

1 teaspoon salt

1/2 teaspoon ground
red pepper (cayenne)

1/4 teaspoon
ground turmeric

3 medium red potatoes
(1 pound), peeled,
cooked and cut into
2-inch pieces (2 cups)

1 cup frozen
green peas

1 cup water

2 tablespoons finely
chopped fresh cilantro

1/2 teaspoon
Spicy Garam Masaala
(page 34)

1. Heat oil in 2-quart saucepan over medium-high heat. Add cumin seed; sizzle 15 to 30 seconds.

2. Add onion; stir-fry 1 to 2 minutes or until golden brown. Stir in tomatoes, salt, ground red pepper and turmeric; stir-fry 1 to 2 minutes or until tomatoes are softened.

3. Stir in remaining ingredients except Spicy Garam Masaala. Heat to boiling; reduce heat to medium. Cover and simmer 5 minutes. Uncover and simmer about 5 minutes longer or until sauce thickens slightly. Stir in Spicy Garam Masaala.

1 Serving: Calories 85 (Calories from Fat 20); Fat 2g (Saturated 0g); Cholesterol 0mg; Sodium 420mg; Carbohydrate 17g (Dietary Fiber 3g); Protein 3g **% Daily Value:** Vitamin A 4%; Vitamin C 14%; Calcium 2%; Iron 4% **Diet Exchanges:** 1/2 Starch, 2 Vegetable

Potatoes with Peas

Raghavan Ki Baaten

☀ If fresh tomatoes are not at hand, use 1 1/2 cups canned chopped tomatoes with juice and reduce the amount of water in the recipe accordingly.

The combination of spices used in this dish represents flavors often found in North Indian homes. This is also a very popular dish in many an Indian restaurant all over the world.

Potatoes with Cauliflower

Aloo Gobi

6 SERVINGS

1/4 cup vegetable oil

1 teaspoon cumin seed

I large onion, finely chopped (1 cup)

5 medium cloves garlic, finely chopped

2 tablespoons finely chopped gingerroot

3 medium red potatoes (1 pound), peeled and cut into 2-inch pieces (2 cups)

1 medium head cauliflower (2 pounds), separated into flowerets

1/2 cup chopped fresh or 1/4 cup crumbled dried fenugreek leaves or 1/2 cup chopped watercress leaves

1/4 cup chopped fresh cilantro

1 tablespoon coriander seed, ground

1 teaspoon cumin seed, ground

1 teaspoon salt

1/2 teaspoon ground red pepper (cayenne)

1/2 teaspoon ground turmeric

1 cup water

2 medium tomatoes, chopped (1 1/2 cups)

1. Heat oil in wok or 3-quart saucepan over medium-high heat. Add cumin seed; sizzle 30 seconds.

2. Add onion, garlic and gingerroot; stir-fry about 5 minutes or until onion is golden brown. Add potatoes; stir-fry 2 minutes. Reduce heat to medium. Cover and cook 5 minutes.

3. Add remaining ingredients except water and tomatoes; stir-fry 2 minutes. Stir in water. Cover and cook about 10 minutes or until vegetables are tender.

4. Stir in tomatoes. Cook 2 to 3 minutes or until tomatoes are hot.

Raghavan Ki Baaten

☀ Fresh, highly aromatic fenugreek leaves look like watercress, but their flavor is far sweeter with a hint of bitterness. They are seasonal and appear in stores usually in the summer months and sometimes in the winter. Dried fenugreek leaves, called kasoori méthi or just méthi, are more readily available, either by mail order or in many of the stores that sell Indian groceries. If neither is available, use watercress leaves or omit from recipe.

1 Serving: Calories 160 (Calories from Fat 70); Fat 8g (Saturated 1g); Cholesterol 0mg; Sodium 430mg; Carbohydrate 23g (Dietary Fiber 5g); Protein 4g **% Daily Value:** Vitamin A 4%; Vitamin C 50%; Calcium 4%; Iron 6% **Diet Exchanges:** 1 Starch, 2 Vegetable, 1 Fat

This recipe is a delicious combination of thoroughly cooked yet still-crunchy bean sprouts and crisped potatoes. Serve it chilled or at room temperature.

Sprouted Mung Bean Salad

6 SERVINGS

1 tablespoon vegetable oil

1 medium white potato, peeled and cut into 1/2-inch cubes (1 cup)

1 package (5 ounces) fresh mung bean sprouts (2 cups)

1 medium tomato, finely chopped (3/4 cup)

Juice of 1 medium lime (2 tablespoons)

1 tablespoon finely chopped fresh cilantro

1/2 teaspoon salt

1 or 2 fresh Thai, serrano or cayenne chilies, finely chopped

1/2 teaspoon Spicy Garam Masaala (page 34)

1. Heat oil in 10-inch nonstick skillet over medium-high heat. Add potato; stir-fry 6 to 8 minutes or until golden brown and crispy.

2. Add bean sprouts; stir-fry 5 minutes. Remove from heat. Cool 10 minutes.

3. Meanwhile, mix remaining ingredients in medium bowl. Stir in cooled potatoes and sprouts.

1 Serving: Calories 40 (Calories from Fat 20); Fat 2g (Saturated 0g); Cholesterol 0mg; Sodium 200mg; Carbohydrate 6g (Dietary Fiber 1g); Protein 1g **% Daily Value:** Vitamin A 2%; Vitamin C 8%; Calcium 0%; Iron 2% **Diet Exchanges:** 1 Vegetable, 1/2 Fat

A good source of vitamin A, sweet potatoes are used in many a South Indian stew and stir-fry. There are many varieties of sweet potato, but the two that are readily available are the pale orange–skinned sweet potato and the darker skinned one that is usually called a yam (although it is not a true yam).

Sweet Potato Curry

4 SERVINGS

1 tablespoon vegetable oil

1 teaspoon black or yellow mustard seed

1/4 teaspoon asafetida (hing)

2 tablespoons dried yellow split peas (chana dal), sorted

1 large sweet potato (1 pound), peeled and cut into 1/2-inch cubes

8 to 10 fresh karhi leaves or 2 tablespoons chopped fresh cilantro

1 teaspoon Tangy Sambhar Powder (page 36)

3/4 teaspoon salt

1/2 cup water

1. Heat oil and mustard seed in wok or deep 12-inch skillet over medium-high heat. Once seed begins to pop, cover wok and wait until popping stops.

2. Add asafetida and split peas; stir-fry about 1 minute or until peas are golden brown. Add remaining ingredients except water; stir-fry 1 to 2 minutes.

3. Stir in water. Heat to boiling; reduce heat. Cover and simmer 5 to 7 minutes or until sweet potato is tender.

1 Serving: Calories 60 (Calories from Fat 25); Fat 3g (Saturated 1g); Cholesterol 0mg; Sodium 450mg; Carbohydrate 9g (Dietary Fiber 3g); Protein 2g **% Daily Value:** Vitamin A 100%; Vitamin C 2%; Calcium 2%; Iron 6% **Diet Exchanges:** 2 Vegetable

Sweet Potato Curry

Raghavan Ki Baaten

☀ You might also want to try this recipe with pumpkin for a comforting fall dish. The pumpkin in India is much smaller than its American cousin. The seeds are often washed, dried and toasted with freshly ground spices and lentils, making a delightful snack.

☀ If asafetida is unavailable, omit from recipe.

Weddings in northern India usually are the best excuse to serve these deliciously smooth and creamy croquettes, since they are a symbol of fertility in the years to come for the new bride and groom. They are slightly laborious to make because multiple steps are involved, but rest assured that all your travails will be well rewarded!

Squash Croquettes in Cream Sauce

4 SERVINGS

Croquettes:

1 medium opa squash, peeled and shredded, or 2 medium zucchini, shredded (1 1/2 cups)

1 teaspoon salt

1/2 cup finely chopped red onion

1 tablespoon finely chopped gingerroot

1 tablespoon chopped fresh cilantro

2 or 3 fresh Thai, serrano or cayenne chilies, finely chopped

1 cup Garbanzo Bean Flour (Bésan), (page 44)

Vegetable oil for deep-frying

Cream Sauce:

1 tablespoon Clarified Butter (Ghee), (page 40) or vegetable oil

1 teaspoon cumin seed

1/2 cup finely chopped red onion

2 medium cloves garlic, finely chopped

1 can (15 ounces) crushed tomatoes, undrained

1 tablespoon coriander seed, ground

1 teaspoon cumin seed, ground

1/2 teaspoon salt

1/4 teaspoon ground turmeric

1/2 cup whipping (heavy) cream

1 teaspoon Garam Masaala (page 32)

1 tablespoon finely chopped fresh cilantro

MAKE CROQUETTES:

1. Mix squash and salt in medium bowl. Let stand 30 minutes.

2. Squeeze squash to drain. Mix squash and remaining croquette ingredients except oil. Shape mixture into eight balls.

3. Heat oil (2 to 3 inches deep) in wok or Dutch oven over medium-high heat until thermometer inserted in oil reads 350°.

4. Carefully drop about 4 croquettes into hot oil and fry 2 to 4 minutes, turning occasionally, until golden brown. Remove with slotted spoon; drain on paper towels. Repeat with remaining croquettes.

MAKE CREAM SAUCE:

1. Heat Clarified Butter in deep 12-inch skillet over medium-high heat. Add whole cumin seed; sizzle 30 seconds.

2. Add onion and garlic; stir-fry 2 to 3 minutes or until onion is golden brown. Stir in tomatoes, ground coriander, ground cumin, salt and turmeric; reduce heat. Partially cover and simmer 5 to 6 minutes or until a thin film of oil forms on the surface.

3. Gently stir in fried croquettes. Cover and simmer 5 to 6 minutes or until croquettes have absorbed the sauce and have softened; remove from heat.

4. Gently stir in whipping cream and Garam Masaala, taking care not to break up the croquettes. Serve sprinkled with cilantro.

1 Serving: Calories 260 (Calories from Fat 160); Fat 18g (Saturated 8g); Cholesterol 40mg; Sodium 1,060mg; Carbohydrate 24g (Dietary Fiber 6g); Protein 7g **% Daily Value:** Vitamin A 20%; Vitamin C 24%; Calcium 10%; Iron 14% **Diet Exchanges:** 5 Vegetable, 3 Fat

Squash Croquettes in Cream Sauce

Raghavan Ki Baaten

☀ Opa squash is a summer squash shaped like a bowling pin. Available in
Indian and Asian grocery stores, it has a thin, light green outer skin. In the
same way that you would prepare a cucumber, peel and slice the squash
lengthwise and discard the seeds in the center. Opa squash has a wonderful, subtle flavor. If unavailable, substitute zucchini, but then there's no
need to peel the skin or remove the seeds before cooking.

A South Indian cook is always judged by how good his or her Avial tastes. The coconut oil in this curry imparts a unique flavor, characteristic of the coastal state of Kerala. Keralites from this southwestern region frequently use coconut oil in their everyday cooking. And the long, dark tresses of a Keralite woman are especially silky as a result of coconut oil conditioning!

Mixed-Vegetable Stew with Coconut

6 SERVINGS

1 1/2 cups water

1 medium white potato, peeled and cut into julienne strips (1/2 cup)

1 medium sweet potato, peeled and cut into julienne strips (1/2 cup)

1 medium carrot, peeled and cut into julienne strips (1/2 cup)

1 small green plantain, peeled and cut into julienne strips (1/2 cup)

1 medium yellow summer squash, cut into julienne strips (1/2 cup)

1 medium zucchini, cut into julienne strips (1/2 cup)

1/2 cup frozen French-style green beans

1 medium drumstick, cut into 2-inch pieces (1 cup), if desired

1/2 teaspoon ground turmeric

1 cup Shredded Fresh Coconut (page 45) or 1/2 cup dried unsweetened shredded coconut

1 teaspoon cumin seed

4 to 6 fresh Thai, serrano or cayenne chilies

8 to 10 fresh karhi leaves or 2 tablespoons chopped fresh cilantro

1 teaspoon coconut oil, if desired

1 teaspoon salt

1. Heat water, all vegetables and turmeric to boiling in 3-quart saucepan; reduce heat. Cover and simmer 6 to 8 minutes or until vegetables are tender.

2. Meanwhile, place coconut, cumin seed and chilies in blender. Cover and blend on medium speed until a smooth paste forms, stopping blender occasionally to scrape sides. (If you need to add water for blender blades to effectively operate, use some of the liquid from saucepan containing vegetables.)

3. Stir coconut mixture and remaining ingredients into vegetable mixture. Simmer uncovered 2 to 3 minutes or until sauce is slightly thickened.

Mixed-Vegetable Stew with Coconut

Raghavan Ki Baaten

☀ Drumstick is a seasonal vegetable and, at times, Indian grocers offer a batch of fresh drumstick in the refrigerated section. They are also usually available in 15- or 16-ounce cans at any Indian grocery store. Half a can, drained, can be used instead of the fresh in this recipe, or if unavailable, use asparagus instead.

☀ Though coconut oil is high in saturated fat, a little goes a long way, as it is quite strong and flavorful. It can be found at Indian grocery stores.

These spicy scrambled eggs are often served with slices of toast made with white bread.

Persian-Influenced Scrambled Eggs

4 SERVINGS

1 tablespoon
vegetable oil

1 teaspoon cumin seed

1 medium onion,
finely chopped
(1/2 cup)

1 tablespoon finely
chopped gingerroot

6 large eggs, beaten

1/2 cup milk

1 teaspoon salt

1 medium tomato,
finely chopped
(3/4 cup)

2 tablespoons finely
chopped fresh cilantro

2 or 3 fresh
Thai, serrano or
cayenne chilies,
finely chopped

4 slices white bread,
toasted

1. Heat oil in 10-inch skillet over medium-high heat. Add cumin seed; sizzle 15 to 20 seconds. Add onion and gingerroot; stir-fry 2 to 3 minutes or until onion is golden brown.

2. Stir in eggs, milk and salt. Cook 3 to 5 minutes, stirring constantly, until eggs are completely cooked. Stir in tomato, cilantro and chilies. Heat 1 to 2 minutes or until tomatoes are hot.

3. Serve topped with toast.

1 Serving: Calories 240 (Calories from Fat 115); Fat 13g (Saturated 4g); Cholesterol 320mg; Sodium 840mg; Carbohydrate 19g (Dietary Fiber 1g); Protein 13g **% Daily Value:** Vitamin A 14%; Vitamin C 8%; Calcium 10%; Iron 12% **Diet Exchanges:** 1 Starch, 1 1/2 Lean Meat, 1 Vegetable, 1 Fat

Persian-Influenced Scrambled Eggs

Raghavan Ki Baaten

☀ In the United States, eggs are often associated just with breakfast; but in Parsee kitchens, this is an ingredient that is prized for other meals as well.

Just when you thought you've run out of ideas for all the leftover hard-cooked eggs from Easter, this tasty concoction from the Parsee kitchen comes to your rescue.

Egg–Tomato Curry

Indu Tamatar Curry

4 SERVINGS

1 tablespoon vegetable oil

1 medium onion, finely chopped (1/2 cup)

2 medium cloves garlic, finely chopped

1 tablespoon sugar

1 teaspoon salt

1 teaspoon cumin seed, ground

1 teaspoon coriander seed, ground

1/2 teaspoon ground red pepper (cayenne)

1/4 teaspoon ground turmeric

4 medium tomatoes, finely chopped (3 cups)

1 cup water

4 large hard-cooked eggs, cut crosswise in half

2 tablespoons finely chopped fresh cilantro

1. Heat oil in 3-quart saucepan over medium-high heat. Add onion and garlic; stir-fry 2 to 3 minutes or until golden brown.

2. Stir in sugar, salt, ground cumin, ground coriander, ground red pepper and turmeric; cook and stir 1 to 2 minutes. Stir in tomatoes and water. Simmer uncovered 5 to 7 minutes or until tomatoes are partially softened.

3. Add eggs. Simmer 2 to 4 minutes longer or until eggs are hot. Gently stir in cilantro.

Raghavan Ki Baaten

☀ **Plates of Steamed Basmati Rice (pages 202 and 203) and fluffy Whole Wheat Unleavened Breads (page 236) are great accompaniments to this robust curry.**

1 Serving: Calories 155 (Calories from Fat 80); Fat 9g (Saturated 2g); Cholesterol 210mg; Sodium 660mg; Carbohydrate 12g (Dietary Fiber 2g); Protein 8g **% Daily Value:** Vitamin A 14%; Vitamin C 20%; Calcium 4%; Iron 8% **Diet Exchanges:** 1 Medium-Fat Meat, 2 Vegetable, 1 Fat

This dish, a staple in many an Indian restaurant, is not an everyday occurrence in North Indian kitchens. Holidays, family gatherings and other special events warrant the extra time spent in the kitchen to make this deliciously robust recipe.

Homemade Cheese with Spinach

Saag Paneer

6 SERVINGS

2 tablespoons vegetable oil

5 medium cloves garlic, finely chopped

2 tablespoons finely chopped gingerroot

1 cup tomato sauce

1 tablespoon coriander seed, ground

1 teaspoon cumin seed, ground

1 teaspoon ground red pepper (cayenne)

1 teaspoon salt

2 packages (10 ounces each) frozen chopped spinach, thawed (do not drain)

2 cups 1/2-inch cubes fried Homemade Cheese (page 42)

1/2 cup whipping (heavy) cream

1 teaspoon Garam Masaala (page 32)

1. Heat oil in 3-quart saucepan over medium-high heat. Add garlic and gingerroot; stir-fry 1 to 2 minutes or until garlic is golden brown.

2. Stir in tomato sauce, ground coriander, ground cumin, ground red pepper and salt; reduce heat to low. Partially cover and simmer 7 to 8 minutes or until thin film of oil starts to form on surface of sauce.

3. Stir in undrained spinach. Cover and simmer 8 to 10 minutes or until spinach turns a light olive green.

4. Stir in Homemade Cheese. Cover and simmer 3 to 4 minutes or until cheese is hot; remove from heat.

5. Stir in whipping cream and Garam Masaala.

Raghavan Ki Baaten

☀ Homemade cheese (paneer) is very simple to make, but it does take 6 to 8 hours to firm up. You can substitute extra-firm tofu if time is of the essence. Drain and fry the tofu in the same manner as fried Handmade Cheese (page 42) is prepared.

1 Serving: Calories 340 (Calories from Fat 200); Fat 22g (Saturated 11g); Cholesterol 65mg; Sodium 860mg; Carbohydrate 24g (Dietary Fiber 3g); Protein 14g **% Daily Value:** Vitamin A 66%; Vitamin C 14%; Calcium 50%; Iron 10% **Diet Exchanges:** 1/2 Medium-Fat Meat, 5 Vegetable, 4 Fat

Yet another northern Indian restaurant staple, this recipe of sweet green peas combined with protein-rich paneer is a substantially satiating side dish.

Homemade Cheese with Peas

Mutter Paneer

6 SERVINGS

1 tablespoon Clarified Butter (Ghee), (page 40) or vegetable oil

1 teaspoon cumin seed

1 cup finely chopped red onion

1 tablespoon finely chopped gingerroot

1 large tomato, finely chopped (1 cup)

1 tablespoon finely chopped fresh cilantro

1 teaspoon salt

1 teaspoon ground red pepper (cayenne)

1 teaspoon Garam Masaala (page 32)

1 bag (16 ounces) frozen green peas

2 cups 1/2-inch cubes fried Homemade Cheese (page 42)

1 1/2 cups water

1. Heat Clarified Butter in 2-quart saucepan over medium-high heat. Add cumin seed; sizzle 15 to 30 seconds.

2. Add onion and gingerroot; stir-fry 1 to 2 minutes or until onion is golden brown.

3. Stir in tomato and cilantro. Cook 1 to 2 minutes or until tomato is softened. Stir in salt, ground red pepper and Garam Masaala. Cook 1 minute.

4. Stir in frozen peas, Homemade Cheese and water. Heat to boiling; reduce heat. Cover and simmer 10 to 12 minutes or until peas are tender and sauce thickens slightly.

1 Serving: Calories 305 (Calories from Fat 160); Fat 18g (Saturated 9g); Cholesterol 50mg; Sodium 590mg; Carbohydrate 25g (Dietary Fiber 3g); Protein 14g **% Daily Value:** Vitamin A 14%; Vitamin C 12%; Calcium 40%; Iron 6% **Diet Exchanges:** 1/2 Medium-Fat Meat, 5 Vegetable, 3 Fat

Homemade Cheese with Peas

Raghavan Ki Baaten

☼ If you make the cheese ahead of time and freeze it, there is no need to thaw it before adding it to the dish. It will thaw and heat through during the 10-minute cooking period.

Chapter Five

Lentils, Beans and Peas

Clockwise from top right: Multi-Lentil Persian Stew with Vegetables (page 168), Kidney Beans with Cardamom-Yogurt Sauce (page 181), Creamed Black Lentils (page 169), Spiced Puffed Breads (page 250)

the Indian World of Legumes

Legumes are a staple in vegetarian and non-vegetarian Indian homes alike, so it is fortunate that India offers more than sixty varieties. Pulses, including lentils, mung beans and peas, are the dried seeds of legumes, which are plants that bear pods containing one row of seeds. The legume category also includes beans and peanuts. Ease of cultivation, long shelf life, low cost and very high nutritional value make them ideal candidates for the Indian table. Combine them with herbs and spices and voilà: There are countless unbeatable combinations. Each legume has its own distinct flavor. So even if the same combination of spices is used to season different legumes, each dish will take on its own unique flavor.

Dal, or *dahl* (pronounced "doll"), the generic Hindi term for all lentil-based preparations, is a must at every meal. Lentils come in three different forms: whole, split with skins intact and split with skins removed. As ingredients, though, usually only the split lentils are called *dal.* For example, split and hulled black lentils are called *urad dal,* while their whole counterparts are *sabud urad.*

Buying and Storing Legumes

Lentils, beans and peas are available at every supermarket, natural-food store, ethnic-food store and Indian grocery store. The common varieties are easy to find, but you may have to make a trip to the Indian grocery store for some of the more unusual ones. Mail-order or Web-site sources are another option if there isn't an Indian store nearby (see pages 20 to 21).

Many natural-food and ethnic-food stores sell legumes in bulk, so customers can buy as much or little as needed. If getting to a specialty store regularly is not an option, you may want to consider buying larger quantities. Purchase lentils in the form called for in the recipe, since lentils of the same variety in a different form won't work as substitutes. For example, mung beans are available whole, split with skins left on and split with no skins (hulled). Each form has a distinct cooking time, texture and flavor and one cannot be substituted for another.

When purchasing legumes, look for bright, uniform color and smooth, unbroken skins, which indicate quality and freshness. Choosing legumes of the same size will result in even cooking. Sort through them before cooking to remove damaged or shriveled legumes and any foreign matter such as small pebbles or sandy grit. Most legumes can be stored indefinitely, but for optimum quality and flavor, use them within one to two years. Store them in the original packaging or transfer to airtight glass or plastic containers, and label contents with the starting storage date. Store in a cool (60° or less), dry location.

Cooking and Eating Legumes

Lentils and split peas cook more quickly than dried beans and peas in their whole form. Check packages for basic cooking directions. Factors such as water hardness, high altitude and age of the legume may increase cooking time, and very old legumes may never soften completely. A pressure cooker is not recommended. Legumes create foam that can clog the pressure valve.

Legumes have the reputation of causing flatulence (intestinal gas), which can occur when the digestive system is unable to fully digest their complex sugars. This can be lessened by draining the soaking liquid used to hydrate dried legumes or by rinsing and draining canned

GARBANZO BEANS
(KABULI CHANNA)

BASMATI RICE
(BASMATI CHAAWAL)

GARBANZO BEAN FLOUR
(BÉSAN/CHANA ATTA)

RED KIDNEY BEANS
(RAJMAH)

CHAPPATI FLOUR
(ROTI KA ATTA)

RED LENTILS
(MASOOR DAL)

HOT WHEAT CEREAL
(RAVA)

RICE FLOUR
(CHAAWAL KA ATTA)

WHOLE GREEN LENTILS
(SABUD MUNG/MOONG)

SPLIT AND HULLED
PIGEON PEAS
(TOOVAR DAL)

SPLIT AND HULLED GREEN
LENTILS *(MUNG/MOONG DAL)*

YELLOW SPLIT PEAS
(CHANA DAL)

SORGHUM FLOUR
(JOWAR KA ATTA)

BLACK-EYED PEAS
(LOBHIA)

GREEN LIMA BEANS
(VAAL NU DAL)

SPLIT AND HULLED
*BLACK LENTILS
(URAD DAL)*

WHITE LIMA BEANS
(VAAL NU DAL)

WHOLE BLACK
LENTILS *(SABUD
URAD)*

legumes. Draining dried or canned beans causes minimal nutritional loss. Certain Indian spices such as Bishop's weed *(ajwain)*, asafetida *(hing)*, turmeric *(haldi)* and gingerroot *(adrak)* are thought to minimize bloating and gas, and either one or a combination is used in many legume-based recipes.

When adding more legumes to your diet, it is recommended that you add them gradually over a period of several weeks to allow your digestive system time to adjust.

Glossary of Lentils, Beans and Peas

Black-eyed peas *(lobhia)*: Native to China, these small off-white peas look like little kidneys with a tiny black circle, their black "eye," on the inside curve.

Garbanzo beans *(kabuli channa)*: Also called chickpeas, these light brown, bumpy beans have a nutty flavor and firm texture. They are also ground into fine flour *(bésan)* and used extensively in Indian cooking.

Lima beans *(vaal)*: Indian lima beans are slightly different than the ones available in the United States. They are off-white in color and look like kidney-shaped butter beans. Lima beans are called butter beans in the southern United States.

Red kidney beans *(rajmah)*: A robust-flavored bean that is used extensively in the North, it is an ideal choice for some of the strong sauces and seasonings from that region. Its hearty texture is welcoming for people who try to eat more meatless meals.

Red lentils *(masoor dal)*: Also known as Egyptian lentils, these beautiful salmon-colored legumes are available in large supermarkets and natural-food stores. They are often combined with the similarly shaped split and hulled green lentils *(mung dal)* in North Indian kitchens to create uniquely flavored stews *(dals)*. Their brilliant color changes to yellow when cooked.

Split and hulled black lentils *(urad dal)*: The name of this lentil is a bit misleading: Once they are split open and the skin is removed, these lentils aren't black at all—they are off-white. Southern Indians use this form exclusively, not only for their crepes, pancakes and dumplings, but also as an important ingredient in many of their spice blends.

Split and hulled green lentils *(mung/moong dal)*: These lentils are actually yellow once they are split and their green skin is discarded. Within 15 minutes of cooking, these easily digestible lentils are tender, making them popular for quick meals. When overcooked, their texture turns to mush.

Split and hulled pigeon peas *(toovar/toor dal)*: *Toovar dal* is packaged in two ways in India: oily and dry. The oily version has a coating of vegetable oil to help prevent insect infestation that can occur due to its sweetness. The dry variety is uncoated. Either one will work in the recipes. If you won't be using them regularly, buy the oily kind, but be sure to wash the oil off before cooking. The dry variety is more common in South India, where they are heavily consumed. Certain spice blends include these peas as a prime ingredient. Almost all of South India's soups and stews are made with these peas. *Toovar dal* is never used in classic North Indian cooking.

Whole black lentils *(sabud urad)*: These tiny, black, oval-shaped legumes are primarily available in stores that sell Indian groceries. *Sabud urad* is used extensively and exclusively in North India, and when cooked, it has a slightly creamy texture.

Whole green lentils *(sabud mung/moong beans)*: Tiny and oval-shaped, like the black lentils *(sabud urad)*, these lentils are forest green and quite versatile. Their cooking time is comparable to whole black lentils, about forty-five minutes to an hour.

Whole pigeon peas *(sabud toovar/toor)*: These peas are used fresh in the northwestern state of Gujarat and are similar in texture to common green peas. *Toovar* peas are oval-shaped and very sweet. When they are split and hulled, they are called *toovar dal*. The dried version is also a delicacy in this region and is more commonly available in Indian grocery stores. Some stores stock the fresh peas in the freezer section.

Yellow split peas *(chana dal)*: Widely available, these deep yellow peas, shaped like thick, tiny contact lenses, are sweet tasting. Because they are split, their cooking time is very short, making them an ideal candidate for a weekday meal. Even when cooked, they retain their firm shape and texture.

Additional Grains and Flours

Basmati rice *(basmati chaawal)*: True basmati rice is grown and cultivated in the foothills of the Himalayas, whose surrounding areas offer uniquely rich soil and a cool climate. Basmati rice has a perfumed, nutty aroma when cooked. (In fact, *bas* refers to aroma.) The long, tender grains swell to extra fluffiness when cooked. Basmati rice can be purchased at Indian grocery stores, specialty foods stores and some supermarkets.

Chappati flour *(geon ka atta)*: Chappati flour is used to make all kinds of breads throughout India, especially the pervasive whole wheat unleavened breads known as rotis or chappatis (page 238). Chappati flour is available at Indian grocery stores and many natural-food stores. The flour is ground from a low-protein wheat grain, so it doesn't form the strong gluten that gives commercial yeast breads their structure. If chappati flour is unavailable, use a combination of whole-wheat flour, all-purpose flour and cake flour in equal proportions for each cup of chappati flour to produce very tender breads. If you use the proportion of one-third whole-wheat flour to two-thirds all-purpose flour, your breads will also be delicious.

Sorghum flour *(jowar ka atta)*: Sorghum is a cereal grass with broad corn-like leaves and clusters of grains at the end of its stalks. It is the third-most produced grain in the United States, but it is rarely used for human consumption here, in spite of the fact that it is extremely nutritious. Third World nations such as India, however, feed their poor with sorghum flour, which is primarily made into bread. Sorghum flour, which is quite dry and dense, is available in Indian grocery stores, some natural-food stores and by mail order. If you're unable to find it, try equal parts of yellow and white cornmeal instead.

Garbanzo bean flour *(bésan)*: Commercially made garbanzo bean flour (also called chickpea flour or gram flour) is available in Indian grocery stores, natural-food stores and in the ethnic-food section of some supermarkets. Garbanzo bean flour has a nutty, slightly tart flavor and a wonderfully crispy texture, especially when it is used to make a batter for fried foods. In India, garbanzo bean flour is used to make a wide variety of appetizers, breads and other foods. It is also sometimes added to a sauce (curry) to thicken it. There is no substitute for this flour, but it can be easily made in your own kitchen using dried garbanzo beans (page 44).

Hot wheat cereal/semolina *(rava/sooji)*: While Americans enjoy a bowl of sweetened hot wheat cereal for breakfast, most Indians prefer to use it as a savory ingredient in appetizers, breads, puddings and many other savory dishes. Hot wheat cereal is processed from the inside of wheat kernels (the endosperm) and is off-white and coarse in texture. The slow-cooking cereal (not the instant variety) is used all across India.

Rice flour *(chaawal ka atta)*: Among the lightest of flours, rice flour is used throughout South India to make a wide array of steamed noodles, dumplings, crepes and batters. It is also used as a thickener in many sauces (curries). Rice flour is available in Asian grocery stores, natural-food stores and in the ethnic foods section of some large supermarkets. Rice flour is so light-textured, in fact, that it was used as the base of face powder in past centuries.

What apple pie is to an American, dhansaak is to a Parsee from Mumbai (Bombay). This combination of legumes (dhan) and vegetables (saak), oftentimes cooked with the addition of pieces of bone-in chicken, is a meal when served with Steamed Basmati Rice (pages 202 and 203).

Multi-Lentil Persian Stew with Vegetables

8 SERVINGS

1/2 cup dried split and hulled pigeon peas (toovar dal) or yellow split peas (chana dal), sorted, rinsed and drained

1/4 cup dried red lentils (masoor dal), sorted, rinsed and drained

2 tablespoons dried yellow split peas (chana dal), sorted, rinsed and drained

2 tablespoons dried split and hulled green lentils (mung dal), sorted, rinsed and drained

6 1/2 cups water

2 medium red onions, cut in half and thinly sliced

1 package (10 ounces) frozen chopped spinach, thawed (do not drain)

2 medium carrots, sliced (1 cup)

1 medium tomato, coarsely chopped (3/4 cup)

1 or 2 fresh Thai, serrano or cayenne chilies, cut lengthwise in half

2 tablespoons Clarified Butter (Ghee), (page 40) or vegetable oil

1 tablespoon grated gingerroot

5 medium cloves garlic, finely chopped

1 tablespoon coriander seed, ground

1 teaspoon salt

1/2 teaspoon ground red pepper (cayenne)

1/2 teaspoon ground cinnamon

1/2 teaspoon ground cloves

1/4 teaspoon ground turmeric

1/4 cup finely chopped fresh cilantro

1 large lime, cut into 8 wedges

1. Place pigeon peas, red lentils, yellow split peas, green lentils, 6 cups of the water, 1/2 cup of the onion, the undrained spinach, carrots, tomato and chilies in 3-quart saucepan. Heat to boiling; reduce heat. Simmer uncovered 15 to 20 minutes, skimming off any foam that floats to the top, until lentils are softened and most of the liquid is absorbed; remove from heat.

2. While lentil mixture is simmering, heat Clarified Butter in 10-inch skillet over medium-high heat. Add remaining 1/2 cup onion, the gingerroot and garlic; stir-fry 2 to 3 minutes, being careful not to burn mixture, until mixture is dark brown.

3. Add remaining ingredients except cilantro and lime to garlic mixture; stir-fry 30 to 60 seconds or until spices have a nutty aroma.

4. Stir in remaining 1/2 cup water. Heat to boiling, scraping brown bits from bottom of skillet. Stir spice mixture into lentil mixture. Simmer uncovered 15 minutes.

5. Serve garnished with cilantro and lime wedges.

Multi-Lentil Persian Stew with Vegetables is pictured on page 163.

1 Serving: Calories 105 (Calories from Fat 35); Fat 4g (Saturated 2g); Cholesterol 10mg; Sodium 320mg; Carbohydrate 17g (Dietary Fiber 6g); Protein 6g **% Daily Value:** Vitamin A 50%; Vitamin C 16%; Calcium 6%; Iron 10% **Diet Exchanges:** 1 Starch, 1/2 Fat

Raghavan Ki Baaten

☼ **Deglazing** is a technique often used by cooks to provide intense flavors in recipes. When ingredients such as onions or vegetables are cooked in a skillet, browned bits tend to stick to the bottom of the pan. Water or other liquid is added to the skillet to loosen those intensely flavored brown bits from the pan.

A staple in North Indian restaurants around the world, these tiny black lentils, similar in shape and size to the mung bean, are used primarily in the North. This recipe will create a broth style of soup that can be served over rice.

Creamed Black Lentils

Makhani Dal

4 SERVINGS

1 cup dried whole black lentils (sabud urad), sorted, rinsed and drained

6 cups water

2 tablespoons Clarified Butter (Ghee), (page 40) or vegetable oil

1 tablespoon finely chopped gingerroot

5 medium cloves garlic, finely chopped

1 cup tomato sauce

1 tablespoon coriander seed, ground

1 teaspoon cumin seed, ground

1/2 teaspoon ground red pepper (cayenne)

1/2 cup whipping (heavy) cream

1/2 teaspoon salt

1/2 teaspoon Garam Masaala (page 32)

Whipping (heavy) cream, if desired

2 tablespoons finely chopped fresh cilantro

Creamed Black Lentils are pictured on page 163.

1. Place lentils and 4 cups of the water in 3-quart saucepan. Heat to boiling; reduce heat. Partially cover and simmer 20 to 25 minutes.

2. Stir in remaining water. Partially cover and simmer 20 to 25 minutes longer or until lentils are tender.

3. While lentils are simmering, heat Clarified Butter in 10-inch skillet over medium heat. Add gingerroot and garlic; stir-fry 1 to 2 minutes or until garlic is golden brown.

4. Stir tomato sauce, ground coriander, ground cumin and ground red pepper into garlic mixture; reduce heat to medium low. Partially cover and simmer about 5 minutes or until a thin film of oil starts to form on surface of sauce. The longer sauce simmers, the more oil will form.

5. Stir tomato mixture into lentils. Partially cover and simmer 10 to 12 minutes to blend flavors; remove from heat. Stir in whipping cream, salt and Garam Masaala.

6. Spoon into serving bowl; drizzle with additional whipping cream and sprinkle with cilantro.

Raghavan Ki Baaten

☀ This dish is also delicious made with dried black beans, but the cooking time will be longer. Heat 1 cup of beans and 4 cups of water to boiling. Boil 2 minutes; remove from heat. Cover and let stand 1 hour. Add more water to cover beans. Heat to boiling; reduce heat. Cover and simmer until beans are tender, 1 to 1 1/2 hours.

1 Serving: Calories 290 (Calories from Fat 145); Fat 16g (Saturated 10g); Cholesterol 50mg; Sodium 680mg; Carbohydrate 34g (Dietary Fiber 12g); Protein 14g **% Daily Value:** Vitamin A 18%; Vitamin C 8%; Calcium 6%; Iron 28% **Diet Exchanges:** 2 Starch, 1 Very Lean Meat, 1 Vegetable, 2 Fat

A comfort food of choice in many homes in southeastern India, this dal's robust flavor comes from a combination of browned gingerroot and nutty mustard seed.

Green Lentils with Ginger

Moong Dal

6 SERVINGS

1 cup dried whole green lentils (sabud mung), sorted, rinsed and drained

4 cups water

1/4 teaspoon ground turmeric

1 tablespoon Clarified Butter (Ghee), (page 40) or vegetable oil

1 teaspoon black or yellow mustard seed

1/4 teaspoon asafetida (hing) or garlic powder

1 tablespoon finely chopped gingerroot

1 medium tomato, finely chopped (3/4 cup)

2 fresh Thai, serrano or cayenne chilies, cut lengthwise in half

1 teaspoon salt

1. Place lentils, water and turmeric in 2-quart saucepan. Heat to boiling; reduce heat. Partially cover and simmer 30 to 35 minutes or until lentils are tender.

2. While lentils are simmering, heat Clarified Butter and mustard seed in 10-inch skillet over medium-high heat. Once seed begins to pop, cover skillet and wait until popping stops.

3. Add asafetida and gingerroot to mustard seed; stir-fry about 30 seconds or until gingerroot is partially brown. Add tomato and chilies; stir-fry 3 to 5 minutes or until tomato is softened.

4. Stir tomato mixture and salt into lentils. Partially cover and simmer 10 minutes.

1 Serving: Calories 135 (Calories from Fat 25); Fat 3g (Saturated 1g); Cholesterol 5mg; Sodium 10mg; Carbohydrate 23g (Dietary Fiber 5g); Protein 9g **% Daily Value:** Vitamin A 10%; Vitamin C 16%; Calcium 8%; Iron 18% **Diet Exchanges:** 1 Starch, 2 Vegetable

Green Lentils with Ginger

Raghavan Ki Baaten

☼ Try any other lentil with the same spice combination for a delightfully different taste sensation, because lentils impart their inherent flavors to the spice mix. Serve with Steamed Basmati Rice (pages 202 and 203).

A bowl of these lentils served with Steamed Basmati Rice (pages 202 and 203) qualifies as South India comfort food. It is not only nutritious, but also is quick to prepare.

Split Green Lentils with Spinach

Keerai Kootu

6 SERVINGS

1 cup dried split and hulled green lentils (mung dal) or red lentils (masoor dal), sorted, rinsed and drained

4 cups water

1 package (10 ounces) frozen chopped spinach, thawed (do not drain)

1 cup Shredded Fresh Coconut (page 45) or 1/2 cup dried unsweetened shredded coconut

1 teaspoon cumin seed, crushed

1 teaspoon salt

2 or 3 fresh Thai, serrano or cayenne chilies, crushed

1 tablespoon Clarified Butter (Ghee), (page 40) or vegetable oil

1 teaspoon black or yellow mustard seed

1. Place lentils and water in 2-quart saucepan. Heat to boiling; reduce heat. Simmer uncovered about 20 minutes or just until lentils are tender.

2. Stir in undrained spinach and remaining ingredients except Clarified Butter and mustard seed. Simmer uncovered 2 minutes.

3. While lentil mixture is simmering, heat Clarified Butter and mustard seed in 6-inch skillet over medium-high heat. Once seed begins to pop, cover skillet and wait until popping stops.

4. Pour hot butter mixture onto lentil mixture; stir well.

Raghavan Ki Baaten

☀ **Whole green lentils are forest green, but the ones to purchase for this recipe are yellow, since they have been split open and the skins removed.**

☀ **To crush cumin seed and chilies, place them in a mortar and pound gently with a pestle. You can also place them in a resealable plastic bag on a cutting board and crush them with a heavy rolling pin.**

1 Serving: Calories 155 (Calories from Fat 65); Fat 7g (Saturated 5g); Cholesterol 6mg; Sodium 430mg; Carbohydrate 22g (Dietary Fiber 9g); Protein 10g **% Daily Value:** Vitamin A 32%; Vitamin C 16%; Calcium 6%; Iron 22% **Diet Exchanges:** 1 Starch, 1 1/2 Vegetable, 1 Fat

Split Green Lentils with Turmeric

Mung Nu Dal

4 SERVINGS

1 cup dried split and hulled green lentils (mung dal), sorted, rinsed and drained

3 cups water

1 tablespoon finely chopped fresh cilantro

1 teaspoon salt

1 teaspoon Spicy Garam Masaala (page 34)

1/2 teaspoon ground red pepper (cayenne)

1/4 teaspoon ground turmeric

1 tablespoon Clarified Butter (Ghee), (page 40) or vegetable oil

1 teaspoon cumin seed

1. Place lentils and water in 3-quart saucepan. Heat to boiling. Stir in remaining ingredients except Clarified Butter and cumin seed; reduce heat. Partially cover and simmer 18 to 20 minutes or until lentils are tender.

2. While lentils are simmering, heat Clarified Butter in 6-inch skillet over medium heat. Add cumin seed; sizzle 30 seconds.

3. Pour hot butter mixture into lentils; stir well.

Raghavan Ki Baaten

☀ Split green lentils are actually yellow. When green lentils (sabud mung) are split open and the skin is removed, the sunny yellow color is exposed. If unavailable, substitute any split lentil or green split peas. Cooking times may vary slightly depending on the lentil used. Split peas will need to cook for 35 to 40 minutes, so plan accordingly.

1 Serving: Calories 150 (Calories from Fat 35); Fat 4g (Saturated 2g); Cholesterol 10mg; Sodium 590mg; Carbohydrate 27g (Dietary Fiber 10g); Protein 12g **% Daily Value:** Vitamin A 2%; Vitamin C 0%; Calcium 2%; Iron 26% **Diet Exchanges:** 1 1/2 Starch, 1 Very Lean Meat

Call this the Gujaratis' version of an old-fashioned hot dish, complete with shoestring potatoes as the quintessential topping. It is a surprisingly simple, flavorful and visually appealing meal all by itself.

Layered Spinach–Lentil–Potato Casserole

Palak saliya Dal

6 SERVINGS

3 1/2 cups water

1 package (10 ounces) frozen chopped spinach, thawed (do not drain)

1 tablespoon finely chopped gingerroot

2 or 3 fresh Thai or cayenne chilies, cut lengthwise in half

1 cup dried split and hulled green lentils (mung dal), sorted, rinsed and drained

1/2 teaspoon ground turmeric

1 teaspoon Spicy Garam Masaala (page 34)

1 teaspoon salt

1 large tomato, chopped (1 cup)

1 can (1.7 ounces) shoestring potatoes (1 cup)

1/2 teaspoon ground red pepper (cayenne)

1. Heat 1/2 cup of the water, spinach, gingerroot and chilies to boiling in 1-quart saucepan. Boil 3 to 5 minutes or until water has evaporated; remove from heat.

2. Place lentils, turmeric and remaining 3 cups water in 2-quart saucepan. Heat to boiling; reduce heat. Partially cover and simmer 18 to 20 minutes or until lentils are tender. Stir in Spicy Garam Masaala and salt.

3. Spoon lentils into serving bowl. Spread spinach over lentils. Top with tomato and shoestring potatoes. Sprinkle with ground red pepper.

1 Serving: Calories 140 (Calories from Fat 25); Fat 3g (Saturated 0g); Cholesterol 0mg; Sodium 490mg; Carbohydrate 27g (Dietary Fiber 9g); Protein 10g **% Daily Value:** Vitamin A 32%; Vitamin C 22%; Calcium 6%; Iron 20% **Diet Exchanges:** 1 Starch, 2 Vegetable, 1 /2 Fat

Layered Spinach-Lentil-Potato Casserole, Whole Wheat Unleavened Breads (page 236)

Raghavan Ki Baaten

☀ An accompaniment of Whole Wheat Unleavened Breads (page 236) along
with a serving of fiery Raw Mango Pickle (page 274) can take you a step
closer to Nirvana.

Dal, a generic term for lentils, is a staple in all Indian homes. Lentils, beans and peas are inexpensive sources of protein and fiber and are found in abundance. In South Indian homes, these split green lentils are cooked for barely 20 minutes, then flavored with a simple combination of halved green chilies, slivers of gingerroot and sweet tomatoes.

Split Green Lentils with Tomatoes

tomatar molagha Dal

6 SERVINGS

1 cup dried split and hulled green lentils (mung dal) or red lentils (masoor dal), sorted, rinsed and drained

3 cups water

2 medium tomatoes, chopped (1 1/2 cups)

2 tablespoons julienne strips gingerroot

2 tablespoons chopped fresh cilantro

1 teaspoon salt

1/4 teaspoon ground turmeric

10 to 12 fresh karhi leaves or 2 or 3 fresh or dried bay leaves

2 or 3 fresh Thai, serrano or cayenne chilies, cut lengthwise in half

1 tablespoon Clarified Butter (Ghee), (page 40) or vegetable oil

1 teaspoon cumin seed

1. Place lentils and water in 2-quart saucepan. Heat to boiling. Stir in remaining ingredients except Clarified Butter and cumin seed; reduce heat. Partially cover and simmer 18 to 20 minutes or until lentils are tender.

2. While lentils are simmering, heat Clarified Butter in 6-inch skillet over medium heat. Add cumin seed; sizzle 30 seconds.

3. Pour hot butter mixture onto lentil mixture; stir well. (If using bay leaves, remove and discard.)

Raghavan Ki Baaten

☀ **When served as is, this dish is a great soup, but when combined with steamed rice or breads, it becomes a substantially satisfying meal.**

1 Serving: Calories 120 (Calories from Fat 25); Fat 3g (Saturated 1g); Cholesterol 6mg; Sodium 400mg; Carbohydrate 22g (Dietary Fiber 8g); Protein 9g **% Daily Value:** Vitamin A 18%; Vitamin C 32%; Calcium 2%; Iron 18% **Diet Exchanges:** 1 Starch, 2 Vegetables

Red lentils, also called Egyptian lentils, are available in natural-food stores and in the ethnic-food section of large supermarkets. These are beautiful salmon-colored legumes that become yellow when cooked.

Red Lentils with Ginger

Masoor Dal

8 SERVINGS

2 cups dried red lentils (masoor dal), sorted, rinsed and drained

4 cups water

1/2 teaspoon ground turmeric

2 tablespoons Clarified Butter (Ghee), (page 40) or vegetable oil

1 teaspoon cumin seed

2 medium red onions, cut in half and thinly sliced

2 tablespoons finely chopped gingerroot

3 fresh Thai, serrano or cayenne chilies, crushed

1 teaspoon salt

2 tablespoons chopped fresh cilantro

1. Place lentils, water and turmeric in 3-quart saucepan. Heat to boiling; reduce heat. Simmer uncovered 15 to 20 minutes, skimming off any foam that floats to the top, until lentils just start to soften and most of the liquid is absorbed; remove from heat.

2. While lentils are simmering, heat Clarified Butter in 10-inch skillet over medium-high heat. Add cumin seed; sizzle 30 seconds. Add onion, gingerroot and chilies; stir-fry 2 to 4 minutes until onion is golden brown.

3. Stir onion mixture and salt into lentils. Simmer uncovered 10 to 15 minutes, stirring occasionally, until lentils are tender. Serve sprinkled with cilantro.

Raghavan Ki Baaten

☀ Leftover cooked dal can be frozen in an airtight container for up to 2 months. Then, reheat, covered, in a microwavable container until warm.

1 Serving: Calories 160 (Calories from Fat 35); Fat 4g (Saturated 2g); Cholesterol 10mg; Sodium 300mg; Carbohydrate 29g (Dietary Fiber 11g); Protein 12g **% Daily Value:** Vitamin A 14%; Vitamin C 20%; Calcium 2%; Iron 26% **Diet Exchanges:** 2 Starch, 1 Very Lean Meat

If a Gujarati was asked to characterize foods from his or her homeland in two words, he or she would say "sweet and hot." Almost all the recipes originating from this northwestern state use a sweetening agent of one form or the other: white cane sugar or a raw form of cane sugar called jaggery (gur).

Lima Beans with Raisins and Onions

6 SERVINGS

1 tablespoon Clarified Butter (Ghee), (page 40) or vegetable oil

1 teaspoon Bishop's weed (ajwain)

1 teaspoon cumin seed

1 tablespoon finely chopped gingerroot

2 large tomatoes, chopped (2 cups)

2 tablespoons coarsely chopped jaggery (gur) or packed brown sugar

1/2 teaspoon ground red pepper (cayenne)

1 teaspoon salt

1 package (10 ounces) frozen lima beans, thawed

2 cups water

1/2 teaspoon ground turmeric

1/4 cup chopped fresh cilantro

1/4 cup golden raisins

1/4 cup finely chopped red onion

1. Heat Clarified Butter in 2-quart saucepan over medium-high heat. Add Bishop's weed and cumin seed; sizzle 10 to 15 seconds.

2. Add gingerroot; stir-fry about 30 seconds or until brown. Stir in tomatoes and jaggery; cook 5 to 7 minutes or until tomatoes are softened.

3. Stir in ground red pepper and salt. Reduce heat; simmer uncovered 1 minute.

4. Stir in lima beans, water and turmeric. Simmer uncovered 15 to 20 minutes or until lima beans are tender and sauce is slightly thickened. Serve sprinkled with cilantro, raisins and onion.

1 Serving: Calories 120 (Calories from Fat 25); Fat 3g (Saturated 1g); Cholesterol 5mg; Sodium 430mg; Carbohydrate 23g (Dietary Fiber 4g); Protein 4g **% Daily Value:** Vitamin A 6%; Vitamin C 14%; Calcium 2%; Iron 8% **Diet Exchanges:** 1 Starch, 2 Vegetable

Lima Beans with Raisins and Onions

Raghavan Ki Baaten

☀ Jaggery (*gur*) is sugar cane juice that is cooked down and dried in large blocks to yield a dark brown mass. Jaggery must be cut with a sharp knife using firm, steady pressure. It has a rich, sweet flavor similar to light molasses. Jaggery is found in Indian grocery stores. Brown sugar or even molasses is a good substitute.

A staple of homes in Delhi and Punjab, this robust kidney bean stew is similar to chili.
A very basic tomato-based curry, when served with steamed rice, becomes a richly satisfying
and nutritionally complete meal.

North Indian Chili

6 SERVINGS

2 tablespoons vegetable oil

1 1/2 cups finely chopped red onion

5 medium cloves garlic, finely chopped

1 tablespoon finely chopped gingerroot

2 large tomatoes, chopped (2 cups)

1 tablespoon coriander seed, ground

1 teaspoon cumin seed, ground

1/2 teaspoon salt

1/2 teaspoon ground red pepper (cayenne)

1/4 teaspoon ground turmeric

2 cans (15 to 16 ounces each) red kidney beans, rinsed and drained

1 cup water

1/2 cup half-and-half

3 tablespoons finely chopped fresh cilantro

1. Heat oil in 2-quart saucepan over medium-high heat. Add 1 cup of the onion, the garlic and gingerroot; stir-fry 3 to 4 minutes or until onion is golden brown.

2. Stir in tomatoes, ground coriander, ground cumin, salt, ground red pepper and turmeric; reduce heat. Simmer uncovered about 5 minutes or until tomatoes are softened.

3. Stir in kidney beans and water. Simmer uncovered 15 to 20 minutes, stirring occasionally, until sauce is thickened; remove from heat.

4. Stir in half-and-half. Served sprinkled with remaining onion and cilantro.

1 Serving: Calories 240 (Calories from Fat 65); Fat 7g (Saturated 2g); Cholesterol 5mg; Sodium 550mg; Carbohydrate 41g (Dietary Fiber 11g); Protein 14g **% Daily Value:** Vitamin A 6%; Vitamin C 14%; Calcium 8%; Iron 28% **Diet Exchanges:** 2 Starch, 2 Vegetable, 1 Fat

Kidney beans (rajmah) are a staple in Punjab, India's heartland and home to its hard-working farmers. The foods of Punjab are glorified in most of the Indian restaurants in the United States that often feature a dish called Rajmah (North Indian Chili, page 180), kidney beans simmered in a robust tomato sauce smoothed with cream. This variation is a refreshing deviation from the norm, using a yogurt base perfumed with cardamom seeds.

Kidney Beans with Cardamom-Yogurt Sauce

Dahi Elaichi Rajmah

6 SERVINGS

1 tablespoon Clarified Butter (Ghee), (page 40) or vegetable oil

1 cup plain yogurt (regular or fat-free)

1 teaspoon cardamom seeds (removed from pods), crushed (page 31)

1/4 teaspoon ground turmeric

1/2 teaspoon ground red pepper (cayenne)

2 cans (15 to 16 ounces each) red kidney beans, rinsed and drained

1 large tomato, chopped (1 cup)

1 cup water

1 teaspoon salt

1/4 cup finely chopped fresh cilantro

Kidney Beans with Cardamom-Yogurt Sauce is pictured on page 163.

1. Heat Clarified Butter in 2-quart saucepan over medium-high heat. Add yogurt, cardamom seeds and turmeric; stir-fry 6 to 8 minutes or until all the water in the yogurt has evaporated.

2. Stir in remaining ingredients except cilantro; reduce heat. Cover and simmer 10 minutes. Remove lid and simmer about 5 minutes longer or until sauce is slightly thickened. Serve sprinkled with cilantro.

Raghavan Ki Baaten

☼ Cardamom pods *(elaichi)* are available in two forms in India. The large black pods are used in the North to flavor many rice-based and meat-based dishes. The black pods are always used whole and impart a smoky, sweet-bitter flavor when stir-fried in hot oil. The green pods are popular in all regions of India, and their seeds are very aromatic and menthol-sweet, making them an ideal choice for many desserts. They are also used as a breath freshener and digestive aid. Use the seeds from green cardamom pods for this recipe.

☼ Note the unique technique used here of stir-frying yogurt in a little Clarified Butter until all the water evaporates to leave behind pleasantly tart curds.

1 Serving: Calories 205 (Calories from Fat 35); Fat 4g (Saturated 2g); Cholesterol 10mg; Sodium 770mg; Carbohydrate 37g (Dietary Fiber 10g); Protein 15g **% Daily Value:** Vitamin A 4%; Vitamin C 6%; Calcium 12%; Iron 24% **Diet Exchanges:** 2 Starch, 1 Very Lean Meat, 1 Vegetable

The northwestern state of Haryana is home to this recipe for garbanzo beans tossed with a unique blend of dry spices and singed with hot oil.

Haryana–Style Garbanzo Beans

6 SERVINGS

2 cans (15 to 16 ounces each) garbanzo beans, rinsed and drained

1 cup water

1 tablespoon mango powder (amchur) or 1 tablespoon lemon or lime juice

1 tablespoon Garam Masaala (page 32)

1 teaspoon dried pomegranate seeds, ground (anardana), or 1 tablespoon lemon or lime juice

1/2 teaspoon regular salt

1/2 teaspoon black salt or 1 teaspoon regular salt

1/4 cup vegetable oil

1/4 cup finely chopped fresh cilantro

1 cup finely chopped red onion

1. Heat garbanzo beans and water to boiling in 2-quart saucepan.

2. Stir in mango powder, Garam Masaala, ground pomegranate seeds, regular salt and black salt; reduce heat. Simmer uncovered 6 to 8 minutes or until almost all of the liquid has evaporated; remove from heat.

3. Heat oil in 6-inch skillet over medium-high heat 2 to 3 minutes or until it almost starts to smoke. Pour hot oil over bean mixture; stir well. Serve sprinkled with cilantro and onion.

1 Serving: Calories 290 (Calories from Fat 115); Fat 13g (Saturated 2g); Cholesterol 0mg; Sodium 590mg; Carbohydrate 42g (Dietary Fiber 12g); Protein 13g **% Daily Value:** Vitamin A 0%; Vitamin C 4%; Calcium 8%; Iron 26% **Diet Exchanges:** 3 Starch, 1 Fat

Haryana-Style Garbanzo Beans, Egg-Flavored Puffy Breads (page 251)

Raghavan Ki Baaten

☀ If you have oil that has been left over after frying other foods (except fish or seafood), use it to season this dish. The more used an oil is, the more flavors it imparts to these beans.

☀ Note the technique of cooking the spices by pouring hot oil over the bean-spice blend. This not only cooks the spices, but it also prevents them from burning. Ground spices are not added directly to hot oil because the instant contact turns them bitter and unpalatable. Whole spices, unlike their ground counterparts, can briefly withstand the hot temperatures.

In the month of October in Tamilian households all across India, during the ten-day festival of Navratri (nine nights), women invite female friends, neighbors and relatives to ring in auspicious times. Men are never invited. Shundal, a warm garbanzo bean salad smothered with roasted chilies and lentils, is traditionally wrapped in "take-home" packets of banana leaves after being blessed by the family priest.

Warm Garbanzo Bean Salad with Roasted Chilies

6 SERVINGS

2 cans (15 to 16 ounces each) garbanzo beans, rinsed and drained

2 cups water

2 teaspoons vegetable oil

3 or 4 dried red Thai, serrano or cayenne chilies

2 tablespoons dried split and hulled black lentils (urad dal) or yellow split peas (chana dal), sorted

1 tablespoon coriander seed

1 teaspoon black or yellow mustard seed

1/4 teaspoon asafetida (hing)

10 to 12 fresh karhi leaves or 2 tablespoons finely chopped fresh cilantro

1 teaspoon salt

1. Heat garbanzo beans and water to boiling in 2-quart saucepan; reduce heat. Simmer uncovered 5 to 7 minutes or until most of the water has evaporated; remove from heat.

2. While beans are simmering, heat 1 teaspoon of the oil in 6-inch skillet over medium heat. Add chilies, lentils and coriander seed; stir-fry 30 to 60 seconds or until chilies blacken and lentils and coriander are reddish brown.

3. Remove spice blend from skillet with slotted spoon; let stand 2 to 4 minutes or until cool. Place spice blend in spice grinder. Grind until finely ground; set aside.

4. Heat remaining 1 teaspoon oil and mustard seed in same 6-inch skillet over medium-high heat. Once seed begins to pop, cover skillet and wait until popping stops.

5. Stir asafetida, karhi leaves and salt into mustard seed. Pour hot oil mixture and ground spice blend over beans; toss well.

1 Serving: Calories 235 (Calories from Fat 55); Fat 6g (Saturated 1g); Cholesterol 0g; Sodium 600mg; Carbohydrate 43g (Dietary Fiber 12g); Protein 14g **% Daily Value:** Vitamin A 16%; Vitamin C 2%; Calcium 8%; Iron 26% **Diet Exchanges:** 3 Starch

Garbanzo beans are known as kabuli channa *in India. During the Moghul regime, prior to colonial days, the sultans had a major influence on the foods and architecture of northern India. They introduced the garbanzo bean along with many spices and nuts to the North.*

Garbanzo Bean Stew with Tomatoes

channa Masaala

6 SERVINGS

1 tablespoon vegetable oil

1 teaspoon cumin seed

1 medium onion, finely chopped (1/2 cup)

1 tablespoon chopped gingerroot

2 medium cloves garlic, finely chopped

2 medium tomatoes, finely chopped (1 1/2 cups)

1 tablespoon mango powder (amchur)

1 teaspoon coriander seed, ground

1 teaspoon cumin seed, ground

1 teaspoon salt

1/2 teaspoon ground red pepper (cayenne)

1/4 teaspoon cardamom seeds, ground

2 cans (15 to 16 ounces each) garbanzo beans, rinsed and drained

1 cup water

2 tablespoons chopped fresh cilantro

2 or 3 fresh Thai, serrano or cayenne chilies, cut lengthwise in half

1 medium lime, cut into wedges

Garbanzo Bean Stew with Tomatoes is pictured on page 244.

1. Heat oil in 2-quart saucepan over medium-high heat. Add cumin seed; sizzle 30 seconds.

2. Add onion, gingerroot and garlic; stir-fry 2 to 3 minutes or until onion is golden brown.

3. Stir in tomatoes, mango powder, ground coriander, ground cumin, salt, ground red pepper and ground cardamom; reduce heat. Partially cover and simmer 4 to 5 minutes, stirring occasionally, until a very thin film of oil glistens on surface of sauce.

4. Stir in garbanzo beans and water. Cover and simmer 8 to 10 minutes or until sauce is slightly thickened. Sprinkle with cilantro; garnish with chilies and lime wedges.

Raghavan Ki Baaten

☼ Restaurants often serve this with its ideal counterpart, Egg-Flavored Puffy Breads (page 251). A great filler food between meals, this combination is also an ample main course for many a treasured brunch.

1 Serving: Calories 230 (Calories from Fat 55); Fat 6g (Saturated 1g); Cholesterol 0mg; Sodium 600mg; Carbohydrate 42g (Dietary Fiber 11g); Protein 13g **% Daily Value:** Vitamin A 14%; Vitamin C 26%; Calcium 8%; Iron 24% **Diet Exchanges:** 2 Starch, 2 Vegetable, 1/2 Fat

The more special an occasion, the more elaborate the Undhiyu. For a very special occasion, it can be a combination of nine vegetables with fried croquettes made with fenugreek-flavored garbanzo bean flour batter. This version does not include the croquettes.

Gujarati-Style Mixed-Vegetable Curry

6 SERVINGS

1 tablespoon vegetable oil

1 teaspoon cumin seed

2 tablespoons sugar

1 tablespoon ground coriander

1 teaspoon salt

1 teaspoon ground cumin

1 teaspoon ground red pepper (cayenne)

1/2 teaspoon ground turmeric

2 medium tomatoes, cut into 1-inch pieces (1 1/2 cups)

2 cups water

2 cups frozen green pigeon peas (sabud toovar) or frozen green peas

1 medium baking potato, peeled and cut into 1-inch cubes (1 1/2 cups)

1 medium sweet potato, peeled and cut into 1-inch cubes (1 1/2 cups)

1 medium carrot, peeled and cut into 1-inch cubes (1/2 cup)

1 small firm, green plantain, peeled and cut into 1-inch cubes (1/2 cup)

1/2 cup flat pea pods (fafda) or snow (Chinese) pea pods

2 tablespoons chopped fresh cilantro

1. Heat oil in 3-quart saucepan over medium heat. Add cumin seed; sizzle 10 to 20 seconds. Stir in sugar, coriander, salt, ground cumin, ground red pepper and turmeric; cook 5 to 10 seconds.

2. Stir in tomatoes. Cook uncovered 1 to 2 minutes, stirring occasionally, until partially warm.

3. Stir in remaining ingredients except cilantro. Heat to boiling; reduce heat. Cover and simmer 10 to 12 minutes or until vegetables are tender. Sprinkle with cilantro.

Raghavan Ki Baaten

☀ The "icing on the cake" comes from incorporating freshly hulled green pigeon peas, a delicacy often found in the frozen section of Indian grocery stores. They are similar in size and color to the green pea, but they are slightly oval in shape. Pigeon peas have a meatier texture with a candy-like sweetness.

☀ Flat green pea pods (fafda) look similar to snow (Chinese) pea pods, but they are not quite as sweet. They are commonly available in the produce section of Indian grocery stores.

1 Serving: Calories 175 (Calories from Fat 25); Fat 3g (Saturated 0g); Cholesterol 0mg; Sodium 410mg; Carbohydrate 38g (Dietary Fiber 7g); Protein 6g **% Daily Value:** Vitamin A 62%; Vitamin C 18%; Calcium 2%; Iron 10% **Diet Exchanges:** 2 Starch, 1 Vegetable

A delicious lentil broth called pepper water (molaha tanri) is served in Tamilian homes all across the nation, and the English were enamored of it during the colonial occupation of India. Thus evolved mulligatawny (rasam), a toned-down rendition of the fiery original. Often served with rice and considered a second rice course in South India, rasam is made 365 days a year with variations galore.

True Mulligatawny

Tomatar Rasam

6 SERVINGS

1/4 cup dried split and hulled pigeon peas (toovar dal) or yellow split peas (chana dal), sorted, rinsed and drained

7 cups water

1 teaspoon tamarind concentrate paste or 1/4 cup lemon juice

1 medium tomato, chopped (3/4 cup)

1/4 cup chopped fresh cilantro

1 tablespoon chopped gingerroot

1 teaspoon salt

1 teaspoon Sambhar Powder (page 35)

1/2 teaspoon asafetida (hing) or garlic powder

12 fresh karhi leaves

2 fresh Thai, serrano or cayenne chilies, cut lengthwise in half

1 tablespoon Clarified Butter (Ghee), (page 40) or vegetable oil

1 teaspoon black or yellow mustard seed

1 teaspoon cumin seed

1/2 teaspoon cumin seed, ground

1/4 teaspoon black peppercorns, ground

1. Heat pigeon peas and 3 cups of the water to boiling in 2-quart saucepan; reduce heat to medium. Partially cover and simmer 30 to 35 minutes or until peas are tender.

2. Place peas and any remaining cooking liquid in blender. Cover and blend on medium speed until smooth; set aside.

3. Dissolve tamarind paste in remaining 4 cups water in same saucepan. Stir in tomato, cilantro, gingerroot, salt, Sambhar Powder, asafetida, karhi leaves and chilies. Heat to boiling; reduce heat to medium. Simmer uncovered about 15 minutes or until tomato is softened.

4. Heat Clarified Butter and mustard seed in 6-inch skillet over medium-high heat. Once seed begins to pop, cover skillet and wait until popping stops. Add whole cumin seed; sizzle 10 seconds.

5. Pour hot butter mixture over tomato mixture. Stir in pea mixture, ground cumin and ground pepper.

Raghavan Ki Baaten

☀ Serve mulligatawny as is for a light soup or with Steamed Basmati Rice (pages 202 and 203) for a heartier meal. If karhi leaves are unavailable, omit from recipe.

1 Serving: Calories 55 (Calories from Fat 25); Fat 3g (Saturated 1g); Cholesterol 5mg; Sodium 400mg; Carbohydrate 7g (Dietary Fiber 2g); Protein 2g **% Daily Value:** Vitamin A 18%; Vitamin C 30%; Calcium 2%; Iron 4% **Diet Exchanges:** 1 Vegetable, 1/2 Fat

What jambalaya is to the Deep South of the United States, sambhar *is to the southern region of India. It is often considered a specialty dish despite the fact that some kind of* sambhar *is made every day of the year.*

Pigeon Pea Stew

6 SERVINGS

1/2 cup dried split and hulled pigeon peas (toovar dal) or yellow split peas (chana dal), sorted, rinsed and drained

7 1/2 cups water

1 teaspoon tamarind concentrate paste or 1/4 cup lemon juice

1 medium green bell pepper, chopped (1 cup)

1 medium tomato, chopped (3/4 cup)

1 tablespoon Sambhar Powder (page 35)

1/2 teaspoon asafetida (hing) or garlic powder

1/4 teaspoon ground turmeric

1 tablespoon vegetable oil

1 tablespoon coriander seed

1/2 cup Shredded Fresh Coconut (page 45) or 1/4 cup dried unsweetened shredded coconut

1 teaspoon black or yellow mustard seed

2 tablespoons chopped fresh cilantro

1 teaspoon salt

12 to 15 fresh karhi leaves

1. Heat pigeon peas and 3 cups of the water to boiling in 3-quart saucepan; reduce heat to medium. Partially cover and simmer 30 to 35 minutes or until peas are tender.

2. Place peas and any remaining cooking liquid in blender. Cover and blend on medium speed until smooth; set aside.

3. Dissolve tamarind paste in 4 cups of the remaining water in same saucepan. Stir in bell pepper, tomato, Sambhar Powder, asafetida and turmeric. Heat to boiling; reduce heat. Simmer uncovered about 15 minutes or until bell pepper and tomatoes are tender.

4. While vegetable mixture is simmering, heat 1 teaspoon of the oil in 6-inch skillet over medium-high heat. Add coriander seed and coconut. Cook 2 to 3 minutes, stirring constantly, until coriander seed is reddish brown and coconut is toasted. Place in blender with remaining 1/2 cup water. Cover and blend on medium speed until smooth. Stir coconut mixture into vegetable mixture.

5. Heat remaining 2 teaspoons oil and mustard seed in same skillet over medium-high heat. Once seed begins to pop, cover skillet and wait until popping stops. Pour hot oil mixture over vegetable mixture; stir in pigeon pea mixture.

6. Stir in cilantro, salt and karhi leaves. Simmer 1 to 2 minutes to blend flavors.

1 Serving: Calories 80 (Calories from Fat 45); Fat 5g (Saturated 2g); Cholesterol 0mg; Sodium 10mg; Carbohydrate 10g (Dietary Fiber 4g); Protein 3g **% Daily Value:** Vitamin A 10%; Vitamin C 18%; Calcium 2%; Iron 4% **Diet Exchanges:** 2 Vegetable, 1/2 Fat

Pigeon Pea Stew, Steamed Basmati Rice (pages 202 and 203)

Raghavan Ki Baaten

☀ If karhi leaves are not at hand, omit from recipe.

☀ When this stew is served with steamed rice, it is always eaten first
as one of three rice courses. The second rice course is the *rasam* (True
Mulligatawny, page 187), and the third culminates in a combination of
rice and buttermilk, often considered essential for smooth digestion.

While Sundays and chicken dinners go hand in hand in many a household in America, lentil dumplings in tamarind sauce take center stage in India's Tamilian kitchens. Serve Spiced Puffed Breads (page 250) or even Steamed Basmati Rice (pages 202 and 203) with this dish.

Lentil Dumplings in Tamarind Sauce

Paruppu Undhai Sambhar

8 SERVINGS

Dumplings:
1 cup dried split and hulled pigeon peas (toovar dal), sorted, rinsed and drained

1 tablespoon dried yellow split peas (chana dal), sorted, rinsed and drained

3 cups warm water

2 or 3 dried red Thai, serrano or cayenne chilies

1 tablespoon chopped gingerroot

12 to 15 fresh karhi leaves, coarsely chopped (1 tablespoon), or 2 tablespoons chopped fresh cilantro

2 tablespoons rice flour or cake flour

1 teaspoon salt

1/4 teaspoon asafetida (hing) or garlic powder

1/4 cup vegetable oil

Sauce:
1 tablespoon tamarind concentrate paste

6 cups warm water

1 tablespoon vegetable oil

1 teaspoon black or yellow mustard seed

1 tablespoon dried yellow split peas (chana dal)

1 teaspoon fenugreek seed (méthi)

12 to 15 fresh karhi leaves or 2 dried bay leaves

2 teaspoons Sambhar Powder (page 35)

1/2 teaspoon asafetida (hing) or garlic powder

1 teaspoon salt

1/4 teaspoon ground turmeric

1/4 cup chopped fresh cilantro

MAKE DUMPLINGS:

1. Place pigeon peas, 1 tablespoon yellow split peas, 3 cups warm water and chilies in large bowl. Soak at room temperature for at least 2 hours but no longer than 12 hours; drain.

2. Place pea mixture and gingerroot in food processor. Cover and process until smooth. Transfer to medium bowl. Stir in karhi leaves, flour, salt and asafetida.

3. Heat oil in wok or Dutch oven over medium heat. Add pea mixture. Cook 2 to 3 minutes, scraping bottom of skillet every 30 seconds to prevent sticking, until mixture looks like soft, dry dough. Spread dough on dinner plate; let stand 10 to 15 minutes or until cool.

4. Divide dough into 16 pieces; shape each piece into a ball. Set aside.

MAKE SAUCE:

1. Dissolve tamarind paste in 6 cups warm water in large bowl.

2. Heat oil and mustard seed in 3-quart saucepan over medium-high heat. Once seed begins to pop, cover saucepan and wait until popping stops. Add yellow split peas and fenugreek seed; stir-fry 20 to 30 seconds or until peas are golden brown.

3. Stir in karhi leaves, Sambhar Powder and asafetida; stir-fry 15 to 30 seconds. Stir in tamarind mixture, salt and turmeric; heat to boiling.

4. Add dumplings; reduce heat to low. Simmer uncovered 8 to 10 minutes without stirring (to prevent dumplings from falling apart) or until sauce is thickened. (If using bay leaves, remove and discard.) Sprinkle with cilantro.

1 Serving: Calories 130 (Calories from Fat 70); Fat 8g (Saturated 1g); Cholesterol 0mg; Sodium 600mg; Carbohydrate 14g (Dietary Fiber 4g); Protein 5g **% Daily Value:** Vitamin A 22%; Vitamin C 0%; Calcium 2%; Iron 6% **Diet Exchanges:** 1 Starch, 1 1/2 Fat

Lentil Dumplings in Tamarind Sauce, Puffy Whole Wheat Breads (page 248), Steamed Basmati Rice (pages 202 and 203)

Raghavan Ki Baaten

☀ Cook the dumpling paste just until it resembles a soft dough, or it will dry out and look like bread crumbs. Dry dough will not hold its shape, and the dumplings will subsequently fall apart in the sauce. The dumplings can be made a day ahead, covered and stored in the refrigerator.

☀ Leave fenugreek seed out of the recipe if unavailable. Because tamarind has such a crucial role in this recipe, there is no substitute for its distinct tartness.

Making stews with pigeon peas is an everyday occurrence in South Indian homes. Certain stews take longer to make, but their flavor reveals rewarding complex layers of flavors with each bite. Stews like this are saved for special events because of the few extra steps involved. The harvest festival of Pongal is an ideal occasion for this sweet-hot ragout.

Eggplant Stew with Coconut

Katarikai Rasavanghy

8 SERVINGS

1 cup dried split and hulled pigeon peas (toovar dal) or yellow split peas (chana dal), sorted, rinsed and drained

6 1/2 cups water

1/4 teaspoon ground turmeric

2 tablespoons sesame oil (light colored) or vegetable oil

1 cup Shredded Fresh Coconut (page 45) or 1/2 cup dried unsweetened shredded coconut

1 tablespoon coriander seed

2 or 3 dried red Thai, serrano or cayenne chilies

1 tablespoon tamarind concentrate paste or juice of 2 medium limes (1/4 cup)

2 tablespoons chopped jaggery (gur) or 2 tablespoons packed brown sugar

1 teaspoon Tangy Sambhar Powder (page 36)

1 teaspoon black or yellow mustard seed

1/4 teaspoon asafetida (hing)

1 medium eggplant (1 1/2 pounds), cut into 1/4-inch cubes

1 medium tomato, chopped (3/4 cup)

12 to 15 fresh karhi leaves or 3 dried bay leaves

1 teaspoon salt

2 tablespoons chopped fresh cilantro

1. Heat pigeon peas, 6 cups of the water and the turmeric to boiling in Dutch oven; reduce heat to medium. Partially cover and simmer 30 to 35 minutes or until peas are tender.

2. While peas are simmering, heat 1 tablespoon of the oil in wok or deep 12-inch skillet over medium-high heat. Add coconut, coriander seed and chilies; stir-fry 2 to 4 minutes or until coconut is golden brown, coriander seed is reddish brown and chilies blacken.

3. Place coconut mixture and remaining 1/2 cup water in blender. Cover and blend on medium speed until a smooth paste forms. Stir paste into peas. Stir in tamarind paste, jaggery and Tangy Sambhar Powder.

4. Heat remaining 1 tablespoon oil and mustard seed in same wok or skillet over medium-high heat. Once seed begins to pop, cover wok and wait until popping stops. Add asafetida and eggplant; stir-fry 5 to 7 minutes or until eggplant is almost tender.

5. Stir tomato, karhi leaves and salt into eggplant mixture. Stir eggplant mixture into peas. Partially cover and simmer 5 to 7 minutes or until eggplant is tender. (If using bay leaves, remove and discard.) Sprinkle with cilantro.

1 Serving: Calories 170 (Calories from Fat 70); Fat 8g (Saturated 4g); Cholesterol 0mg; Sodium 310mg; Carbohydrate 25g (Dietary Fiber 8g); Protein 7g **% Daily Value:** Vitamin A 12%; Vitamin C 4%; Calcium 2%; Iron 10% **Diet Exchanges:** 1 Starch, 2 Vegetable, 1 Fat

Lucknow is a prominent Muslim city, located in one of the largest states in North Central India, Uttar Pradesh. It is home to many artists and poets who still preserve Moghul India's ancient traditions through the language of Urdu, one of the sweetest and most poetic of all languages. What is also sweet is the abundant use of red onions in many of Lucknow's dishes. The sweetness of yellow split peas is further enhanced with a bounty of red onions, slowly cooked until caramelized.

Yellow Split Peas with Caramelized Onions

Lucknowi Chana Dal

4 SERVINGS

1 cup dried yellow split peas (chana dal), sorted, rinsed and drained

6 cups water

1/4 teaspoon ground turmeric

2 tablespoons Clarified Butter (Ghee), (page 40) or vegetable oil

6 medium red onions, cut in half and thinly sliced

1 teaspoon cumin seed, crushed

2 or 3 fresh Thai, serrano or cayenne chilies, crushed

1/2 teaspoon salt

2 tablespoons chopped fresh cilantro

1. Heat yellow split peas, 6 cups water and the turmeric to boiling in Dutch oven; reduce heat. Partially cover and simmer 25 to 30 minutes, skimming off any foam that floats to the top, until peas are softened.

2. While peas are simmering, heat Clarified Butter in 10-inch skillet over medium-high heat. Add onions. Cook about 10 minutes, stirring occasionally, until onions are golden brown.

3. Add crushed cumin and chilies to onions; stir-fry 2 to 3 minutes or until chilies have a pungent aroma.

4. Stir onion mixture and salt into peas. Partially cover and simmer 2 to 3 minutes to blend flavors. Sprinkle with cilantro.

1 Serving: Calories 210 (Calories from Fat 65); Fat 7g (Saturated 4g); Cholesterol 15mg; Sodium 300mg; Carbohydrate 37g (Dietary Fiber 12g); Protein 12g **% Daily Value:** Vitamin A 16%; Vitamin C 24%; Calcium 4%; Iron 12% **Diet Exchanges:** 2 Starch, 1 Vegetable, 1 Fat

Kootu is Tamil for coconut-based stews that are usually made with either yellow split peas (chana dal) or the much sweeter split and hulled pigeon peas (toovar dal).

Green Bean–Yellow Split Pea Stew

Kotovangai Kootu

6 SERVINGS

1 cup dried yellow split peas (chana dal), sorted, rinsed and drained

3 cups water

1/4 teaspoon ground turmeric

8 ounces yard-long green beans, cut into 2 1/2-inch pieces

2 tablespoons Clarified Butter (Ghee), (page 40) or vegetable oil

3 or 4 dried red Thai, serrano or cayenne chilies

1 tablespoon coriander seed

1 teaspoon black or yellow mustard seed

1/2 cup Shredded Fresh Coconut (page 45) or 1/4 cup dried unsweetened shredded coconut

1 teaspoon salt

10 to 12 fresh karhi leaves or 2 to 3 dried bay leaves

Steamed Basmati Rice (pages 202 and 203), if desired

1. Heat yellow split peas, water and turmeric to boiling in 3-quart saucepan; reduce heat. Partially cover and simmer 10 to 12 minutes, skimming off any foam that floats to the top, until peas are partially softened.

2. Stir in green beans. Partially cover and simmer 12 to 15 minutes or until peas are tender.

3. While peas and beans are simmering, heat 1 tablespoon of the Clarified Butter in 6-inch skillet over medium-high heat. Add chilies; roast about 30 seconds or until slightly blackened. Remove chilies from butter.

4. Add coriander seed to same butter; roast 5 to 10 seconds or until reddish brown. Remove coriander seed from butter; mix with chilies.

5. Place chilies and coriander seed in spice grinder or mortar. Grind or crush with pestle until coarsely ground.

6. Heat remaining 1 tablespoon Clarified Butter and mustard seed in same skillet over medium-high heat. Once seed begins to pop, cover skillet and wait until popping stops.

7. Stir butter-seed mixture, coconut, salt, karhi leaves and ground spice blend into pea and bean mixture. Cover and simmer 2 to 4 minutes to blend flavors. (If using bay leaves, remove and discard.) Serve with rice.

1 Serving: Calories 160 (Calories from Fat 70); Fat 8g (Saturated 5g); Cholesterol 10mg; Sodium 410mg; Carbohydrate 23g (Dietary Fiber 9g); Protein 8g **% Daily Value:** Vitamin A 28%; Vitamin C 2%; Calcium 4%; Iron 12% **Diet Exchanges:** 1 Starch, 2 Vegetable, 1 Fat

Green Bean–Yellow Split Pea Stew

Raghavan Ki Baaten

☀ *Kotorangai* is a yard-long green bean (see page 117) used extensively in
the southeastern region of India. If they are available at a store near you,
use them in a heartbeat. If unavailable, use a 9-ounce box of frozen
French-style green beans, rinsed under running water to separate; drained.

Here's a hearty South Indian stew to warm your stomach and soul during any down days. A bowl of piping-hot Steamed Basmati Rice (pages 202 and 203) is a must to mop up the thick sauce.

Squash-Coconut Stew

Shorakai Kootu

6 SERVINGS

1 cup dried yellow split peas (chana dal), sorted, rinsed and drained

3 cups warm water

2 teaspoons Tangy Sambhar Powder (page 36)

1/4 teaspoon asafetida (hing) or garlic powder

1/4 teaspoon ground turmeric

1 medium opa squash, peeled and seeded, or 2 medium yellow summer squash (1 pound), cut into 1/4-inch cubes

1/2 cup Shredded Fresh Coconut (page 45) or 1/4 cup dried unsweetened shredded coconut

1 tablespoon Clarified Butter (Ghee), (page 40) or vegetable oil

1 teaspoon black or yellow mustard seed

1 tablespoon dried split and hulled black lentils (urad dal)

12 fresh karhi leaves or 1/4 cup chopped fresh cilantro

1 teaspoon salt

1. Heat yellow split peas, warm water, Tangy Sambhar Powder, asafetida and turmeric to boiling in 3-quart saucepan; reduce heat. Partially cover and simmer 10 to 12 minutes, skimming off any foam that floats to the top, until peas are partially softened.

2. Stir in squash and coconut. Partially cover and simmer 12 to 15 minutes or until squash and peas are tender.

3. While squash mixture is simmering, heat Clarified Butter and mustard seed in 6-inch skillet over medium-high heat. Once seed begins to pop, cover skillet and wait until popping stops. Add lentils; stir-fry about 30 seconds or until golden brown.

4. Stir butter mixture, karhi leaves and salt into squash mixture. Cover and simmer 2 to 4 minutes to blend flavors.

Raghavan Ki Baaten

☀ If split and hulled black lentils are unavailable, just eliminate them from the recipe.

1 Serving: Calories 130 (Calories from Fat 45); Fat 5g (Saturated 3g); Cholesterol 5mg; Sodium 400mg; Carbohydrate 21g (Dietary Fiber 8g); Protein 8g **% Daily Value:** Vitamin A 4%; Vitamin C 6%; Calcium 2%; Iron 8% **Diet Exchanges:** 1 Starch, 1 Vegetable, 1/2 Fat

This Maharashtrian delicacy is very addicting! In addition to being visually stunning, it offers solace to the palate and soul. It is especially satisfying when served with Griddle Breads with Clarified Butter (page 238).

Sprouted Mung Beans with Coconut Milk

Mung Chi Dal

4 SERVINGS

1/2 cup hot water	1/2 teaspoon salt
12 slices dried mangosteen	1/2 teaspoon ground red pepper (cayenne)
1 tablespoon vegetable oil	1/4 teaspoon ground turmeric
10 medium cloves garlic, finely chopped (2 tablespoons)	1 can (14 ounces) unsweetened coconut milk
1 package (5 ounces) fresh mung bean sprouts (2 cups)	3 tablespoons chopped fresh cilantro

1. Pour hot water over mangosteen slices in small bowl; let stand 30 minutes or until soft. Drain; reserve water. Finely chop mangosteen; set aside.

2. Heat oil in 2-quart saucepan over medium-high heat; add garlic. Stir-fry 1 to 2 minutes until golden brown. Add sprouts, salt, ground red pepper, and turmeric; stir-fry 1 to 2 minutes.

3. Stir in coconut milk, mangosteen, reserved water, and 2 tablespoons of the cilantro. Heat to boiling; reduce heat. Simmer uncovered 10 to 15 minutes, stirring occasionally, until sauce slightly thickens. Serve sprinkled with remaining cilantro.

Raghavan Ki Baaten

☀ The bean sprouts used in India are just partially sprouted, and are quite different in texture and flavor than the fully sprouted beans used in Chinese cooking. If you wish to use partially sprouted ones instead, you can grow them in your kitchen: Rinse a cup of whole mung beans 4 to 6 times, draining after each rinse. Cover with warm water and soak 6 to 8 hours, or overnight; drain. Wrap beans loosely in a clean, damp, light kitchen towel. Lay towel in a colander and place colander in large mixing bowl. Keep in warm dark place (such as under the sink) 24 hours, spraying with water every 4 hours, until beans partially sprout.

☀ Dried mangosteen slices (*kokum*) are available in Indian grocery stores. Soak the mangosteen slices in hot water for this Maharashtrian recipe. If unavailable, use 1/4 cup chopped tangerine sections mixed with 1/2 teaspoon packed brown sugar. No need to soak in hot water. Just stir tangerine, brown sugar and 1/2 cup hot water into sprout mixture.

1 Serving: Calories 185 (Calories from Fat 125); Fat 14g (Saturated 16g); Cholesterol 15mg; Sodium 490mg; Carbohydrate 14g (Dietary Fiber 3g); Protein 4g **% Daily Value:** Vitamin A 4%; Vitamin C 10%; Calcium 2%; Iron 4% **Diet Exchanges:** 3 Vegetable, 1 1/2 Fat

When one thinks of black-eyed peas and greens, the Deep South of the United States comes to mind—quite the reverse in India. The midwestern state of Punjab pays tribute to black-eyed peas (lobhia), which offer a rich source of energy to the workers who till the soil. The combination of beans, dairy and greens makes this dish not only a powerhouse of nutrients, but also downright delicious.

Black-Eyed Peas with Greens

Lobhia Di Saag

6 SERVINGS

2 tablespoons Clarified Butter (Ghee), (page 40) or vegetable oil

1 tablespoon cumin seed

10 medium cloves garlic, finely chopped

1 large tomato, chopped (1 cup)

1 tablespoon Garam Masaala (page 32)

2 cups water

4 cups freshly cooked black-eyed peas or 2 cans (15 to 16 ounces each) black-eyed peas, rinsed and drained

1 teaspoon salt

1 cup plain yogurt (regular or fat-free)

1 tablespoon grated gingerroot

8 cups chopped mustard greens (1 large bunch)

1/2 teaspoon salt

1. Heat 1 tablespoon of the Clarified Butter in 2-quart saucepan over medium-high heat. Add cumin seed; sizzle 30 seconds. Add garlic; cook 1 minute, stirring frequently, until golden brown.

2. Stir in tomato and Garam Masaala. Cook 3 to 5 minutes, stirring occasionally, until tomato is softened. Stir in water, black-eyed peas and 1 teaspoon salt. Heat to boiling; reduce heat to medium. Simmer uncovered 15 to 20 minutes or until sauce is thickened.

3. Beat yogurt with wire whisk or spoon until smooth; stir into tomato mixture. Cook 2 minutes; remove from heat.

4. Heat remaining 1 tablespoon Clarified Butter in wok or deep 12-inch skillet over medium-high heat. Add gingerroot; stir-fry about 30 seconds or until partially brown.

5. Add greens; stir-fry 2 to 4 minutes or until greens are wilted and cooking liquid has evaporated. Stir in remaining 1/2 teaspoon salt.

6. To serve, place peas in serving bowl and top with cooked greens.

1 Serving: Calories 180 (Calories from Fat 55); Fat 6g (Saturated 3g); Cholesterol 15mg; Sodium 660mg; Carbohydrate 31g (Dietary Fiber 8g); Protein 8g **% Daily Value:** Vitamin A 48%; Vitamin C 18%; Calcium 28%; Iron 20% **Diet Exchanges:** 1 Starch, 3 Vegetable, 1/2 Fat

Black-Eyed Peas with Greens

Raghavan Ki Baaten

☀ *Saag* is Hindi for greens. *Sarson ka saag* are mustard greens, and *palak ka saag* signify spinach greens. Even though this recipe calls for mustard greens, feel free to substitute spinach, kale or even collard greens.

Chapter Six

Rice and Grains

From top: Seafood Pilaf with Saffron (page 206), Minted Black-Eyed Peas and Rice Casserole (page 208), Coconut Rice Noodles (page 228)

True basmati rice is grown and cultivated in the foothills of the mighty Himalaya Mountains, whose surrounding areas offer uniquely rich soil and a cool climate. Basmati rice has a perfumed, nutty aroma when cooked. (In fact, bas refers to aroma.) The long, tender basmati grains swell up and reveal an extra fluffiness, quite unlike regular long-grain rice.

Steamed Basmati Rice— Covered-Pan Method

Saada Chaawal

4 SERVINGS

1 cup uncooked basmati or regular long-grain rice

1 1/2 cups cold water

1. Place rice in 1-quart saucepan; add enough cold water to cover rice. Rub rice gently between fingers; drain. Repeat 4 or 5 times until water is clear; drain.

2. Add 1 1/2 cups cold water; soak 30 minutes.

3. Heat water and rice to boiling, stirring once; reduce heat to medium-high. Cook uncovered 5 to 6 minutes, stirring occasionally, until most of the water has evaporated.

4. Reduce heat to low. Cover and cook 5 minutes; remove from heat. Let stand covered 5 to 10 minutes.

5. Gently fluff rice with fork or spoon to release steam.

Raghavan Ki Baaten

☀ In this method, rice is soaked in water for a half hour and then brought to a boil, uncovered. Once almost all the water has evaporated, by which time the rice is 75 percent cooked, the pan is covered and the rice continues to cook. Then the pan is removed from the heat and stands, imprisoning the steam and causing the remaining uncooked rice grains to gently swell and become tender. Once you have followed this recipe, rest assured you will always make perfect steamed rice from then on.

☀ Store uncooked basmati rice in an airtight container in a cool, dry place up to 1 year.

☀ I cover and refrigerate cooked rice up to 5 days or freeze it in an airtight container for a month. It's easy to reheat by covering with boiling water and immediately draining off the water.

1 Serving: Calories 170 (Calories from Fat 0); Fat 0g (Saturated 0g); Cholesterol 0mg; Sodium 0mg; Carbohydrate 40g (Dietary Fiber 1g); Protein 4g **% Daily Value:** Vitamin A 0%; Vitamin C 0%; Calcium 0%; Iron 8% **Diet Exchanges:** 2 Starch

This method of cooking rice is less complicated than the covered-pan method, but you still have to watch over it to avoid overcooking. In this method, the rice is not soaked in water but is cooked much like we cook pasta, in plenty of boiling water.

Steamed Basmati Rice–Open-Pan Method

Saada Chaawal

4 SERVINGS

1 cup uncooked basmati or regular long-grain rice

8 cups water

1. Place rice in medium bowl; add enough cold water to cover rice. Rub rice gently between fingers; drain. Repeat 4 or 5 times until water is clear; drain.

2. Heat 8 cups water to boiling in 3-quart saucepan; add rice. Boil uncovered 5 to 7 minutes, stirring occasionally, until rice is tender. Drain; rinse under cold running water to stop cooking.

Raghavan Ki Baaten

☀ Refrigerate cooked rice for up to 5 days or freeze in an airtight container for up to a month. I sometimes reheat it by placing it in a microwavable container and microwave, covered, 1 or 2 minutes or until warm.

☀ There are two reasons why I wash rice before cooking: I find that long-grain rice, such as basmati, is fluffier if the starch is washed off the grains before it is cooked; and I like to wash off any dust that might be on bulk rice or rice in cloth bags.

1 Serving: Calories 170 (Calories from Fat 0); Fat 0g (Saturated 0g); Cholesterol 0mg; Sodium 0mg; Carbohydrate 40g (Dietary Fiber 1g); Protein 4g **% Daily Value:** Vitamin A 0%; Vitamin C 0%; Calcium 0%; Iron 8% **Diet Exchanges:** 2 Starch

At the onset of spring, the weather in Kashmir is ideal for that prized fungus known as the morel. Strong, rich and earthy-flavored, these mushrooms find an ideal match in perfumed basmati rice.

Basmati Rice with Mushrooms

Gucchi Pulao

4 SERVINGS

1 cup uncooked basmati or regular long-grain rice

2 tablespoons Clarified Butter (Ghee), (page 40) or vegetable oil

4 cardamom pods

1/2 pound morel mushrooms, coarsely chopped

1 1/2 cups cold water

1 teaspoon salt

1 cup chopped fresh or 1/2 cup crumbled dried fenugreek leaves (méthi)

1. Place rice in medium bowl; add enough cold water to cover rice. Rub rice gently between fingers; drain. Repeat 4 or 5 times until water is clear; drain. Cover rice with cold water; soak 30 minutes. Drain; set aside.

2. Heat Clarified Butter in 2-quart saucepan over medium-high heat. Add cardamom pods; sizzle 30 seconds. Add mushrooms; stir-fry 2 to 3 minutes or until tender.

3. Add rice; gently stir-fry 1 to 2 minutes, taking care not to break tender rice grains. Stir in 1 1/2 cups cold water and the salt. Heat to boiling, stirring once; reduce heat to medium-high. Cook uncovered 5 to 6 minutes, stirring occasionally, until almost all the water has evaporated.

4. Spread fenugreek evenly over top of rice; reduce heat to low. Cover and cook 5 minutes; remove from heat. Let rice stand covered 10 to 15 minutes.

5. Gently fluff rice with fork or spoon to release steam. Serve with cardamom pods left in to continue to flavor the rice, but do not eat them.

Raghavan Ki Baaten

☀ **Morels can make a dent in your pocketbook, so feel free to use crimini, oyster, portabella, shiitake or any combination of mushrooms that you like instead.**

☀ **If fresh or dried fenugreek leaves are unavailable, substitute watercress leaves.**

1 Serving: Calories 250 (Calories from Fat 65); Fat 7g (Saturated 4g); Cholesterol 15mg; Sodium 600mg; Carbohydrate 43g (Dietary Fiber 1g); Protein 5g **% Daily Value:** Vitamin A 8%; Vitamin C 4%; Calcium 2%; Iron 12% **Diet Exchanges:** 2 Starch, 2 Vegetable, 1 Fat

Green peas (mutter) are seasonal in India. During the onset of monsoon season, open-air markets in Mumbai (Bombay) and New Delhi are inundated with giant, plump pea pods. Many a kitchen on a Sunday perfumes the air with the aroma of cumin seed sizzling in ghee, offering a deliciously sweet backdrop for the green peas. Nowadays, frozen green peas are perennial, and restaurants offer this classic rice pilaf from Delhi as standard fare.

Basmati Rice with Green Peas

Mutter Pulao

6 SERVINGS

1 cup uncooked basmati or regular long-grain rice

2 tablespoons Clarified Butter (Ghee), (page 40) or vegetable oil

1 teaspoon cumin seed

1/2 teaspoon black peppercorns

4 cardamom pods

4 whole cloves

2 three-inch sticks cinnamon

2 dried bay leaves

1 medium onion, cut in half and thinly sliced

1 1/2 cups cold water

1 teaspoon salt

1 cup frozen green peas

1/4 cup chopped fresh mint leaves

1. Place rice in medium bowl; add enough cold water to cover rice. Rub rice gently between fingers; drain. Repeat 4 or 5 times until water is clear; drain. Cover rice with cold water; soak 30 minutes. Drain; set aside.

2. Heat Clarified Butter in heavy 2-quart saucepan over medium-high heat. Add cumin seed, peppercorns, cardamom pods, cloves, cinnamon sticks and bay leaves; sizzle 30 seconds. Add onion; stir-fry 2 to 3 minutes or until onion is partially brown.

3. Add rice; gently stir-fry 1 to 2 minutes, taking care not to break tender rice grains. Stir in 1 1/2 cups cold water and the salt. Heat to boiling, stirring once; reduce heat to medium-high. Cook uncovered 5 to 6 minutes, stirring occasionally, until almost all the water has evaporated.

4. Spread green peas and mint over top of rice; reduce heat to low. Cover and cook 5 minutes; remove from heat. Let rice stand covered 10 to 15 minutes.

5. Fluff rice with fork or spoon to release steam. Serve with peppercorns, cardamom pods, cloves, cinnamon sticks and bay leaves left in, but do not eat them.

Raghavan Ki Baaten

☀ Rice pilafs (pulaos) in India are generally served with the whole spices present. This not only makes for an appealing presentation, but they continue to flavor the rice. Do not eat the whole cloves, black peppercorns, bay leaves, cinnamon sticks or cardamom pods.

1 Serving: Calories 180 (Calories from Fat 45); Fat 5g (Saturated 3g); Cholesterol 10mg; Sodium 410mg; Carbohydrate 32g (Dietary Fiber 2g); Protein 4g **% Daily Value:** Vitamin A 6%; Vitamin C 2%; Calcium 2%; Iron 10% **Diet Exchanges:** 1 Starch, 3 Vegetable, 1/2 Fat

When you travel to Goa, just south of Mumbai (Bombay), you cannot help but notice the abundance of ornate churches with their Spanish-style architecture. This state is home to many a Jesuit, and influences of Portuguese rule still linger. Aromas of vinegar, coconut milk, cashews, chilies and garlic emanate from Goan kitchens and permeate many a seafood preparation made with the bountiful fruits of the Arabian Sea.

Seafood Pilaf with Saffron

Goan Pulao

6 SERVINGS

1 cup uncooked basmati or regular long-grain rice

1/2 pound mussels in shells

1/2 pound uncooked extra-jumbo shrimp (8 to 10), peeled and deveined

1/2 pound sea or bay scallops

1 cup Shredded Fresh Coconut (page 45) or 1/2 cup dried unsweetened shredded coconut

1/3 cup white vinegar

1/2 teaspoon salt

8 medium cloves garlic

4 or 5 fresh Thai, serrano or cayenne chilies

2 tablespoons vegetable oil

1/4 cup raw whole cashews

1 teaspoon cumin seed

2 dried bay leaves

2 three-inch sticks cinnamon

2 medium red onions, cut in half and thinly sliced

1/2 pound fresh green beans, cut into 1-inch pieces

2 1/2 cups cold water

1/2 teaspoon saffron threads

1/2 teaspoon salt

Seafood Pilaf with Saffron is pictured on page 201.

1. Place rice in medium bowl; add enough cold water to cover rice. Rub rice gently between fingers; drain. Repeat 4 or 5 times until water is clear; drain. Cover rice with cold water; soak 30 minutes. Drain; set aside.

2. While rice is soaking, discard any broken-shell or open (dead) mussels. Scrub remaining mussels in cold water, removing any barnacles with a dull paring knife. Remove beards. Place mussels in large container. Cover with cool water. Agitate water with hand, then drain and discard water. Repeat several times until water runs clear; drain.

3. Rinse and drain shrimp and scallops. Place shrimp, scallops and mussels in medium bowl.

4. Place coconut, vinegar, salt, garlic and chilies in blender. Cover and blend on medium speed until smooth. Pour over seafood mixture; mix well. Cover and refrigerate 20 minutes.

5. Heat oil in Dutch oven over medium-high heat. Add cashews; stir-fry 15 to 30 seconds or until cashews are golden brown. Remove with slotted spoon; drain on paper towels.

6. Add cumin seed, bay leaves and cinnamon sticks to oil; sizzle 15 to 30 seconds. Mix in onions; stir-fry 3 to 4 minutes or until onions are golden brown.

7. Stir in green beans and 1/4 cup of the cold water; reduce heat. Cover and cook about 5 minutes or until beans are partially cooked.

1 Serving: Calories 310 (Calories from Fat 15); Fat 13g (Saturated 5g); Cholesterol 25mg; Sodium 500mg; Carbohydrate 39g (Dietary Fiber 4g); Protein 13g **% Daily Value:** Vitamin A 6%; Vitamin C 10%; Calcium 8%; Iron 26% **Diet Exchanges:** 2 Starch, 1/2 Lean Meat, 2 Vegetable, 2 Fat

8. Add rice; gently stir-fry 1 to 2 minutes, taking care not to break tender rice grains. Stir in remaining 2 1/4 cups cold water, the saffron and salt. Heat to boiling, stirring once; reduce heat to medium-high. Cook uncovered 5 to 6 minutes, stirring occasionally, until almost all the water has evaporated.

9. Drain seafood; discard marinade. Arrange mussels, shrimp and scallops evenly over top of rice; push mussels in the rice. Cover and cook 10 minutes; remove from heat. Let stand covered 4 to 6 minutes. Discard any unopened mussels.

10. Fluff pilaf with fork or spoon to release steam. Serve sprinkled with roasted cashews. Serve with bay leaves and cinnamon sticks left in, but do not eat them

Fish stall in the open-air market, Bombay.

Raghavan Ki Baaten

☼ The resemblance to the Spanish shellfish paella is uncanny in this rice pilaf that includes succulent shrimp, scallops and mussels in a saffron-perfumed bed of basmati rice. This version, though, is quite soft in texture.

☼ I like to use fresh green beans, but when they aren't at their peak, crisp and tender, I use a 9-ounce box of frozen cut green beans instead.

Call it a casserole, call it a hot dish, but don't call it mundane! This nutritiously complete meal-in-a-dish combines the earthy flavor of black-eyed peas with the cool freshness of mint, all intertwined with highly aromatic basmati rice.

Minted Black-Eyed Peas and Rice Casserole

6 SERVINGS

1 cup uncooked basmati or regular long-grain rice

2 tablespoons vegetable oil

2 three-inch sticks cinnamon

2 dried bay leaves

1 medium red onion, cut in half and thinly sliced

1 medium tomato, chopped (3/4 cup)

1 can (15 to 16 ounces) black-eyed peas, drained and rinsed

1 teaspoon Garam Masaala (page 32)

1 teaspoon salt

2 1/2 cups cold water

1 cup chopped fresh mint leaves

Minted Black-Eyed Peas and Rice Casserole is pictured on page 201.

1. Place rice in medium bowl; add enough cold water to cover rice. Rub rice gently between fingers; drain. Repeat 4 or 5 times until water is clear; drain. Cover rice with cold water; soak 30 minutes. Drain; set aside.

2. Heat oil in heavy 2-quart saucepan over medium-high heat. Add cinnamon sticks and bay leaves; sizzle 15 to 20 seconds or until cinnamon sticks swell up. Add onion; stir-fry 2 to 3 minutes or until onion is partially brown.

3. Stir in tomato. Simmer uncovered 3 to 4 minutes or until softened. Stir in black-eyed peas, Garam Masaala and salt.

4. Add rice; gently stir-fry 1 minute, taking care not to break tender rice grains. Stir in 2 1/2 cups cold water. Heat to boiling, stirring once; reduce heat to medium-high. Cook uncovered 5 to 6 minutes, stirring occasionally, until almost all the water has evaporated.

5. Spread mint over top of rice; reduce heat to low. Cover and cook 5 minutes; remove from heat. Let rice stand covered 10 to 15 minutes. Fluff rice with fork or spoon to release steam.

☼ The frozen-foods section of your grocery store often has packages of black-eyed peas. Use a 16-ounce package of frozen black-eyed peas for this recipe; there is no need to thaw them first. Sometimes I use them instead of canned.

1 Serving: Calories 235 (Calories from Fat 45); Fat 5g (Saturated 1g); Cholesterol 0mg; Sodium 540mg; Carbohydrate 44g (Dietary Fiber 6g); Protein 9g **% Daily Value:** Vitamin A 4%; Vitamin C 4%; Calcium 4%; Iron 18% **Diet Exchanges:** 2 Starch, 3 Vegetable

From the western state of Maharashtra hails this version of fried rice, a substantial lunch when accompanied by a bowl of plain yogurt.

Spiced Basmati Rice with Peanuts

Masaala Bhat

6 SERVINGS

1 tablespoon Clarified Butter (Ghee), (page 40) or vegetable oil

1 teaspoon cumin seed

1 medium onion, finely chopped (1/2 cup)

1/3 cup dry-roasted unsalted peanuts

2 or 3 fresh Thai, serrano or cayenne chilies, finely chopped

1 cup cooked basmati or regular long-grain rice

1 cup frozen green peas, thawed

1 medium tomato, finely chopped (3/4 cup)

2 tablespoons finely chopped fresh cilantro

1 teaspoon salt

1 teaspoon Spicy Garam Masaala (page 34)

1/4 teaspoon ground turmeric

1. Heat Clarified Butter in wok or deep 12-inch skillet over medium high heat. Add cumin seed; sizzle 15 to 20 seconds.

2. Add onion, peanuts and chilies; stir-fry 2 to 3 minutes or until onion is golden brown.

3. Add remaining ingredients; stir-fry 3 to 5 minutes or until rice, peas and tomato are warm.

Raghavan Ki Baaten

☼ When I have leftover steamed vegetables, I use them as an alternative to the peas and tomato. This is also a great recipe for using up any leftover cooked rice you might have tucked away in the refrigerator.

1 Serving: Calories 120 (Calories from Fat 55); Fat 6g (Saturated 2g); Cholesterol 5mg; Sodium 420mg; Carbohydrate 15g (Dietary Fiber 2g); Protein 4g **% Daily Value:** Vitamin A 4%; Vitamin C 6%; Calcium 2%; Iron 6% **Diet Exchanges:** 1 Starch, 1 Fat

Saffron, the world's most expensive spice, finds an ideal partner in basmati, the royal rice. Saffron is the stigma of the crocus flower (crocus sativa), a delicate purple blossom. About 5,000 flowers must be handpicked to produce a single ounce of saffron. A little saffron goes a long way—a few threads will permeate the entire dish with a pungent aroma and rich yellow hue.

Basmati Rice with Saffron

Zaffrani Pulao

6 SERVINGS

1 cup uncooked basmati or regular long-grain rice

2 tablespoons vegetable oil

1/4 cup raw whole cashews

1/4 cup golden raisins

1 teaspoon cumin seed

1/2 teaspoon black peppercorns

5 cardamom pods

6 whole cloves

2 bay leaves

2 three-inch sticks cinnamon

2 medium red onions, cut in half and thinly sliced

1 1/2 cups cold water

1/2 teaspoon saffron threads

1 teaspoon salt

1. Place rice in medium bowl; add enough cold water to cover rice. Rub rice gently between fingers; drain. Repeat 4 or 5 times until water is clear; drain. Cover rice with cold water; soak 30 minutes. Drain; set aside.

2. Heat oil in 2-quart saucepan over medium-high heat. Add cashews; stir-fry 10 to 20 seconds or until cashews are golden brown. Remove with slotted spoon; drain on paper towels.

3. Add raisins to hot oil; stir-fry 20 to 30 seconds or until raisins plump up. Remove with slotted spoon; add to cashews to drain.

4. Add cumin seed, peppercorns, cardamom pods, cloves, bay leaves and cinnamon sticks to hot oil; sizzle 15 to 30 seconds. Mix in onions; stir-fry 3 to 4 minutes or until onions are golden brown.

5. Add rice; gently stir-fry 1 minute, taking care not to break tender rice grains. Stir in 1 1/2 cups cold water, the saffron and salt. Heat to boiling, stirring once; reduce heat to medium-high. Cook uncovered 5 to 6 minutes, stirring occasionally, until almost all the water has evaporated.

6. Reduce heat to low. Cover and cook 5 minutes; remove from heat. Let rice stand covered 10 to 15 minutes.

7. Fluff rice with fork or spoon to release steam. Serve sprinkled with roasted cashews and raisins. Serve with peppercorns, cardamom pods, cloves, bay leaves and cinnamon sticks left in to continue to flavor the rice, but do not eat them.

1 Serving: Calories 230 (Calories from Fat 70); Fat 8g (Saturated 1g); Cholesterol 0mg; Sodium 400mg; Carbohydrate 37g (Dietary Fiber 2g); Protein 4g **% Daily Value:** Vitamin A 0%; Vitamin C 2%; Calcium 0%; Iron 10% **Diet Exchanges:** 2 Starch, 1/2 Fruit, 1 Fat

Basmati Rice with Saffron

Raghavan Ki Baaten

☀ Refrain from buying powdered saffron, as it might not be pure. Store saffron threads in their original airtight container in a cool, dry area.

☀ Note the technique of flavoring oil with cashews and raisins. The nutty sweetness richly flavors the rice along with the whole spices. Pay extra attention when roasting cashews and raisins because they turn light brown almost instantly in hot oil.

☀ Rice pilafs (pulaos) in India are generally served with the whole spices used in cooking. The spices not only make for an appealing presentation but also continue to flavor the rice. We don't eat them, but push them aside while eating the rice.

The rice harvest season in southern India falls in October and November. One of the days is set aside as a day of rest for the stomach. As the sun gently caresses the western sky, mothers all across this region prepare large batches of rice and divide them into three equal parts. One is flavored with limes and cashews, the second is tempered with toasted coconut (page 213), and the third is mellowed with smooth, plain yogurt (page 214).

Lime–Cashew Rice Pilaf

4 SERVINGS

1 cup uncooked basmati or regular long-grain rice

1 1/2 cups cold water

2 tablespoons vegetable oil

1 teaspoon black or yellow mustard seed

1/4 cup raw whole cashews

1/4 cup dried yellow split peas (chana dal)

Juice of 2 medium limes (1/4 cup)

1 teaspoon salt

1/4 teaspoon ground turmeric

10 to 12 fresh karhi leaves or 2 tablespoons chopped fresh cilantro

2 or 3 fresh Thai, serrano or cayenne chilies, cut lengthwise in half

1. Place rice in 1 1/2-quart saucepan; add enough cold water to cover rice. Rub rice gently between fingers; drain. Repeat 4 or 5 times until water is clear; drain. Cover rice with cold water; soak 30 minutes. Drain; return to pan.

2. Heat rice and 1 1/2 cups cold water to boiling, stirring once; reduce heat to medium-high. Cook uncovered 5 to 6 minutes, stirring occasionally, until almost all the water has evaporated.

3. Reduce heat to low. Cover and cook 5 minutes; remove from heat. Let rice stand covered 10 to 15 minutes.

4. Meanwhile, heat oil and mustard seed in 10-inch skillet over medium-high heat. Once seed begins to pop, cover skillet and wait until popping stops.

5. Add cashews and yellow split peas; stir-fry about 1 minute or until cashews and peas are golden brown; remove from heat. Stir in remaining ingredients. Add to cooked rice; toss well.

1 Serving: Calories 325 (Calories from Fat 110); Fat 12g (Saturated 2g); Cholesterol 0mg; Sodium 600mg; Carbohydrate 50g (Dietary Fiber 4g); Protein 8g **% Daily Value:** Vitamin A 2%; Vitamin C 6%; Calcium 2%; Iron 14% **Diet Exchanges:** 3 Starch, 1 Vegetable, 1 1/2 Fat

Shallots have an interesting onion-garlic flavor and are widely used in southern Indian recipes.

Coconut Rice Pilaf

4 SERVINGS

1 cup uncooked basmati or regular long-grain rice

1 1/2 cups cold water

1 tablespoon vegetable oil

1 teaspoon black or yellow mustard seed

1/4 cup dried split and hulled black lentils (urad dal) or yellow split peas (chana dal)

1/4 cup raw whole cashews

8 medium shallots, thinly sliced

2 or 3 dried red Thai, serrano or cayenne chilies

10 to 12 fresh karhi leaves

1/2 cup Shredded Fresh Coconut (page 45) or 1/4 cup dried unsweetened shredded coconut

1 teaspoon salt

1. Place rice in 1 1/2-quart saucepan; add enough cold water to cover rice. Rub rice gently between fingers; drain. Repeat 4 or 5 times until water is clear; drain. Cover rice with cold water; soak 30 minutes. Drain; return to pan.

2. Heat rice and 1 1/2 cups cold water to boiling, stirring once; reduce heat to medium-high. Cook uncovered 5 to 6 minutes, stirring occasionally, until almost all the water has evaporated.

3. Reduce heat to low. Cover and cook 5 minutes; remove from heat. Let rice stand covered 10 to 15 minutes.

4. Meanwhile, heat oil and mustard seed in 10-inch skillet over medium-high heat. Once seed begins to pop, cover skillet and wait until popping stops.

5. Add black lentils and cashews; stir-fry about 1 minute or until lentils and cashews are golden brown. Add shallots and chilies; stir-fry 1 to 2 minutes or until shallots are partially brown.

6. Mix in karhi leaves and coconut. Cook 1 to 2 minutes, stirring constantly, until coconut is golden brown. Add coconut mixture and salt to cooked rice; toss well.

1 Serving: Calories 340 (Calories from Fat 110); Fat 12g (Saturated 4g); Cholesterol 0mg; Sodium 600mg; Carbohydrate 54g (Dietary Fiber 5g); Protein 9g **% Daily Value:** Vitamin A 4%; Vitamin C 2%; Calcium 4%; Iron 20% **Diet Exchanges:** 3 Starch, 1/2 Fruit, 2 Fat

Yogurt Rice Pilaf

6 SERVINGS

1 cup uncooked basmati or regular long-grain rice

1 1/2 cups cold water

1 tablespoon vegetable oil

1 teaspoon black or yellow mustard seed

1 cup plain yogurt (regular or fat-free)

1/2 teaspoon salt

2 or 3 fresh Thai, serrano or cayenne chilies, cut lengthwise in half

10 to 12 fresh karhi leaves

1. Place rice in 1 1/2-quart saucepan; add enough cold water to cover rice. Rub rice gently between fingers; drain. Repeat 4 or 5 times until water is clear; drain. Cover rice with cold water; soak 30 minutes. Drain; return to pan.

2. Heat rice and 1 1/2 cups cold water to boiling, stirring once; reduce heat to medium-high. Cook uncovered 5 to 6 minutes, stirring occasionally, until almost all the water has evaporated.

3. Reduce heat to low. Cover and cook 5 minutes; remove from heat. Let rice stand covered 10 to 15 minutes.

4. Meanwhile, heat oil and mustard seed in 6-inch skillet over medium-high heat. Once seed begins to pop, cover skillet and wait until popping stops; remove from heat.

5. Mix remaining ingredients in medium bowl. Stir in oil mixture. Add cooked rice; toss well.

1 Serving: Calories 165 (Calories from Fat 25); Fat 3g (Saturated 1g); Cholesterol 0mg; Sodium 230mg; Carbohydrate 30g (Dietary Fiber 0g); Protein 5g **% Daily Value:** Vitamin A 2%; Vitamin C 2%; Calcium 8%; Iron 6% **Diet Exchanges:** 2 Starch

Yogurt Rice Pilaf

Raghavan Ki Baaten

☀ Yogurt is essential to the conclusion of many a South Indian meal.
Soothing and mellow, it not only is thought to aid digestion, but it also
helps to alleviate the chilies' attack on the palate. The next time you
eat something fiery hot, remember to either drink some milk or eat a small
bowl of plain yogurt to help ease the burning in your mouth!

Basmati Rice with Eggplant

6 SERVINGS

1 cup uncooked basmati or regular long-grain rice

1 1/2 cups cold water

2 tablespoons Clarified Butter (Ghee), (page 40) or vegetable oil

1/4 cup dried split and hulled black lentils (urad dal) or yellow split peas (chana dal)

1/4 cup dried yellow split peas (chana dal)

1/4 cup raw whole cashews

1 tablespoon coriander seed

3 or 4 dried red Thai, serrano or cayenne chilies

1 teaspoon black or yellow mustard seed

1/4 teaspoon asafetida (hing)

4 cups 1/2-inch cubes eggplant

12 to 15 fresh karhi leaves

1 teaspoon salt

1. Place rice in 1-quart saucepan; add enough cold water to cover rice. Rub rice gently between fingers; drain. Repeat 4 or 5 times until water is clear; drain. Cover rice with cold water; soak 30 minutes. Drain; return to pan.

2. Heat rice and 1 1/2 cups cold water to boiling, stirring once; reduce heat to medium-high. Cook uncovered 5 to 6 minutes, stirring occasionally, until almost all the water has evaporated.

3. Reduce heat to low. Cover and cook 5 minutes; remove from heat. Let rice stand covered 10 to 15 minutes.

4. Meanwhile, heat 1 tablespoon of the Clarified Butter in wok or deep 12-inch skillet over medium-high heat. Add black lentils, yellow split peas, cashews, coriander seed and chilies; stir-fry 1 to 2 minutes or until lentils and cashews are golden brown. Transfer mixture to plate; cool 4 to 5 minutes.

5. Place lentil mixture in spice grinder. Grind until finely ground.

6. Heat remaining 1 tablespoon Clarified Butter and mustard seed in same wok or skillet over medium-high heat. Once seed begins to pop, cover wok and wait until popping stops.

7. Add asafetida and eggplant to mustard seed; stir-fry 2 to 4 minutes or until eggplant is partially cooked. Stir in karhi leaves and ground mixture; stir-fry 1 minute. Reduce heat to low, cover and cook 4 to 6 minutes or until eggplant is tender.

8. Spoon cooked rice into large bowl. Stir in eggplant mixture and salt.

1 Serving: Calories 235 (Calories from Fat 65); Fat 7g (Saturated 3g); Cholesterol 10mg; Sodium 400mg; Carbohydrate 41g (Dietary Fiber 6g); Protein 8g **% Daily Value:** Vitamin A 6%; Vitamin C 0%; Calcium 2%; Iron 16% **Diet Exchanges:** 2 Starch, 2 Vegetable, 1 Fat

Raghavan Ki Baaten

☀ Karhi leaves are essential to many a southern Indian recipe and are available fresh in Indian grocery stores. The dried leaves, though more commonly available, are not as flavorful as the fresh ones. If unavailable, omit from recipe.

☀ If asafetida is not at hand, eliminate from recipe.

☀ Uncooked basmati rice is very tender. Be careful when rinsing it so you don't split the grain.

Layered Rice-Potato Pilaf

Raghavan Ki Baaten

☀ This colorfully layered rice casserole looks complex and time-consuming to make but is actually quite easy. It is a great do-ahead recipe for entertaining that can be rewarmed in a microwave or oven before serving.

Biryanis are casseroles primarily originating from India's northern states, and they are as varied as the households that enjoy them. Biryanis have three main elements to them: rice, meat and/or vegetable in a sauce (curry), and nuts and raisins. And there are plenty of permutations and combinations!

Layered Rice–Potato Pilaf

Aloo Biryani

8 SERVINGS

Potato Dumplings:
3 medium red potatoes (1 pound), peeled and cooked

1/2 cup Garbanzo Bean Flour (Bésan), (page 44)

1 teaspoon Spicy Garam Masaala (page 34)

1/2 teaspoon salt

1/2 teaspoon ground turmeric

1/2 teaspoon ground red pepper (cayenne)

1/4 cup finely chopped fresh cilantro

Vegetable oil for deep-frying

1 cup plain yogurt (regular or fat-free)

Rice:
1 1/2 cups uncooked basmati or regular long-grain rice

3 tablespoons vegetable oil

1/2 cup raw whole cashews

1/2 cup golden raisins

1 teaspoon cumin seed

2 three-inch sticks cinnamon

6 cardamom pods

2 medium red onions, cut in half and thinly sliced

2 1/2 cups cold water

1 teaspoon salt

1 teaspoon paprika

1/2 teaspoon ground turmeric

MAKE POTATO DUMPLINGS:

1. Mash potatoes in medium bowl. Stir in remaining ingredients for dumplings except 2 tablespoons of the cilantro, the oil and yogurt. Divide into 12 pieces. Shape each piece into a ball; set aside.

2. Heat oil (2 to 3 inches deep) in wok or Dutch oven over medium-high heat until thermometer inserted in oil reads 350°.

3. Carefully drop 4 to 5 balls into hot oil and fry 3 to 4 minutes, turning occasionally, until golden brown. Remove with slotted spoon; drain on paper towels. Repeat with remaining balls.

4. Beat yogurt in medium bowl, using wire whisk, until smooth. Gently mix in fried dumplings and remaining 2 tablespoons cilantro; set aside.

MAKE RICE:

1. Place rice in medium bowl; add enough cold water to cover rice. Rub rice gently between fingers; drain. Repeat 4 or 5 times until water is clear; drain. Cover rice with cold water; soak 30 minutes. Drain; set aside.

2. Heat oil in 3-quart saucepan over medium-high heat. Add cashews; stir-fry 10 to 20 seconds or until cashews are golden brown. Remove with slotted spoon; drain on paper towels.

3. Add raisins to hot oil; stir-fry 20 to 30 seconds or until raisins plump up. Remove with slotted spoon; add to cashews to drain.

4. Add cumin seed, cinnamon sticks and cardamom pods to hot oil; sizzle 15 to 30 seconds. Mix in onions; stir-fry 3 to 4 minutes or until onions are golden brown.

continues

1 Serving: Calories 370 (Calories from Fat 115); Fat 13g (Saturated 2g); Cholesterol 0mg; Sodium 470mg; Carbohydrate 57g (Dietary Fiber 4g); Protein 8g **% Daily Value:** Vitamin A 0%; Vitamin C 4%; Calcium 10%; Iron 14% **Diet Exchanges:** 3 Starch, 2 Vegetable, 2 Fat

**Rice fields,
Uttar Pradesh.**

continued

5. Add rice; gently stir-fry 1 minute, taking care not to break tender rice grains. Stir in 2 1/2 cups cold water and the salt. Heat to boiling, stirring once; reduce heat to medium-high. Cook uncovered 5 to 6 minutes, stirring occasionally, until almost all the water has evaporated; remove from heat.

6. Divide partially cooked rice in half. Mix paprika into one half and turmeric into the other half; set aside.

ASSEMBLE PILAF:

1. Heat oven to 350°. Spray 3-quart glass casserole with cooking spray.

2. Spread turmeric rice evenly in casserole. Arrange dumplings with yogurt sauce as second layer. Top with paprika rice as third layer.

3. Place casserole in larger baking pan. Pour hot water into pan until 2 inches deep to prevent rice from becoming crisp. Cover and bake 40 to 45 minutes or until top layer of rice is tender.

4. Serve sprinkled with roasted cashews and raisins. Serve with cinnamon sticks and cardamom pods left in to continue to flavor pilaf, but do not eat them.

Pongal is a festival celebrating the harvest season during the end of summer in southern India. As a tribute to Mother Earth to thank her for fertile soil after the cultivation of the rice crop, the village women prepare large vats of rice-lentil porridge. They season it with a simple combination of coarsely ground black peppercorns and cumin seed.

Rice-Lentil Porridge

Ven Pongal

6 SERVINGS

1 cup uncooked basmati or regular long-grain rice

1 cup dried split and hulled green lentils (mung dal) or red lentils (masoor dal)

4 cups cold water

1 teaspoon salt

2 tablespoons Clarified Butter (Ghee), (page 40) or vegetable oil

1 tablespoon cumin seed

1 teaspoon black peppercorns

12 to 15 fresh karhi leaves or 2 tablespoons chopped fresh cilantro

1. Place rice and lentils in 2 1/2 quart saucepan; add enough cold water to cover rice and lentils. Rub rice and lentils gently between fingers; drain. Repeat 4 or 5 times until water is clear; drain. Add 4 cups cold water; soak 30 minutes.

2. Stir salt into rice and lentils. Heat to boiling, stirring once; reduce heat to medium-high. Cook uncovered 5 to 6 minutes, stirring occasionally, until almost all the water has evaporated.

3. Reduce heat to low. Cover and cook 5 minutes; remove from heat. Let rice mixture stand covered 5 to 10 minutes.

4. Meanwhile, heat Clarified Butter in 6-inch skillet over medium-high heat. Add cumin seed and peppercorns; sizzle 15 to 30 seconds or until cumin seed is reddish brown and has a nutty aroma.

5. Remove cumin seed and peppercorns from hot oil; place in spice grinder or mortar. Grind until coarsely ground.

6. Add karhi leaves to hot oil; sizzle 5 seconds. Stir oil-karhi mixture and ground spices into rice-lentil porridge.

1 **Serving:** Calories 250 (Calories from Fat 45); Fat 5g (Saturated 3g); Cholesterol 10mg; Sodium 400mg; Carbohydrate 45g (Dietary Fiber 7g); Protein 11g **% Daily Value:** Vitamin A 4%; Vitamin C 0%; Calcium 4%; Iron 26% **Diet Exchanges:** 3 Starch, 1/2 Fat

A soul-satisfying rice pilaf, this recipe is testimony to the subtleties of spice blends and techniques. They create a myriad of flavors that will sing in your mouth. A signature dish of certain communities in the North, this biryani is always reserved for a special occasion.

Curried Lamb-Rice Casserole

Gosht Biryani

6 SERVINGS

Lamb Curry:
2 tablespoons vegetable oil

1/2 cup finely chopped red onion

2 tablespoons finely chopped gingerroot

5 medium cloves garlic, finely chopped

1/2 cup tomato sauce

1 tablespoon coriander seed, ground

1 teaspoon cumin seed, ground

1/2 teaspoon salt

1/2 teaspoon ground red pepper (cayenne)

1/4 teaspoon ground turmeric

3/4 cup water

1 pound boneless lamb cut into 2-inch cubes

Rice:
1 cup uncooked basmati or regular long-grain rice

3 tablespoons vegetable oil

1/2 cup raw whole cashews

1/2 cup golden raisins

1 teaspoon cumin seed

2 three-inch sticks cinnamon

4 cardamom pods

2 medium red onions, cut in half and thinly sliced

2 1/2 cups cold water

1 teaspoon salt

1/2 teaspoon ground turmeric

Chutney:
1 cup chopped fresh cilantro

1 medium tomato, chopped (3/4 cup)

3/4 cup chopped fresh mint leaves

1 medium onion, chopped (1/2 cup)

1 teaspoon salt

2 medium cloves garlic

1 or 2 fresh Thai, serrano or cayenne chilies

MAKE LAMB CURRY:

1. Heat oil in 1-quart saucepan over medium-high heat. Add onion, gingerroot and garlic; stir-fry about 5 minutes or until onion is golden brown.

2. Stir in tomato sauce, ground coriander, ground cumin, salt, ground red pepper and turmeric; reduce heat. Partially cover and simmer about 5 minutes or until a thin film of oil starts to form on surface of sauce. (The longer sauce simmers, the more oil will form.)

3. Stir in water and lamb. Partially cover and simmer 35 to 40 minutes, stirring occasionally, until lamb is slightly pink in center; remove from heat.

MAKE RICE:

1. Place rice in medium bowl; add enough cold water to cover rice. Rub rice gently between fingers; drain. Repeat 4 or 5 times until water is clear; drain. Cover rice with cold water; soak 30 minutes. Drain; set aside.

2. Heat oil in 3-quart saucepan over medium-high heat. Add cashews; stir-fry 10 to 20 seconds or until cashews are golden brown. Remove with slotted spoon; drain on paper towels.

3. Add raisins to hot oil; stir-fry 20 to 30 seconds or until raisins plump up. Remove with slotted spoon; add to cashews to drain.

4. Add cumin seed, cinnamon sticks and cardamom pods to hot oil; sizzle 15 to 30 seconds. Mix in onions; stir-fry 3 to 4 minutes or until onions are golden brown.

1 Serving: Calories 450 (Calories from Fat 180); Fat 20g (Saturated 4g); Cholesterol 40mg; Sodium 1,150mg; Carbohydrate 51g (Dietary Fiber 4g); Protein 20g **% Daily Value:** Vitamin A 6%; Vitamin C 12%; Calcium 6%; Iron 22% **Diet Exchanges:** 3 Starch, 1 Lean Meat, 1 Vegetable, 3 Fat

5. Add rice; gently stir-fry 1 minute, taking care not to break tender rice grains. Stir in 2 1/2 cups cold water and the salt. Heat to boiling, stirring once; reduce heat to medium-high. Cook uncovered 5 to 6 minutes, stirring occasionally, until almost all the water has evaporated; remove from heat. Stir in turmeric; set aside.

MAKE CHUTNEY:

1. Place all ingredients for chutney in food processor.

2. Cover and process until smooth.

ASSEMBLE CASSEROLE:

1. Heat oven to 350°. Spray 3-quart glass casserole with cooking spray.

2. Spread rice evenly in casserole. Arrange lamb curry as second layer. Top with chutney as third layer.

3. Place casserole in larger baking pan. Pour hot water into pan until 2 inches deep to prevent rice from becoming crisp when exposed to dry heat. Cover and bake 40 to 45 minutes or until rice is cooked and lamb is tender.

4. Serve sprinkled with roasted cashews and raisins. Serve with cinnamon sticks and cardamom pods left in to continue to flavor rice, but do not eat them.

Raghavan Ki Baaten

☀ I bake this tasty lamb dish in a water bath because it keeps it creamy and it holds together when served. Without the water bath, the edges become too brown and dry and the top becomes too crusty. This extra step is worth the effort.

☀ This makes for a great do-ahead meal. The casserole can be assembled and baked a day ahead and reheated in the microwave before serving. Oftentimes, the flavors evolve over time and leftovers take on a wonderful new flavor. Serve this dish with a simple salad and a bowl of plain, unsweetened yogurt.

Kichidis are as diverse as their regions of origin. An adaptation of this humble porridge became kedgeree, *a popular English breakfast dish of rice with flaked fish and eggs. Ayurveda, a branch of medicine that uses herbs and spices to maintain the body's balance, considers* kichidis *soothing to the digestive system and recommends serving them with a bowl of plain yogurt.*

Rice–Lentil Porridge with Caramelized Onions

8 SERVINGS

1 cup uncooked basmati or regular long-grain rice

1 cup dried split and hulled green lentils (mung dal)

3 cups cold water

1 package (10 ounces) frozen chopped spinach, thawed (do not drain)

1 teaspoon salt

1/2 teaspoon ground turmeric

2 tablespoons Clarified Butter (Ghee), (page 40) or vegetable oil

1 teaspoon cumin seed

2 medium red onions, cut in half and thinly sliced

1 tablespoon finely chopped gingerroot

1/3 cup water

1 teaspoon black peppercorns, crushed

1. Place rice and lentils in 3 1/2-quart saucepan; add enough cold water to cover rice and lentils. Rub rice and lentils gently between fingers; drain. Repeat 4 or 5 times until water is clear; drain. Stir in 3 cups cold water, undrained spinach, salt and turmeric.

2. Heat rice mixture to boiling, stirring once; reduce heat to medium-high. Cook uncovered 5 to 6 minutes, stirring occasionally, until almost all the water has evaporated; reduce heat to medium. Cover and simmer 10 minutes.

3. Meanwhile, heat Clarified Butter in 10-inch skillet over medium-high heat. Add cumin seed; sizzle 15 to 20 seconds or until seed is reddish brown and has a nutty aroma. Add onions and gingerroot; stir-fry 4 to 6 minutes or until onions are lightly browned. Stir in 1/3 cup water.

4. Spread onion mixture and crushed peppercorns over rice-lentil porridge. Cover and simmer 1 to 2 minutes; remove from heat. Let porridge stand covered 5 minutes. Gently fluff porridge with fork or spoon to release steam.

1 Serving: Calories 130 (Calories from Fat 35); Fat 4g (Saturated 2g); Cholesterol 10mg; Sodium 320mg; Carbohydrate 22g (Dietary Fiber 6g); Protein 8g **% Daily Value:** Vitamin A 20%; Vitamin C 4%; Calcium 6%; Iron 16% **Diet Exchanges:** 1 Starch, 1 Vegetable, 1/2 Fat

Rice-Lentil Porridge with Caramelized Onions, Spicy Lemon Pickle (page 272)

Raghavan Ki Baaten

☼ To crush black peppercorns, I place them in a mortar and pound them
gently with a pestle until just cracked. If a mortar and pestle are not at
hand, place the peppercorns in a heavy-duty resealable plastic bag
and crush them with a rolling pin.

This is often considered picnic food in Tamilian households all across India. These southeastern natives make fresh rice noodles (sevai) to take on picnics and long road trips. In a laboriously precise process, hand-cranked noodle machines yield strands that melt in your mouth.

Lime-Flavored Rice Noodles with Cashews

6 SERVINGS

2 quarts water

1 pound fresh (refrig-
erated) or dried rice
noodles, cut into
3-inch pieces

2 tablespoons
vegetable oil

1 teaspoon black or
yellow mustard seed

1/4 teaspoon asafetida
(hing)

1/4 cup dried yellow
split peas (chana dal)

1/4 cup raw
whole cashews

Juice of 2 medium
limes (1/4 cup)

1 teaspoon salt

1/4 teaspoon ground
turmeric

8 to 10 fresh karhi
leaves or 2 table-
spoons chopped
fresh cilantro

2 or 3 fresh
Thai, serrano or
cayenne chilies, cut
lengthwise in half

1. Heat water to boiling in 3-quart saucepan; remove from heat. Add fresh noodles; soak 30 seconds (do not soak longer). Drain; rinse with cold water. If using dried noodles, cook according to package directions. Set aside.

2. Heat oil and mustard seed in wok or 12-inch skillet over medium-high heat. Once seed begins to pop, cover wok and wait until popping stops.

3. Add asafetida, yellow split peas and cashews; stir-fry about 1 minute or until peas and cashews are golden brown.

4. Add remaining ingredients and cooked rice noodles; toss 1 to 2 minutes or until noodles are heated.

1 Serving: Calories 265 (Calories from Fat 65); Fat 7g (Saturated 1g); Cholesterol 0mg; Sodium 400mg; Carbohydrate 48g (Dietary Fiber 3g); Protein 5g **% Daily Value:** Vitamin A 14%; Vitamin C 26%; Calcium 2%; Iron 10% **Diet Exchanges:** 3 Starch, 1 Fat

Lime-Flavored Rice Noodles with Cashews

Raghavan Ki Baaten

☀ Rice noodles are found in Asian grocery stores and some large supermarkets. If you cannot find fresh rice noodles for this recipe, the flavors
and textures of dried cooked noodles are quite similar to the "real deal."
Do not overcook rice noodles because they will become mushy. Immediately
drain noodles in a colander, and run cold water through them to stop the
cooking process.

☀ If asafetida is unavailable, eliminate from recipe.

South Indians have a knack for giving each dish a distinctive flavor, even though many similar ingredients are used. Here's an example: Rice noodles, coconut, cashews and dried chilies are some of the ingredients of Rice Noodles with Pepper (page 229) as well, but this recipe produces a unique savory sensation. Stir-frying the coconut until it is toasted creates a whole new taste.

Coconut Rice Noodles

Thenga Sevai

6 SERVINGS

2 quarts water

1 pound fresh (refrigerated) or dried rice noodles, cut into 3-inch pieces

2 tablespoons vegetable oil

1 teaspoon black or yellow mustard seed

2 tablespoons dried split and hulled black lentils (urad dal) or yellow split peas (chana dal)

1/4 cup raw whole cashews

8 medium shallots, thinly sliced

3 or 4 dried red Thai, serrano or cayenne chilies

18 to 20 fresh karhi leaves

1 cup Shredded Fresh Coconut (page 45) or 1/2 cup dried unsweetened shredded coconut

1 teaspoon salt

1. Heat water to boiling in 3-quart saucepan; remove from heat. Add fresh noodles; soak 30 seconds (do not soak longer). Drain; rinse with cold water. If using dried noodles, cook according to package directions. Set aside.

2. Heat oil and mustard seed in wok or 12-inch skillet over medium-high heat. Once seed begins to pop, cover skillet and wait until popping stops.

3. Add black lentils and cashews; stir-fry about 1 minute or until lentils and cashews are golden brown. Add shallots and chilies; stir-fry 1 to 2 minutes or until shallots are partially brown.

4. Add karhi leaves and coconut; stir-fry 1 to 2 minutes or until coconut is golden brown.

5. Add cooked rice noodles and salt; toss 1 to 2 minutes or until noodles are heated.

Raghavan Ki Baaten

☀ **Karhi leaves are available fresh at any store that sells Indian groceries. If unavailable, omit from recipe.**

1 Serving: Calories 300 (Calories from Fat 100); Fat 11g (Saturated 5g); Cholesterol 0mg; Sodium 400mg; Carbohydrate 49g (Dietary Fiber 4g); Protein 5g **% Daily Value:** Vitamin A 6%; Vitamin C 2%; Calcium 2%; Iron 12% **Diet Exchanges:** 2 Starch, 1 Fruit, 1 1/2 Fat

Rice Noodles with Pepper

Podi Sevai

4 SERVINGS

1/4 cup raw cashew pieces

1/4 cup dried yellow split peas (chana dal)

1 teaspoon cumin seed

1 teaspoon black peppercorns

1 dried red Thai, serrano or cayenne chili

1/2 cup Shredded Fresh Coconut (page 45) or 1/4 cup dried unsweetened shredded coconut

1 tablespoon sesame oil (light colored)

1 teaspoon salt

12 to 15 fresh karhi leaves or 2 tablespoons chopped fresh cilantro

2 quarts water

1 pound fresh (refrigerated) or dried rice noodles, cut into 3-inch pieces

1. Heat 6-inch skillet over medium-high heat. Add cashews, yellow split peas, cumin seed, peppercorns and chili; stir-fry 3 to 4 minutes, until cashews and split peas are golden brown. Transfer to small bowl; let stand 3 to 5 minutes or until cool.

2. Place roasted spice blend in spice grinder. Grind until finely ground; set aside.

3. Mix coconut, oil, salt and karhi leaves; set aside.

4. Heat water to boiling in 3-quart saucepan; remove from heat. Add fresh noodles; soak 30 seconds (do not soak longer). Drain; rinse with cold water. If using dried noodles, cook according to package directions.

5. Place noodles in serving bowl. Add ground spice blend and coconut mixture; toss well.

Raghavan Ki Baaten

☀ The light-colored sesame oil used in this recipe is different than the darker oil common to Chinese cooking. The Asian oil, made with toasted sesame seed, is reddish brown and has a strong nutty flavor. Unrefined or "light" sesame oil, pressed from untoasted sesame seed, is available in Indian grocery stores. Unrefined sesame oil may also be labeled as just "sesame oil," but I refer to it as "sesame oil (light colored)" here. If unavailable, for every tablespoon of light-colored sesame oil, substitute 1/2 teaspoon dark-colored sesame oil mixed with enough vegetable oil to equal the same amount.

1 Serving: Calories 390 (Calories from Fat 100); Fat 11g (Saturated 4g); Cholesterol 0mg; Sodium 600mg; Carbohydrate 71g (Dietary Fiber 5g); Protein 7g **% Daily Value:** Vitamin A 4%; Vitamin C 0%; Calcium 4%; Iron 18% **Diet Exchanges:** 3 Starch, 1 1/2 Fruit, 1 1/2 Fat

It truly is amazing what you can do with something as simple as hot wheat cereal, a favorite ingredient in South Indian kitchens. This spiced and nutty recipe combines hot wheat cereal with vegetables, elevating its position from an oftentimes bland breakfast food to a hearty accompaniment or even a light main course.

Spiced Creamy Wheat with Cashews

8 SERVINGS

2 tablespoons vegetable oil

1 teaspoon black or yellow mustard seed

1/4 cup raw cashew pieces

2 tablespoons dried split and hulled black lentils (urad dal)

2 tablespoons dried yellow split peas (chana dal)

1 medium onion, finely chopped (1/2 cup)

1 tablespoon finely chopped gingerroot

3 cups water

2 medium red potatoes, peeled and cut into 1/4-inch cubes (1 cup)

1 cup frozen green peas

2 or 3 fresh Thai, serrano or cayenne chilies, finely chopped

1 teaspoon salt

1/2 teaspoon ground turmeric

15 fresh karhi leaves

1 cup uncooked hot wheat cereal (not instant)

1 medium tomato, chopped (3/4 cup)

2 tablespoons chopped fresh cilantro

1. Heat oil and mustard seed in 2-quart saucepan or wok over medium-high heat. Once seed begins to pop, cover saucepan and wait until popping stops.

2. Add cashews, black lentils and yellow split peas; stir-fry about 30 seconds or until lentils and cashews are golden brown. Add onion and gingerroot; stir-fry 2 to 3 minutes or until onion is golden brown.

3. Stir in remaining ingredients except hot wheat cereal, tomato and cilantro. Heat to boiling; reduce heat. Cover and simmer 5 to 6 minutes or until potatoes are tender.

4. Stir in uncooked hot wheat cereal. Cover and simmer 3 to 4 minutes or until all water is absorbed. Stir in tomato and cilantro. Cover and simmer 1 to 2 minutes or until tomato is warm.

1 Serving: Calories 175 (Calories from Fat 45); Fat 5g (Saturated 1g); Cholesterol 0mg; Sodium 320mg; Carbohydrate 30g (Dietary Fiber 4g); Protein 6g **% Daily Value:** Vitamin A 4%; Vitamin C 8%; Calcium 4%; Iron 40% **Diet Exchanges:** 2 Starch, 1/2 Fat

Spiced Creamy Wheat with Cashews

Raghavan Ki Baaten

☼ Hot wheat cereal or farina (*sooji* or *rava* in Tamil), is widely available in supermarkets, but make sure you **do not** use the instant kind for this recipe.

☼ I like to serve this dish by itself or as a base for bowls of Pigeon Pea Stew (page 188).

☼ If split and hulled black lentils are unavailable, increase the amount of yellow split peas to 1/4 cup. Eliminate karhi leaves if none is at hand.

Plain tapioca pearls are transformed into a mouth-tingling, robust-flavored meal when combined with potatoes and peanuts. Mothers in Maharashtra treat their families to large bowls of sabudana kichidi.

Tapioca Pearls with Peanuts and Potatoes

sabudana kichidi

6 SERVINGS

1 cup uncooked tapioca pearls (sabudana)

3/4 cup hot water

1 tablespoon peanut or vegetable oil

1 teaspoon cumin seed

1 medium onion, finely chopped (1/2 cup)

1 medium baking potato, peeled and cut into 1/2-inch cubes (1 1/2 cups)

1/4 teaspoon ground turmeric

1/2 cup dry-roasted unsalted peanuts

1/4 cup finely chopped fresh cilantro

1 tablespoon sugar

1 teaspoon salt

2 or 3 fresh Thai, serrano or cayenne chilies, finely chopped

1. Rinse tapioca in large bowl; add enough cold water to cover tapioca. Rub tapioca gently between fingers; drain. Repeat 4 or 5 times until water is clear; drain. Add 1/4 cup of the hot water; soak about 30 minutes or until pearls swell up and soften. Drain; set aside.

2. Heat oil in wok or 12-inch skillet over medium-high heat. Add cumin seed; sizzle 10 to 15 seconds.

3. Add onion; stir-fry 1 to 2 minutes or until partially brown. Add potato and turmeric; stir-fry 1 to 2 minutes.

4. Stir in remaining 1/2 cup hot water; reduce heat. Cover and simmer 5 to 6 minutes or until potatoes are tender.

5. Stir in remaining ingredients. Cook 1 to 2 minutes, stirring occasionally, until peanuts are warm.

6. Stir in tapioca. Cook 2 to 4 minutes, stirring constantly, until tapioca is warm.

1 Serving: Calories 210 (Calories from Fat 70); Fat 8g (Saturated 1g); Cholesterol 0mg; Sodium 400mg; Carbohydrate 33g (Dietary Fiber 2g); Protein 4g **% Daily Value:** Vitamin A 2%; Vitamin C 4%; Calcium 2%; Iron 4% **Diet Exchanges:** 2 Starch, 1 Fat

Tapioca Pearls with Peanuts and Potatoes (uncooked multi-color pearl tapioca and pearl tapioca in bowls)

Raghavan Ki Baaten

☀ The softened tapioca, when cooked, exhibits its starchy consistency, similar to sticky rice, and offers an interesting texture contrast to the crunchy peanuts.

Chapter Seven

Breads

From Top: Egg-Flavored Puffy Breads (page 251), Multi-Lentil Pancakes (page 258), Yogurt with Fresh Mint (page 271), Stuffed Rice-Lentil Crepes (page 260)

Nothing is more basic, simple and pervasive in kitchens across India than griddle breads made with whole wheat (chappati) *flour, salt and water. Interchangeably known as rotis or* chappatis, *these breads are torn into bite-size pieces, wrapped around morsels of food and devoured—making them an excellent substitute for flatware too!*

Whole Wheat Unleavened Breads

Rotis

8 BREADS (4 SERVINGS)

2 cups chappati flour

1/2 teaspoon salt

1/4 to 1/2 cup warm water

Clarified Butter (Ghee), melted, (page 40) or melted butter for brushing

1. Mix flour and salt in medium bowl. Stir in warm water, 2 tablespoons at a time, until a fairly stiff dough forms.

2. Knead dough in bowl or on lightly floured surface 2 to 3 minutes or until dough becomes smooth and pliable. Brush dough with Clarified Butter and cover with plastic wrap; set aside 10 to 15 minutes. (At this point, dough can be covered and refrigerated up to 24 hours. When ready to roll, let dough stand at room temperature 30 minutes so it becomes soft and easy to handle.)

3. Divide dough into 8 equal pieces; return them to bowl and cover. Heat heavy 8-inch skillet over medium heat.

4. Working with one piece of dough at a time, roll into 6-inch circle on lightly floured surface. Cook dough in skillet 2 to 4 minutes, turning once, until brown spots start to form on bottom and bubbles start to appear on surface. Remove from skillet; brush with butter. Repeat with remaining dough.

5. Wrap cooked breads in aluminum foil to keep warm while cooking remaining dough.

2 Breads: Calories 140 (Calories from Fat 25); Fat 3g (Saturated 1g); Cholesterol 5mg; Sodium 300mg; Carbohydrate 25g (Dietary Fiber 2g); Protein 5g **% Daily Value:** Vitamin A 2%; Vitamin C 0%; Calcium 0%; Iron 10% **Diet Exchanges:** 1 1/2 Starch, 1/2 Fat

Whole Wheat Unleavened Breads, Gujarati-Style Mixed-Vegetable Curry (page 186)

Raghavan Ki Baaten

☀ Chappati flour is available in natural-food stores and Indian grocery stores. The flour is ground from a low-protein wheat grain, so it doesn't form the strong gluten that gives commercial yeast breads their structure. If chappati flour is unavailable, use an equal amount of whole wheat flour, all-purpose flour and cake flour for each cup of chappati flour.

☀ I freeze cooked rotis up to 2 months tightly wrapped in aluminum foil. Reheat them by placing the foil pack of frozen rotis in a 200° oven for 10 to 15 minutes, or until warm.

Warm, buttery, flaky! How can you go wrong with fresh griddle breads liberally brushed with nutty Clarified Butter? Because of the slightly laborious process, paranthas are not an everyday occurrence, but the end result is worth the effort.

Griddle Breads with Clarified Butter

Paranthas

8 BREADS (8 SERVINGS)

3 cups chappati flour

1 teaspoon salt

1/4 cup melted Clarified Butter (Ghee), (page 40) or vegetable oil

About 1/2 cup warm water

Clarified Butter (Ghee), melted, or melted butter for brushing

1. Mix flour and salt in medium bowl. Add 1/4 cup Clarified Butter. Rub flour and butter between palms and fingers about 1 minute or until mixture looks like coarse crumbs. Stir in warm water, 2 tablespoons at a time, until dough leaves side of bowl and forms a ball. The dough should not be sticky or dry.

2. Knead dough in bowl or on lightly floured surface 2 to 3 minutes or until dough becomes smooth and pliable. Brush dough with Clarified Butter and cover with plastic wrap; set aside 30 minutes. (At this point, dough can be covered and refrigerated up to 24 hours. When ready to roll, let dough stand at room temperature 30 minutes so it becomes soft and easy to handle.)

3. Divide dough into 8 equal pieces; return them to bowl and cover.

4. Working with one piece of dough at a time, roll into 6-inch circle on lightly floured surface. Brush top of dough with Clarified Butter. Lift dough from one end and roll up tightly. Shape roll into a coil. Roll coil into 6-inch circle. Repeat with remaining dough.

Raghavan Ki Baaten

☼ **If chappati flour is unavailable, use an equal amount of whole wheat flour, all-purpose flour and cake flour for each cup of chappati flour.**

1 Bread: Calories 255 (Calories from Fat 80); Fat 9g (Saturated 5g); Cholesterol 20mg; Sodium 300mg; Carbohydrate 38g (Dietary Fiber 2g); Protein 8g **% Daily Value:** Vitamin A 6%; Vitamin C 0%; Calcium 0%; Iron 16% **Diet Exchanges:** 2 1/2 Starch, 1 Fat

5. Heat ungreased heavy 10-inch skillet over medium heat. Cook one circle of dough 1 to 2 minutes or until brown spots appear on bottom. Turn over and brush cooked side with butter, then turn buttered side down and cook 1 to 2 minutes. Brush top with butter, then turn buttered side down and cook 30 seconds. Turn again and cook 30 seconds. Repeat with remaining dough.

6. Wrap cooked breads in aluminum foil to keep warm while cooking remaining dough.

Shaping Griddle Breads

Shape circle of dough into a roll.   Shape roll into a coil.   Roll coil into a 6-inch circle.

This aromatic bread is very dense and has a chewy texture.

Fenugreek-Scented Griddle Breads

méthi Paranthas

8 BREADS (8 SERVINGS)

2 cups chappati flour

2 tablespoons
Garbanzo Bean Flour
(Bésan), (page 44)

1 teaspoon salt

1 tablespoon melted
Clarified Butter
(Ghee), (page 40)
or vegetable oil

1 cup finely chopped
fresh or 1/2 cup
crumbled dried
fenugreek leaves
(méthi)

2 tablespoons mango
powder (amchur) or
1 tablespoon grated
lemon or lime peel

1 teaspoon ground
red pepper (cayenne)

About 3/4 cup
warm water

Clarified Butter
(Ghee), melted,
or melted butter
for brushing

1. Mix flours and salt in medium bowl. Add 1 tablespoon Clarified Butter. Rub flour and butter between palms and fingers about 1 minute or until mixture looks like coarse crumbs. Stir in fenugreek, mango powder and ground red pepper. Stir in warm water, 2 tablespoons at a time, until dough leaves side of bowl and forms a ball. The dough should not be sticky or dry.

2. Knead dough in bowl or on lightly floured surface 2 to 3 minutes or until dough becomes smooth and pliable. Brush dough with Clarified Butter and cover with plastic wrap; set aside 30 minutes. (At this point, dough can be covered and refrigerated up to 24 hours. When ready to roll, let dough stand at room temperature 30 minutes so it becomes soft and easy to handle.)

3. Divide dough into 8 equal pieces; return them to bowl and cover. Heat ungreased heavy 10-inch skillet over medium heat.

4. Working with one piece of dough at a time, roll into 6-inch circle on lightly floured surface. Cook dough 1 to 2 minutes or until brown spots appear on bottom. Turn over and brush cooked side with butter, then turn buttered side down and cook 1 to 2 minutes. Brush top with butter, then turn buttered side down and cook 30 seconds. Turn again and cook 30 seconds. Repeat with remaining dough.

5. Wrap cooked breads in aluminum foil to keep warm while cooking remaining dough.

1 Bread: Calories 145 (Calories from Fat 25); Fat 3g (Saturated 2g); Cholesterol 5mg; Sodium 300mg; Carbohydrate 26g (Dietary Fiber 2g); Protein 5g **% Daily Value:** Vitamin A 4%; Vitamin C 2%; Calcium 0%; Iron 10% **Diet Exchanges:** 1 1/2 Starch, 1/2 Fat

Fenugreek-Scented Griddle Breads, Red Lentils with Ginger (page 177)

Raghavan Ki Baaten

☀ Highly perfumed fenugreek leaves have a subtle, pleasantly bitter flavor.
Because this bread's flavor primarily comes from these leaves, there is
unfortunately no substitute for the fenugreek. The dried leaves are
available at Indian grocery stores, where you can also find the fresh ones
in season.

☀ If chappati flour is unavailable, use an equal amount of whole wheat flour,
all-purpose flour and cake flour for each cup of chappati flour.

A pleasantly pungent parantha, this bread is consumed in northern Indian households on many an occasion. Daikon, a long Japanese white radish, often available in supermarkets in the United States, has a pungency level between that of the garden-variety red radish and strong horseradish. I have used shredded vegetables such as red radishes, red or green cabbage or carrots in place of the daikon, with excellent results.

Griddle Breads with Daikon

mooli Paranthas

8 BREADS (8 SERVINGS)

2 cups shredded daikon or radishes

1 1/2 teaspoons salt

2 cups chappati flour

2 tablespoons Garbanzo Bean Flour (Bésan), (page 44)

1 tablespoon melted Clarified Butter (Ghee), (page 40) or vegetable oil

2 tablespoons mango powder (amchur) or 1 tablespoon grated lemon or lime peel

2 tablespoons chopped fresh cilantro

1 teaspoon cumin seed, ground

About 1/2 cup warm water

Clarified Butter (Ghee), melted, or melted butter for brushing

1. Mix daikon and salt in medium bowl; set aside 30 minutes.

2. Completely squeeze water out of daikon, using hands. Mix daikon and remaining ingredients except water and Clarified Butter for brushing in medium bowl. Stir in warm water, 2 tablespoons at a time, until dough leaves side of bowl and forms a ball. The dough should not be sticky or dry.

3. Knead dough in bowl or on lightly floured surface 2 to 3 minutes or until dough becomes smooth and pliable. Brush dough with Clarified Butter and cover with plastic wrap; set aside 30 minutes. (At this point, dough can be covered and refrigerated up to 24 hours. When ready to roll, let dough stand at room temperature 30 minutes so it becomes soft and easy to handle.)

4. Divide dough into 8 equal pieces; return them to bowl and cover. Heat heavy 10-inch skillet over medium heat.

5. Working with one piece of dough at a time, roll into 6-inch circle on lightly floured surface. Cook dough 1 to 2 minutes or until brown spots appear on bottom. Turn over and brush cooked side with butter, then turn buttered side down and cook 1 to 2 minutes. Brush top with butter, then turn buttered side down and cook 30 seconds. Turn again and cook 30 seconds. Repeat with remaining dough.

6. Wrap cooked breads in aluminum foil to keep warm while cooking remaining dough.

Raghavan Ki Baaten

☀ **If chappati flour is unavailable, use an equal amount of whole wheat flour, all-purpose flour and cake flour for each cup of chappati flour.**

Part of a poor villager's diet in the western state of Maharashtra, these breads are simply delicious when served with Roasted-Garlic Chutney (page 286). The number of chilies called for here might seem alarming! But sorghum flour is quite dry and dense, so extra chilies are necessary to even be noticeable. If using cornmeal, decrease to 4 chilies.

Sorghum Griddle Breads

Bhaakra

8 BREADS (8 SERVINGS)

2 cups sorghum flour (jowar ka atta)

1 teaspoon salt

2 tablespoons melted Clarified Butter (Ghee), (page 40) or vegetable oil

1/4 cup chopped fresh cilantro

1 tablespoon finely chopped gingerroot

8 to 10 fresh Thai, serrano or cayenne chilies

About 2/3 cup water

Clarified Butter (Ghee), melted, or melted butter for brushing

1. Mix flour and salt in medium bowl. Add 2 tablespoons Clarified Butter. Rub flour and butter between palms and fingers about 1 minute or until mixture looks like coarse crumbs.

2. Place cilantro, gingerroot and chilies in food processor. Cover and process until coarsely ground. Stir into flour mixture. Stir in water, 2 tablespoons at a time, until dough leaves side of bowl and forms a fairly stiff ball. The dough should not be sticky or dry.

3. Knead dough on lightly floured surface 2 to 3 minutes or until dough just holds together. (Due to its low protein content, sorghum dough will never hold together as well as dough made from regular flour milled from wheat.)

4. Divide dough into 8 equal pieces; return them to bowl and cover. Heat 10-inch skillet over medium heat.

5. Working with one piece of dough at a time, pat each into 5- to 6-inch circle between palms of hands. Cook dough 4 to 6 minutes, turning once, until golden brown. Brush one side with Clarified Butter. Repeat with remaining dough.

6. Wrap cooked breads in aluminum foil to keep warm while cooking remaining dough.

Raghavan Ki Baaten

☀ **Sorghum** is a cereal grass with broad corn-like leaves and clusters of grains at the end of its stalks. It is the third-most produced grain in the United States, but it is never used for human consumption here, in spite of the fact that it is extremely nutritious. Third World nations such as India feed their poor with sorghum flour (*jowar ka atta*). Sorghum flour is widely available in Indian grocery stores. If you're unable to get it, try equal parts of yellow and white cornmeal instead.

1 Bread: Calories 155 (Calories from Fat 45); Fat 5g (Saturated 3g); Cholesterol 10mg; Sodium 300mg; Carbohydrate 27g (Dietary Fiber 3g); Protein 3g **% Daily Value:** Vitamin A 6%; Vitamin C 4%; Calcium 0%; Iron 8% **Diet Exchanges:** 1 1/2 Starch, 1 Fat

Potato-Filled Whole Wheat Breads, Garbanzo Bean Stew with Tomatoes (page 185)

Raghavan Ki Baaten

☀ These hearty breads are a great treat for a weekend brunch. The dough can be made the day before to save time in the morning. Just remember to take it out of the refrigerator about 30 minutes before rolling so it is easy to handle.

☀ If chappati flour is unavailable, use an equal amount of whole wheat flour, all-purpose flour and cake flour for each cup of chappati flour.

This is a special-occasion bread in North Indian households, as it is slightly time-consuming to prepare. But the effort is well rewarded, especially when the breads are served with a soothing accompaniment of Yogurt with Fresh Mint (page 271).

Potato-Filled Whole Wheat Breads

Aloo Paranthas

6 BREADS (6 SERVINGS)

Dough:
3 cups chappati flour

3/4 teaspoon salt

1/4 cup melted Clarified Butter (Ghee), (page 40) or vegetable oil

About 1/2 cup warm water

Clarified Butter (Ghee), melted, or melted butter for brushing

Filling:
3 medium potatoes (1 pound), peeled and cooked

1/2 cup chopped fresh cilantro

1 tablespoon finely chopped gingerroot

4 or 5 fresh Thai, serrano or cayenne chilies

1 teaspoon salt

3/4 teaspoon Garam Masaala (page 32)

MAKE DOUGH:

1. Mix flour and salt in medium bowl. Add 1/4 cup Clarified Butter. Rub flour and butter between palms and fingers about 1 minute or until mixture looks like coarse crumbs. Stir in warm water, 2 tablespoons at a time, until dough leaves side of bowl and forms a ball. The dough should not be sticky or dry.

2. Knead dough in bowl or on lightly floured surface 2 to 3 minutes or until dough becomes smooth and pliable. Brush dough with Clarified Butter and cover with plastic wrap; set aside 30 minutes. (At this point, dough can be covered and refrigerated up to 24 hours. When ready to roll, let dough stand at room temperature 30 minutes so it becomes soft and easy to handle.)

3. Divide dough into 6 equal pieces; return them to bowl and cover.

MAKE FILLING:

1. Mash potatoes in medium bowl until smooth.

2. Place cilantro, gingerroot and chilies in food processor. Cover and process until coarsely ground. Add cilantro mixture, salt and Garam Masaala to potatoes; mix well.

3. Divide filling into 6 equal parts. Shape each part into a ball; set aside.

continues

1 Bread: Calories 375 (Calories from Fat 110); Fat 12g (Saturated 6g); Cholesterol 25mg; Sodium 690mg; Carbohydrate 61g (Dietary Fiber 5g); Protein 11g **% Daily Value:** Vitamin A 16%; Vitamin C 6%; Calcium 0%; Iron 12% **Diet Exchanges:** 4 Starch, 1 Fat

Separating rice
from the chaff
in the wind,
Uttar Pradesh.

continued

ASSEMBLE BREADS:

1. Heat heavy 10-inch skillet over medium heat. Working with one piece of dough at a time, roll into 6-inch circle on lightly floured surface. Place ball of filling on center of dough. Bring edges of dough up over filling; pinch edges to seal. Place seam side down. Gently pat or roll into 6-inch circle (dough may crack).

2. Cook filled dough in skillet 1 to 2 minutes or until brown. Turn over and brush cooked side with butter, then turn buttered side down and cook 1 to 2 minutes. Turn over again and brush top with butter, then turn buttered side down and cook 30 seconds. Turn again and cook 30 seconds. Repeat with remaining dough.

3. Wrap cooked breads in aluminum foil to keep warm while cooking remaining dough.

Shaping Filled Breads

Bring edges of dough up over filling.   Pinch edges together to seal.   Place seam side down and pat into circle.

Although ubiquitous throughout India and surprisingly simple to prepare, these pooris are usually reserved for special occasions. They are never consumed on a daily basis, since they are deep-fried and oil is an expensive commodity in the average household.

Puffy Whole Wheat Breads

Pooris

10 BREADS (5 SERVINGS)

2 cups chappati flour

1/2 teaspoon salt

2 tablespoons vegetable oil

About 1/2 cup warm water

Vegetable oil for brushing and deep-frying

1. Mix flour and salt in medium bowl. Add 2 tablespoons oil. Rub flour and oil between palms and fingers about 1 minute or until mixture looks like coarse crumbs. Stir in warm water, 2 tablespoons at a time, until dough leaves side of bowl and forms a ball. The dough should not be sticky or dry.

2. Knead dough in bowl or on lightly floured surface 2 to 3 minutes or until dough becomes smooth and pliable. Brush dough with oil and cover with plastic wrap; set aside 30 minutes. (At this point, dough can be covered and refrigerated up to 24 hours. When ready to roll, let dough stand at room temperature 30 minutes so it becomes soft and easy to handle.)

3. Heat oil (2 to 3 inches deep) in wok or Dutch oven over medium-high heat until thermometer inserted in oil reads 350°.

4. Divide dough into 10 equal pieces; return them to bowl and cover.

5. Working with one piece of dough at a time, roll into 3- to 4-inch circle on lightly floured surface. Carefully place dough in hot oil. With back of slotted spoon, gently submerge dough in oil until it puffs up. Turn once; fry about 30 seconds or until golden brown.

6. Remove from oil with slotted spoon; drain on paper towels. Repeat with remaining dough. Serve immediately.

2 Breads: Calories 215 (Calories from Fat 70); Fat 8g (Saturated 1g); Cholesterol 0mg; Sodium 240mg; Carbohydrate 35g (Dietary Fiber 6g); Protein 7g **% Daily Value:** Vitamin A 0%; Vitamin C 0%; Calcium 2%; Iron 10% **Diet Exchanges:** 2 Starch, 1 Fat

Puffy Whole Wheat Breads, Cardamom-Scented Yogurt Cheese (page 310)

Raghavan Ki Baaten

☀ I find it is very important to roll the dough evenly and carefully without a tear. Letting the dough rest makes it easier to work with.

☀ It is fun to see the *pooris* puff up in hot oil. The technique of submerging the dough while frying creates a burst of steam that fails to escape, yielding the *pooris'* characteristic puffy appearance. The hot air trapped inside cooks the dough within seconds.

☀ If chappati flour is unavailable, use an equal amount of whole wheat flour, all-purpose flour and cake flour for each cup of chappati flour.

Masaala is Hindi for "spicy" (as in "well seasoned"), and variations of these pooris are found in many a kitchen across India. These spiced pooris will not puff up as much as their plain cousins (page 248). The addition of flavorful onion makes the dough heavier, preventing the breads from expanding as spectacularly.

Spiced Puffed Breads

Masaala Pooris

10 BREADS (5 SERVINGS)

2 cups chappati flour

2 tablespoons finely chopped red onion

2 tablespoons finely chopped fresh cilantro

1 teaspoon cumin seed

1/2 teaspoon salt

1/2 teaspoon ground red pepper (cayenne)

1/4 teaspoon ground turmeric

2 fresh Thai, serrano or cayenne chilies, finely chopped

2 tablespoons vegetable oil

About 1/3 cup warm water

Vegetable oil for brushing and deep-frying

1. Mix all ingredients except the 2 tablespoons oil and water in medium bowl. Add 2 tablespoons oil. Rub flour mixture and oil between palms and fingers about 1 minute or until mixture looks like coarse crumbs. Stir in warm water, 2 tablespoons at a time, until dough leaves side of bowl and forms a ball. The dough should not be sticky or dry.

2. Knead dough in bowl or on lightly floured surface 2 to 3 minutes or until dough becomes smooth and pliable. Brush dough with oil and cover with plastic wrap; set aside 30 minutes. (At this point, dough can be covered and refrigerated up to 24 hours. When ready to roll, let dough stand at room temperature 30 minutes so it becomes soft and easy to handle.)

3. Heat oil (2 to 3 inches deep) in wok or Dutch oven over medium-high heat until thermometer inserted in oil reads 350°.

4. Divide dough into 10 equal pieces; return them to bowl and cover.

5. Working with one piece of dough at a time, roll into 3- to 4-inch circle on lightly floured surface. Carefully place dough in hot oil. With back of slotted spoon, gently submerge dough in oil until it puffs up. Turn once; fry about 30 seconds or until golden brown.

6. Remove from oil with slotted spoon; drain on paper towels. Repeat with remaining dough. Serve immediately.

2 Breads: Calories 240 (Calories from Fat 55); Fat 6g (Saturated 1g); Cholesterol 0mg; Sodium 120mg; Carbohydrate 40g (Dietary Fiber 2g); Protein 8g **% Daily Value:** Vitamin A 4%; Vitamin C 6%; Calcium 0%; Iron 10% **Diet Exchanges:** 2 1/2 Starch, 1 Fat

Raghavan Ki Baaten

☀ **If chappati flour is unavailable, use an equal amount of whole wheat flour, all-purpose flour and cake flour for each cup of chappati flour.**

This rich-tasting bread is usually served in Indian restaurants with Garbanzo Bean Stew with Tomatoes (page 185). Strongly resembling Native American fry breads, bhaturas are very filling. If you do not eat eggs, omit from recipe.

Egg-Flavored Puffy Breads

4 BREADS (8 SERVINGS)

3 cups all-purpose flour

1 tablespoon sugar

1 teaspoon salt

1 teaspoon baking powder

1/2 teaspoon baking soda

1/2 cup milk, slightly warmed

2 tablespoons vegetable oil

1 egg, slightly beaten

About 1/4 cup warm water

Clarified Butter (Ghee), melted, (page 40) or melted butter for brushing

Vegetable oil for deep-frying

Egg-Flavored Puffy Breads are pictured on page 235.

1. Sift together flour, sugar, salt, baking powder and baking soda in large bowl. Mix warm milk, oil and egg; stir into flour mixture. Stir in warm water, 2 tablespoons at a time, until dough leaves side of bowl and forms a fairly stiff ball. The dough should not be sticky or dry.

2. Knead dough in bowl or on lightly floured surface 2 to 3 minutes or until dough becomes smooth and pliable. Brush dough with Clarified Butter and cover with plastic wrap; set aside 30 minutes. (At this point, dough can be covered and refrigerated up to 24 hours. When ready to roll, let dough stand at room temperature 30 minutes so it becomes soft and easy to handle.)

3. Divide dough into 4 equal pieces. Shape each into a ball; brush with butter. Cover and let stand 20 to 30 minutes.

4. Heat oil (2 to 3 inches deep) in wok or Dutch oven over medium-high heat until thermometer inserted in oil reads 350°.

5. Working with one piece of dough at a time, roll into 6- to 8-inch circle on lightly floured surface. Carefully place dough in hot oil. With back of slotted spoon, gently submerge dough in oil until it puffs up. Turn once; fry about 30 seconds or until golden brown.

6. Remove from oil with slotted spoon; drain on paper towels. Repeat with remaining dough. Cut each bread in half to serve. Serve immediately.

1/2 Bread: Calories 245 (Calories from Fat 70); Fat 8g (Saturated 2g); Cholesterol 30mg; Sodium 450mg; Carbohydrate 38g (Dietary Fiber 1g); Protein 6g **% Daily Value:** Vitamin A 2%; Vitamin C 0%; Calcium 6%; Iron 12% **Diet Exchanges:** 2 1/2 Starch, 1 Fat

If you have never seen the way naans *are prepared, take a peek the next time you are at your favorite Indian restaurant: The chef slaps a piece of dough between his hands, stretching it into that familiar tear shape. Working quickly, he reaches into the* tandoor *(clay-lined oven) and slaps the dough against its inner wall. Within seconds, the dough puffs up and forms brown spots. He peels the bread away from the wall with a flat-edged skewer and brushes it with clarified butter. "Heaven on earth," you say, as you eat it with your favorite curry.*

Tandoori Breads

4 BREADS (8 SERVINGS)

3 cups
all-purpose flour

1 tablespoon sugar

2 teaspoons
baking powder

1 teaspoon salt

1/2 teaspoon
baking soda

1/2 cup milk,
slightly warmed

2 tablespoons
vegetable oil

About 1/4 cup
warm water

Clarified Butter
(Ghee), melted
(page 40), or melted
butter for brushing

1. Sift together flour, sugar, baking powder, salt and baking soda in large bowl. Mix warm milk and oil; stir into flour mixture. Stir in warm water, 2 tablespoons at a time, until dough leaves side of bowl and forms a fairly stiff ball. The dough should not be sticky or dry.

2. Knead dough in bowl or on lightly floured surface 2 to 3 minutes or until dough becomes smooth and pliable. Brush dough with Clarified Butter and cover with plastic wrap; set aside 30 minutes. (At this point, dough can be covered and refrigerated up to 24 hours. When ready to roll, let dough stand at room temperature 30 minutes so it becomes soft and easy to handle.)

3. Place round or square pizza stone on grill rack. Heat coals or gas grill to medium-high for direct heat. If using gas grill, set heat to medium-high.

4. Divide dough into 4 equal pieces. Shape each into a ball; brush with butter. Cover and let stand 20 to 30 minutes.

5. Working with one piece of dough at a time, roll into 8-inch circle or teardrop shape, about 1/4 inch thick, on lightly floured surface, taking care not to tear dough. Repeat with remaining dough.

6. Place dough on hot pizza stone and cook 1 to 2 minutes or until brown spots form and bubbles start to appear on surface. Turn; cook 30 seconds. Remove bread with spatula; brush with butter.

7. Wrap cooked breads in aluminum foil to keep warm while cooking remaining dough. Cut each bread in half to serve.

1/2 Bread: Calories 215 (Calories from Fat 45); Fat 5g (Saturated 1g); Cholesterol 5mg; Sodium 500mg; Carbohydrate 38g (Dietary Fiber 1g); Protein 5g **% Daily Value:** Vitamin A 2%; Vitamin C 0%; Calcium 8%; Iron 12% **Diet Exchanges:** 2 1/2 Starch

Tandoori Breads

Raghavan Ki Baaten

☀ Not everyone in India has a tandoor in his or her kitchen. But there are
ways to replicate the smoky flavor and crispy texture of naan in your very
own backyard—using your grill. The essential piece of equipment you
may need to purchase (if you don't already own one) is a pizza stone. You
can also buy unglazed quarry or terra-cotta tiles at the hardware store.
Once you follow the recipe instructions, you may very well be convinced
that you indeed have a tandoor of your very own.

Naan, though native to Northern India, is the most well-known, well-liked and, well, just popular bread of India. The naan dough is often used as a base to create simple and delicious variations. Here, spiced onion is stuffed between two naans and baked to perfection to yield kulcha. This bread not only makes an excellent accessory to many a curry but also is delicious served on its own.

Onion-Filled Tandoori Breads

Pyaaz Kulcha

2 BREADS (8 SERVINGS)

Dough:
3 cups all-purpose flour

1 tablespoon sugar

2 teaspoons baking powder

1 teaspoon salt

1/2 teaspoon baking soda

1/2 cup milk, slightly warmed

2 tablespoons vegetable oil

About 1/4 cup warm water

Clarified Butter (Ghee), melted, (page 40) or melted butter for brushing

Filling:
1 cup finely chopped red onion

1/4 cup finely chopped fresh cilantro

2 to 4 fresh Thai, serrano or cayenne chilies, finely chopped

1/2 teaspoon salt

MAKE DOUGH:

1. Sift together flour, sugar, baking powder, salt and baking soda in large bowl. Mix warm milk and oil; stir into flour mixture. Stir in warm water, 2 tablespoons at a time, until dough leaves side of bowl and forms a fairly stiff ball. The dough should not be sticky or dry.

2. Knead dough in bowl or on lightly floured surface 2 to 3 minutes or until dough becomes smooth and pliable. Brush dough with Clarified Butter and cover with plastic wrap; set aside 30 minutes. (At this point, dough can be covered and refrigerated up to 24 hours. When ready to roll, let dough stand at room temperature 30 minutes so it becomes soft and easy to handle.)

3. Place round or square pizza stone on grill rack. Heat coals or gas grill for direct heat. If using gas grill, set heat to medium-high.

4. Divide dough into 4 equal pieces. Shape each into a ball; brush with butter. Cover and let stand 20 to 30 minutes.

1/4 Bread: Calories 225 (Calories from Fat 45); Fat 5g (Saturated 1g); Cholesterol 5mg; Sodium 500mg; Carbohydrate 41g (Dietary Fiber 2g); Protein 6g **% Daily Value:** Vitamin A 6%; Vitamin C 10%; Calcium 10%; Iron 14% **Diet Exchanges:** 2 1/2 Starch, 1/2 Fat

MAKE FILLING:

Mix all ingredients in small bowl.

ASSEMBLE BREADS:

1. Working with one piece of dough at a time, roll into 8-inch circle or teardrop shape on lightly floured surface, taking care not to tear dough.

2. Spread half of the filling evenly over one circle within 1/2 inch of the edge. Place another circle on top; press edges firmly to seal. Repeat with remaining dough.

3. Place dough on hot pizza stone and cook 1 to 2 minutes or until brown spots form and bubbles start to appear on surface. Turn; cook 30 to 60 seconds. Remove bread with spatula; brush with butter.

4. Wrap cooked bread in aluminum foil to keep warm while cooking remaining dough. Cut each bread into fourths to serve.

Raghavan Ki Baaten

☀ Kulchas can be baked, cooled and kept in the refrigerator tightly covered for up to 2 days or frozen up to 1 month. Reheat frozen ones without thawing, or the bread may become soggy. Wrap the frozen bread in aluminum foil and heat in a 200° oven for 10 to 15 minutes or until warm.

As the recipe name suggests, these fluffy pancakes have a remarkable resemblance to omelets—but without the eggs! They can be served as an accompaniment to a curry or savored on their own for a delicious brunch.

"Mock" Omelets

8 PANCAKES (4 SERVINGS)

1 cup Garbanzo Bean
Flour (Bésan),
(page 44)

1/2 teaspoon salt

1/4 teaspoon
ground turmeric

About 3/4 cup water

1/2 cup finely
chopped red onion

1 medium tomato,
finely chopped
(3/4 cup)

1 tablespoon finely
chopped fresh cilantro

1 or 2 fresh
Thai, serrano or
cayenne chilies,
finely chopped

Vegetable oil for
pan-frying

1. Sift flour into medium bowl. Stir in salt and turmeric.

2. Add water, 2 tablespoons at a time, beating with wire whisk to form a smooth pancake-like batter. Stir in remaining ingredients except oil.

3. Brush 1/4 teaspoon oil in 8-inch nonstick skillet or a griddle; heat over medium heat. Pour 1/4 cup batter into skillet and quickly spread with back of spoon to form 4-inch circle. Cook 2 to 4 minutes, turning once, until brown on both sides.

4. Repeat with remaining batter, brushing skillet with oil as needed. Wrap pancakes in aluminum foil to keep warm while cooking remaining batter.

2 Pancakes: Calories 80 (Calories from Fat 20); Fat 2g (Saturated 0g);
Cholesterol 0mg; Sodium 300mg; Carbohydrate 15g (Dietary Fiber 4g);
Protein 4g **% Daily Value:** Vitamin A 8%; Vitamin C 14%; Calcium 2%;
Iron 8% **Diet Exchanges:** 1 Starch

"Mock" Omelets, Sweet-and-Hot Mango Pickle (page 273)

Raghavan Ki Baaten

☀ The rich flavor of these pancakes comes from garbanzo bean flour (*bésan*).
It is widely available in natural-food stores and Indian grocery stores, or
you can make your own (page 44).

A protein powerhouse, these southeastern pancakes are delicious as is, or served as they often are with a piece of jaggery. The intensely sweet raw cane sugar offers a pleasing contrast to the chilies' potency. If not at hand, try mixing 1 tablespoon packed brown sugar with 2 tablespoons Clarified Butter (Ghee), (page 40) for a heavenly spread. I also enjoy these pancakes with Yogurt with Fresh Mint (page 271).

Multi-Lentil Pancakes

12 PANCAKES (6 SERVINGS)

1 cup dried split and hulled pigeon peas (toovar dal), sorted and rinsed

1/2 cup dried yellow split peas (chana dal), sorted and rinsed

1/2 cup dried split and hulled black lentils (urad dal), sorted and rinsed

1/2 cup dried split and hulled green lentils (mung dal), sorted and rinsed

1/2 cup uncooked basmati or regular long-grain rice

6 cups warm water

4 to 6 dried red Thai, serrano or cayenne chilies

2 cups warm water

2 or 3 fresh Thai, serrano or cayenne chilies

1/4 cup fresh karhi leaves or cilantro, coarsely chopped

1 1/2 teaspoons salt

1/2 teaspoon asafetida (hing) or garlic powder

Vegetable oil for brushing

Multi-Lentil Pancakes are pictured on page 235.

1. Place peas, lentils, rice, 6 cups of the warm water, dried chilies and fresh chilies in large bowl. Let stand at room temperature at least 4 hours but no longer than 24 hours; drain.

2. Place 1/2 cup of the warm water and 2 cups of the lentil mixture in blender. Cover and blend on medium speed until smooth. The batter will be quite thick and feel slightly gritty. Pour batter into large bowl. Repeat with remaining warm water and lentil mixture. If necessary, thin batter with additional 1/2 cup warm water so mixture forms a thick pancake-like batter.

3. Stir karhi leaves, salt and asafetida into batter. Batter can be covered and refrigerated up to 3 days or frozen in airtight container up to 1 month. Thaw frozen batter in refrigerator at least 8 hours before using.

4. Brush 1/2 teaspoon oil in 10-inch nonstick skillet or a griddle; heat over medium heat. For each pancake, pour 1/4 cup batter into skillet and quickly spread with back of spoon to form 6- to 8-inch circle. (If batter doesn't spread evenly, stir in a small amount of water to thin.) Cook 2 to 4 minutes, turning once, until brown on both sides.

5. Repeat with remaining batter. Wrap pancakes in aluminum foil to keep warm while cooking remaining batter.

☀ The combination of flavors that arise from the dried peas and lentils is unique—there aren't really any good substitutions.

☀ For best results, use a cast-iron or nonstick skillet. If the skillet gets too hot, the batter will clump up and not spread evenly. If that begins to happen, remove the skillet from the heat and cool a few minutes before making more pancakes.

2 Pancakes: Calories 125 (Calories from Fat 20); Fat 2g (Saturated 0g); Cholesterol 0mg; Sodium 300mg; Carbohydrate 26g (Dietary Fiber 8g); Protein 9g **% Daily Value:** Vitamin A 10%; Vitamin C 6%; Calcium 2%; Iron 14% **Diet Exchanges:** 1 1/2 Starch

This quick bread from southern India packs intense flavors in each crepe. This is usually eaten with pickles or chutneys (pages 272 to 289), but it is equally delicious unadorned.

Wheat Crepes
Rava Dosas

6 CREPES (6 SERVINGS)

1/2 cup all-purpose flour

1/2 cup rice flour

1/2 cup uncooked hot wheat cereal

1 teaspoon salt

1 2/3 cups warm water

2 tablespoons finely chopped fresh cilantro

2 or 3 fresh Thai, serrano or cayenne chilies, finely chopped

1 teaspoon vegetable oil

1 teaspoon black or yellow mustard seed

1 teaspoon cumin seed

Vegetable oil for brushing

1. Mix all-purpose flour, rice flour, uncooked hot wheat cereal and salt in medium bowl.

2. Beat in warm water, using wire whisk, until smooth and batter is thin. Stir in cilantro and chilies; set aside.

3. Heat 1 teaspoon oil and mustard seed in 6-inch nonstick skillet over medium-high heat. Once seed begins to pop, cover skillet and wait until popping stops. Add cumin seed; sizzle 10 seconds. Pour hot oil mixture into batter; mix well.

4. Brush 1/4 teaspoon oil in 6-inch or larger crepe pan or skillet; heat over medium heat. For each crepe, pour 1/4 cup batter into skillet. Immediately rotate skillet until thin layer of batter covers bottom. (If batter doesn't spread evenly, stir in a small amount of water into remaining batter to thin.) Cook 1 to 2 minutes or until top surface is opaque and side of crepe starts to pull away from pan. Run wide spatula around edge to loosen; turn and cook other side 1 minute.

5. Repeat with remaining batter. Stack crepes, placing waxed paper between each and wrap in aluminum foil to keep warm while cooking remaining batter.

Raghavan Ki Baaten

☼ If the skillet gets too hot, the crepe batter will clump up and not spread evenly; if that happens, remove the skillet from the heat and cool a few minutes before making additional crepes. Wiping the inside of a hot skillet with a clean dish towel soaked in cold water will instantly lower the temperature, but be careful not to burn your fingers.

1 Crepe: Calories 170 (Calories from Fat 35); Fat 4g (Saturated 1g); Cholesterol 0mg; Sodium 400mg; Carbohydrate 31g (Dietary Fiber 1g); Protein 4g **% Daily Value:** Vitamin A 6%; Vitamin C 12%; Calcium 2 %; Iron 28% **Diet Exchanges:** 2 Starch

Ask any Indian the first thing that comes to mind when thinking of South Indian foods, and the response is instant—masaala dosai. These puffy crepes, often served with Pigeon Pea Stew (page 188) and Coconut Chutney (page 285), grace South Indian kitchens, restaurants and communal eating places. Making these crepes can be an art, and professional chefs oftentimes make them as large as two feet in diameter.

Stuffed Rice-Lentil Crepes

Masaala Dosai

8 CREPES (8 SERVINGS)

Batter:
3 cups uncooked basmati or regular long-grain rice, rinsed

1 cup dried split and hulled black lentils (urad dal), sorted and rinsed

8 cups warm water

1/2 teaspoon fenugreek seed (méthi)

2 cups warm water

2 teaspoons salt

Vegetable oil for brushing

Filling:
2 tablespoons vegetable oil

1 teaspoon black or yellow mustard seed

3 tablespoons dried yellow split peas (chana dal), sorted

3 tablespoons raw cashew pieces

1/4 teaspoon asafetida (hing)

1/4 teaspoon ground turmeric

1 cup water

3 medium red potatoes (1 pound), peeled, cooked and cut into 1-inch pieces

1 large tomato, cut into 1-inch pieces (1 cup)

1/4 cup chopped fresh cilantro

2 tablespoons julienne strips gingerroot

1/2 teaspoon salt

4 fresh Thai, serrano or cayenne chilies, cut lengthwise in half

10 to 12 fresh karhi leaves

MAKE BATTER:

1. Place rice, lentils, 8 cups of the warm water and fenugreek seed in large bowl. Let stand at room temperature at least 4 hours but no longer than 24 hours; drain.

2. Place 1/2 cup of the warm water and 2 cups of the rice mixture in blender. Cover and blend on medium speed until smooth. The batter will be quite thick and feel slightly gritty. Pour batter into large bowl. Repeat with remaining 1 1/2 cups warm water and rice mixture. If necessary, thin batter with additional 1/2 cup warm water so mixture forms a thick pancake-like batter.

3. Stir salt and additional 1/2 cup warm water into batter. Cover with plastic wrap and let stand at room temperature about 24 hours or until batter ferments, bubbles up and develops a sourdough aroma.

MAKE FILLING:

1. Heat oil and mustard seed in wok or deep 12-inch skillet over medium-high heat. Once seed begins to pop, cover wok and wait until popping stops. Add yellow split peas and cashews; stir-fry about 1 minute or until golden brown.

2. Stir in asafetida and turmeric. Stir in remaining filling ingredients; reduce heat. Cover and simmer 5 to 7 minutes or until water is absorbed; remove from heat.

1 Crepe: Calories 460 (Calories from Fat 70); Fat 8g (Saturated 1g); Cholesterol 0mg; Sodium 750mg; Carbohydrate 89g (Dietary Fiber 9g); Protein 16g **% Daily Value:** Vitamin A 14%; Vitamin C 26%; Calcium 6%; Iron 32% **Diet Exchanges:** 6 Starch

MAKE CREPES:

1. Brush 1/2 teaspoon oil in 12-inch nonstick skillet or crepe pan; heat over medium heat. For each crepe, pour 1/2 cup batter into skillet and quickly spread with back of spoon to form 8-inch circle. (If batter doesn't spread evenly, stir a small amount of water into remaining batter to thin.) Cook 2 to 4 minutes, turning once, until brown on both sides.

2. Repeat with remaining batter. Stack crepes, placing waxed paper between each and wrap in aluminum foil to keep warm while cooking remaining batter.

3. To serve, place 1/2 cup filling on center of each crepe; fold crepe to cover filling.

Raghavan Ki Baaten

☼ The batter's fermentation is crucial to the flavor and texture of these crepes. A slightly warm oven with its light left on expedites the process.

☼ There is no substitute for split and hulled black lentils; if fenugreek, asafetida or karhi leaves are unavailable, eliminate from recipe.

☼ Use the largest skillet you have in the house. I use a 15-inch *lefse* (a Scandinavian bread griddle) for these crepes. If the skillet gets too hot, the crepe batter will clump up and not spread evenly. If that happens, remove the skillet from the heat to cool a few minutes before making additional crepes. Wiping the hot skillet with a clean dish towel soaked in cold water will instantly lower the temperature, but be careful not to burn your fingers.

☼ If you have more batter than filling, you can make plain crepes to serve as a bread with meals. Leftover batter can be covered and refrigerated up to 3 days or frozen in an airtight container up to 1 month. Thaw frozen batter in refrigerator at least 8 hours before using.

Uttapams are thick pancakes made from the same batter used for Stuffed Rice-Lentil Crepes (page 260). Uttapams are often stuffed with spiced onions and served with Coconut Chutney (page 285) for a midafternoon snack or light dinner. Fresh karhi leaves enhance the filling, but if they are not at hand, eliminate from recipe.

Rice-Lentil Pancakes with Spiced Onions

Uttappam

10 PANCAKES (10 SERVINGS)

Batter:
3 cups uncooked basmati or regular long-grain rice, rinsed

1 cup dried split and hulled black lentils (urad dal), sorted and rinsed

8 cups warm water

1/2 teaspoon fenugreek seed (méthi)

2 cups warm water

2 teaspoons salt

Vegetable oil for brushing

Filling:
2 cups finely chopped red onion

1/2 cup finely chopped fresh cilantro

1/2 cup chopped fresh karhi leaves

1 teaspoon salt

4 to 6 fresh Thai, serrano or cayenne chilies, finely chopped

MAKE BATTER:

1. Place rice, lentils, 8 cups of the warm water and fenugreek seed in large bowl. Let stand at room temperature at least 4 hours but no longer than 24 hours; drain.

2. Place 1/2 cup of the remaining warm water and 2 cups of the rice mixture in blender. Cover and blend on medium speed until smooth. The batter will be quite thick and feel slightly gritty. Pour batter into large bowl. Repeat with remaining 1 1/2 cups warm water and rice mixture. (If necessary, thin batter with additional 1/2 cup warm water so mixture forms a thick pancake-like batter.)

3. Stir salt into batter. Cover with plastic wrap and let stand at room temperature about 24 hours or until batter ferments, bubbles up and develops a sourdough aroma.

MAKE FILLING:

Mix all filling ingredients in medium bowl; set aside.

MAKE PANCAKES:

1. Brush 1 teaspoon oil in 12-inch nonstick skillet or a griddle; heat over medium heat. For each pancake, pour 1/2 cup batter into skillet and quickly spread with back of spoon to form 8-inch circle. Cook 2 to 4 minutes, turning once, until brown on both sides.

2. Repeat with remaining batter. Stack pancakes, placing waxed paper between each and wrap in aluminum foil to keep warm while cooking remaining batter.

3. To serve, spread 1/2 cup filling over each pancake.

1 Pancake: Calories 280 (Calories from Fat 20); Fat 2g (Saturated 0g); Cholesterol 0mg; Sodium 710mg; Carbohydrate 62g (Dietary Fiber 6g); Protein 10g **% Daily Value:** Vitamin A 10%; Vitamin C 16%; Calcium 4%; Iron 22% **Diet Exchanges:** 3 Starch, 3 Vegetable

Rice-Lentil Pancakes with Spiced Onions, Coconut Chutney (page 285)

Raghavan Ki Baaten

☀ To test whether the batter has fermented enough, cook a coin-size pancake.
Once the batter starts to cook, little holes should appear on the surface,
similar to a buttermilk pancake. If the skillet gets too hot, the batter will
clump up and spread unevenly, so cool the skillet a few minutes before
making more pancakes. Wiping the hot skillet with a clean dish towel
soaked in cold water will instantly lower the temperature, but be careful
not to burn your fingers.

Chapter Eight

Chutneys, Pickles and Condiments

From top: Tamarind Chutney with Cashews (page 289), Yogurt with Fresh Mint (page 271), Spicy Lemon Pickle (page 272)

Chopped Tomato Salad

Tamatar Nu Salade

4 SERVINGS

3 medium tomatoes
(1 pound), chopped

1/4 cup dry-roasted
unsalted peanuts,
coarsely chopped

1/4 cup finely chopped
fresh cilantro

1 tablespoon sugar

2 or 3 fresh
Thai, serrano or
cayenne chilies,
finely chopped

1/2 teaspoon salt

1 tablespoon
vegetable oil

1 teaspoon black or
yellow mustard seed

1. Mix all ingredients except oil and mustard seed in medium bowl.

2. Heat oil and mustard seed in 6-inch skillet over medium-high heat. Once seed begins to pop, cover skillet and wait until popping stops.

3. Pour hot oil mixture over tomato mixture; toss well.

1 Serving: Calories 115 (Calories from Fat 70); Fat 8g (Saturated 1g);
Cholesterol 0mg; Sodium 300mg; Carbohydrate 9g (Dietary Fiber 2g);
Protein 3g **% Daily Value:** Vitamin A 6%; Vitamin C 16%; Calcium
2%; Iron 4% **Diet Exchanges:** 2 Vegetable, 1 1/2 Fat

Chopped Tomato Salad

Raghavan Ki Baaten

☀ Make this recipe only when you have access to lush, ripe tomatoes. Hydroponic tomatoes, though expensive, are tasty. Use an assortment of colored tomatoes if available. This flavorful tomato salad is excellent as an accompaniment to any meal or served on crisp greens for a light, refreshing summer dish.

Raitas are yogurt-based accompaniments that act as a cooling agent for the palate when eating spicy foods. Apples are native to Kashmir, home state of the Himalaya Mountains. This raita combines cool, creamy yogurt with the sweet-tart taste of apple and the nutty flavor of roasted cumin seed. Enjoy this as an accompaniment to any of the breads in this book.

Yogurt with Apples

3 CUPS YOGURT MIXTURE (12 SERVINGS)

2 cups plain yogurt (1 pound), (regular or fat-free)

1/4 cup water

1 medium unpeeled tart eating apple, coarsely chopped (1 cup)

1 tablespoon finely chopped fresh cilantro

1 tablespoon roasted cumin seed (page 31)

1/2 teaspoon salt

1/4 teaspoon ground red pepper (cayenne)

1. Beat yogurt and water in medium bowl, using wire whisk, until well blended. Stir in remaining ingredients.

2. Refrigerate at least 30 minutes to blend flavors. Cover and refrigerate any remaining yogurt mixture up to 2 weeks.

1/4 Cup: Calories 35 (Calories from Fat 10); Fat 1g (Saturated 0g); Cholesterol 0mg; Sodium 125mg; Carbohydrate 5g (Dietary Fiber 0g); Protein 2g **% Daily Value:** Vitamin A 0%; Vitamin C 2%; Calcium 8%; Iron 2% **Diet Exchanges:** 1/2 Fruit

Yogurt with Apples, Fenugreek-Scented Griddle Breads (page 240)

Raghavan Ki Baaten

☀ *Raita* is an easy recipe and one that is fun to vary creatively. Try other fresh seasonal fruits for a nice flavor change. Some of my favorites are chopped bananas, pears and peaches—but use what appeals to you.

Ever eaten a full-course meal from a large banana leaf while sitting cross-legged on the ground? It's an everyday occurrence for millions of South Indians. An array of chutneys, pickles and yogurt-based relishes, such as this stewed-tomato accompaniment, are ladled onto the banana leaf. The soothing yogurt provides welcome armor against some of the fiery chili-based dishes yet to come. Add this recipe to any Indian meal you serve.

Yogurt with Stewed Tomatoes

Pachadi

8 SERVINGS

1 cup plain yogurt (regular or fat-free)

1/4 cup water

1 tablespoon vegetable oil

1 teaspoon black or yellow mustard seed

1/8 teaspoon asafetida (hing)

1 medium tomato, finely chopped (3/4 cup)

1 or 2 fresh Thai, serrano or cayenne chilies, finely chopped

1 tablespoon finely chopped fresh cilantro

1/2 teaspoon salt

1. Beat yogurt and water in medium bowl, using wire whisk, until well blended; set aside.

2. Heat oil and mustard seed in 8-inch skillet over medium-high heat. Once seed begins to pop, cover skillet and wait until popping stops.

3. Add remaining ingredients. Cook 2 to 3 minutes, stirring occasionally, until tomato is softened.

4. Fold tomato mixture into yogurt. Serve immediately or chill. Cover and refrigerate any remaining yogurt mixture up to 2 days.

Raghavan Ki Baaten

☀ **If asafetida is unavailable, omit from recipe.**

1/4 Cup: Calories 40 (Calories from Fat 20); Fat 2g (Saturated 1g); Cholesterol 0mg; Sodium 170mg; Carbohydrate 3g (Dietary Fiber 0g); Protein 2g **% Daily Value:** Vitamin A 2%; Vitamin C 2%; Calcium 6%; Iron 0% **Diet Exchanges:** 1/2 Vegetable, 1/2 Fat

Combine three key ingredients—yogurt, cucumber and mint—to create a dish that is cool and soothing to your lips and easy on your hips! It is a welcome dip for any of the breads in this book.

Yogurt with Fresh Mint

Pudhina Raita

2 CUPS (8 SERVINGS)

1 cup plain yogurt (regular or fat-free)

1 large cucumber (1/2 pound), peeled, seeded and shredded

1/2 cup chopped fresh mint leaves

1/2 teaspoon salt

1/2 teaspoon coarsely ground black pepper

1. Beat yogurt in medium bowl, using wire whisk, until smooth. Stir in remaining ingredients.

2. Refrigerate at least 1 hour to blend flavors. Cover and refrigerate any remaining yogurt mixture up to 2 weeks.

1/4 Cup: Calories 30 (Calories from Fat 10); Fat 1g (Saturated 0g); Cholesterol 0mg; Sodium 320mg; Carbohydrate 3g (Dietary Fiber 0g); Protein 2g **% Daily Value:** Vitamin A 2%; Vitamin C 4%; Calcium 6%; Iron 0% **Diet Exchanges:** 1 Vegetable

Raghavan Ki Baaten

☀ **1 cup shredded raw carrots (about 2 medium) can be substituted for the cucumber.**

Indians pickle just about any vegetable, fruit, berry and nut. Pickles are intended to pack strong flavors in small quantities, so they are never consumed by spoonfuls. They are meant to enhance breads, rice and other mellow-flavored items during a meal. The majority of pickles are spicy hot, containing a high proportion of ground red pepper (cayenne). Others are milder, but all pickles are laced with spices.

Spicy Lemon Pickle

Limboo Urughai

ABOUT 2 CUPS PICKLE (32 SERVINGS)

2 medium lemons, each cut into 16 wedges

1 cup water

1 tablespoon salt

2 tablespoons ground red pepper (cayenne)

1/4 cup vegetable oil

1 teaspoon black or yellow mustard seed

1/2 teaspoon asafetida (hing) or garlic powder

1/2 teaspoon roasted fenugreek seed (page 31), ground

1. Heat lemon wedges, water and salt to boiling in 2-quart saucepan; reduce heat. Simmer uncovered 12 to 15 minutes or until lemons are tender and water has almost evaporated; remove from heat. Stir in ground red pepper.

2. Heat oil and mustard seed in 6-inch skillet over medium-high heat. Once seed begins to pop, cover skillet and wait until popping stops. Add hot oil mixture and remaining ingredients to lemons; mix well.

3. Cool pickle 20 to 30 minutes. Tightly cover and store in refrigerator up to 2 weeks.

Raghavan Ki Baaten

☼ The lemons found in India are much smaller and juicier than their American cousins. At times, your local Indian grocery store might stock this variety, so buy them in a hurry before they disappear. The usual kind available in your supermarket will work just fine, too.

1 Tablespoon: Calories 20 (Calories from Fat 20); Fat 2g (Saturated 0g); Cholesterol 0mg; Sodium 220mg; Carbohydrate 1g (Dietary Fiber 0g); Protein 0g **% Daily Value:** Vitamin A 0%; Vitamin C 2%; Calcium 0%; Iron 0% **Diet Exchanges:** 1 Serving is free

When you sample any Indian pickle, you will marvel at how complex the flavors are. This one is sweet and only mildly hot. This pickle tastes great served with any of the bread recipes in chapter 7. But one of my favorite ways to eat it is with slices of buttered toast at breakfast. Try it sometime!

Sweet-and-Hot Mango Pickle

Maangai Pachadi

3 1/2 CUPS PICKLE (56 SERVINGS)

4 cups water

1 cup sugar

2 large green mangoes, peeled, pitted and shredded (3 cups)

1 teaspoon ground red pepper (cayenne)

1. Heat water and sugar to boiling in 3-quart saucepan.

2. Stir in mangoes; reduce heat to medium. Cook uncovered about 1 hour, stirring occasionally, until all water has evaporated and sugar syrup is thickened; remove from heat. Stir in ground red pepper.

3. Cool pickle 20 to 30 minutes. Tightly cover and store in refrigerator up to 2 weeks.

Raghavan Ki Baaten

☀ Green mangos are quite firm and can be peeled and cut much like a vegetable. First, remove the skin using a vegetable peeler. Then cut the mango lengthwise as close to the seed as possible. Cut the other half of the mango from the seed. Continue to cut off any flesh that remains on the seed, and discard the seed. The mango flesh can be cut into very thin sticks or grated on the large holes of a grater.

1 Tablespoon: Calories 20 (Calories from Fat 0); Fat 0g (Saturated 0g); Cholesterol 0mg; Sodium 0mg; Carbohydrate 5g (Dietary Fiber 0g); Protein 0g **% Daily Value:** Vitamin A 4%; Vitamin C 2%; Calcium 0%; Iron 0% **Diet Exchanges:** 1 Serving is free

Fiery, robust, pleasantly tart—these are some of the words that will pass through your mind as you indulge in this pickle. It is a specialty of the town of Chidambaram in southeastern India, home of the monumental stone-carved temple dedicated to Nataraja, the dancing reincarnation of Lord Shiva. This pickle will not only dance in your mouth, it will sing too!

Raw Mango Pickle

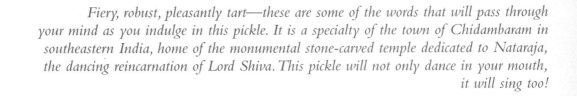

3 CUPS PICKLE (48 SERVINGS)

2 large green mangoes, peeled, pitted and cut into 1/2-inch cubes (3 cups)

1/4 cup ground red pepper (cayenne)

1 tablespoon salt

1/2 teaspoon asafetida (hing)

1/3 cup vegetable oil

2 teaspoons black or yellow mustard seed

1. Mix mangoes, ground red pepper, salt and asafetida in medium bowl.

2. Heat oil and mustard seed in 6-inch skillet over medium-high heat. Once seed begins to pop, cover skillet and wait until popping stops.

3. Pour hot oil mixture over mango mixture; toss well.

4. Cool pickle 20 to 30 minutes. Tightly cover and store in refrigerator up to 2 weeks.

1 Tablespoon: Calories 15 (Calories from Fat 10); Fat 1g (Saturated 0g); Cholesterol 0mg; Sodium 150mg; Carbohydrate 2g (Dietary Fiber 0g); Protein 0g **% Daily Value:** Vitamin A 4%; Vitamin C 2%; Calcium 0%; Iron 0% **Diet Exchanges:** 1 Serving is free

Raw Mango Pickle

Raghavan Ki Baaten

☀ Green mangos are quite firm and can be peeled and cut much like a vegetable. First, remove the skin using a vegetable peeler. Then cut the mango lengthwise as close to the seed as possible. Cut the other half of the mango from the seed. Continue to cut off any flesh that remains on the seed, and discard the seed. The mango flesh can be cut into very thin sticks or grated on the large holes of a grater.

☀ Images of being enslaved at the stove for long hours may have prevented you from making condiments like pickles before. This recipe proves just the opposite: that you can achieve miracles with green mangoes, oil and spices—without spending hours in the kitchen!

☀ If asafetida is unavailable, eliminate from recipe.

This potent pickle is an absolute delight—if you like things hot! Typical southern Indian comfort food is a meal of Yogurt Rice Pilaf (page 214) served with a dollop of this pickle. The pilaf offers a mellow backdrop to the pickle's fiery flavor.

Grated Mango Pickle

maangai tokku

3 3/4 CUPS PICKLE (60 SERVINGS)

1 cup vegetable oil

1 tablespoon black or yellow mustard seed

2 large green mangoes, peeled, pitted and shredded (3 cups)

1/2 cup ground red pepper (cayenne)

1 tablespoon salt

1 teaspoon asafetida (hing) or garlic powder

1/2 teaspoon ground turmeric

1/2 teaspoon roasted fenugreek seed, ground or yellow mustard seed

1. Heat oil and mustard seed in wok or deep 12-inch skillet over medium-high heat. Once seed begins to pop, cover wok and wait until popping stops. Remove skillet from heat; cool 2 to 3 minutes.

2. Reduce heat to medium. Add mangoes to oil. Cook uncovered 10 to 12 minutes, stirring occasionally, until mangoes are tender.

3. Stir in remaining ingredients. Cook uncovered 2 to 4 minutes, stirring occasionally, to blend flavors; remove from heat.

4. Cool pickle 20 to 30 minutes. Tightly cover and store in refrigerator up to 2 weeks.

Raghavan Ki Baaten

☀ Green mangos are quite firm and can be peeled and cut much like a vegetable. First, remove the skin using a vegetable peeler. Then cut the mango lengthwise as close to the seed as possible. Cut the other half of the mango from the seed. Continue to cut off any flesh that remains on the seed, and discard the seed. The mango flesh can be cut into very thin sticks or grated on the large holes of a grater.

☀ The oil is essential to the character of this recipe. Pay attention to the oil temperature; you do not want it very hot or it can burn the mangoes and turn them bitter. And no, the measurement for ground red pepper (cayenne) is not a typo—you really do need 1/2 cup!

1 Tablespoon: Calories 35 (Calories from Fat 25); Fat 3g (Saturated 0g); Cholesterol 0mg; Sodium 120mg; Carbohydrate 2g (Dietary Fiber 0g); Protein 0g **% Daily Value:** Vitamin A 6%; Vitamin C 2%; Calcium 0%; Iron 0% **Diet Exchanges:** 1/2 Vegetable, 1/2 Fat

In India, red onions are cheaper than yellow ones, which is quite the opposite case in the United States. For this chutney, when a pungent flavor (raw onion) is combined with tart (tamarind) and hot (chilies), the result is nothing short of miraculous. Surprisingly, this chutney, made with red onion actually turns out green.

Red Onion Chutney

Vengayam Thuviyal

ABOUT 2 CUPS CHUTNEY (32 SERVINGS)

1 cup coarsely chopped red onions

1/2 cup water

2 tablespoons chopped fresh cilantro

1 teaspoon salt

1 teaspoon tamarind concentrate paste or juice of 1 medium lime (2 tablespoons)

2 or 3 fresh Thai, serrano or cayenne chilies

1. Place all ingredients in blender. Cover and blend on medium speed until smooth. (Chutney will thicken as it stands; if it becomes too thick, stir in additional water until it reaches the consistency of a thick pesto.)

2. Tightly cover and store in refrigerator up to 1 week.

Raghavan Ki Baaten

☀ Serve this chutney with **Puffy Whole Wheat Breads (page 248)** for a scrumptious lunch. It also perks up a bowl of steamed rice; just add a cup of plain yogurt for a simple but complete meal. (I find it to be an excellent alternative when faced with another sandwich for lunch!)

1 Tablespoon: Calories 5 (Calories from Fat 0); Fat 0g (Saturated 0g); Cholesterol 0mg; Sodium 75mg; Carbohydrate 1g (Dietary Fiber 0g); Protein 0g **% Daily Value:** Vitamin A 0%; Vitamin C 2%; Calcium 0%; Iron 0% **Diet Exchanges:** 1 Serving is free

An old phrase in Kerala says "If nature gave you coconut trees, make thénga thuviyal." The picturesque state of Kerala is home to white-sand beaches fringed with coconut palms, offering numerous opportunities for making this recipe—and for taking plenty of postcard-perfect photos.

Roasted-Coconut Chutney

thénga thuviyal

ABOUT 1 CUP CHUTNEY (16 SERVINGS)

2 tablespoons sesame oil (light colored) or vegetable oil

1 teaspoon black or yellow mustard seed

2 tablespoons dried split and hulled black lentils (urad dal), sorted

4 dried red Thai, serrano or cayenne chilies

1 cup Shredded Fresh Coconut (page 45) or 1/2 cup dried unsweetened shredded coconut

1/2 teaspoon asafetida (hing) or garlic powder

2 fresh Thai, serrano or cayenne chilies

10 to 12 fresh karhi leaves

1/2 cup water

2 tablespoons chopped fresh cilantro

1 teaspoon salt

1 teaspoon sugar

1 teaspoon chopped dried tamarind pulp or 1/4 teaspoon tamarind concentrate paste or juice of 1 medium lime (2 tablespoons)

1. Heat oil and mustard seed in wok or 10-inch skillet over medium-high heat. Once seed begins to pop, cover wok and wait until popping stops.

2. Add lentils and dried chilies; stir-fry 30 to 60 seconds or until lentils are golden brown and chilies blacken slightly. Add coconut, asafetida, fresh chilies and karhi leaves; stir-fry 3 to 5 minutes or until coconut is dark brown.

3. Place coconut mixture and remaining ingredients in blender. Cover and blend on medium speed until a smooth paste forms.

4. Tightly cover and store in refrigerator up to 10 days.

1 Tablespoon: Calories 15 (Calories from Fat 10); Fat 1g (Saturated 0g); Cholesterol 0mg; Sodium 150mg; Carbohydrate 2g (Dietary Fiber 0g); Protein 0g   **% Daily Value:** Vitamin A 4%; Vitamin C 2%; Calcium 0%; Iron 0%   **Diet Exchanges:** 1 Serving is free

Roasted-Coconut Chutney

Raghavan Ki Baaten

☀ If karhi leaves are unavailable, eliminate from recipe.

☀ This thuviyal will continue to thicken as it stands. Use as much water as needed to return it to its original pesto-ike consistency.

Considered an essential condiment for wedding banquets and other religious meals in the South, this roasted chutney occupies a pivotal corner of the banana leaf on which communal meals are served.

Roasted–Yellow Split Pea Chutney

Paruppu Thuviyal

ABOUT 1 2/3 CUPS CHUTNEY (26 SERVINGS)

1 tablespoon vegetable oil

1/2 cup dried yellow split peas (chana dal), sorted

1 cup water

1/2 cup Shredded Fresh Coconut (page 45) or 1/4 cup dried unsweetened shredded coconut

2 or 3 fresh Thai, serrano or cayenne chilies

2 or 3 dried red Thai, serrano or cayenne chilies

1 teaspoon salt

1 teaspoon black or yellow mustard seed

1. Heat 1 teaspoon of the oil in 8-inch skillet over medium-high heat. Add yellow split peas. Cook 1 to 2 minutes, stirring constantly, until peas are golden brown.

2. Place roasted peas and remaining ingredients except remaining oil and mustard seed in blender. Cover and blend on medium speed until smooth. Transfer to small bowl; set aside. (Chutney will thicken as it stands; if it becomes too thick, stir in additional water until it reaches desired consistency.)

3. Heat remaining 2 teaspoons oil and mustard seed in same skillet over medium-high heat. Once seed begins to pop, cover skillet and wait until popping stops. Pour hot oil mixture over chutney; mix well.

4. Tightly cover and store in refrigerator up to 3 days.

1 Tablespoon: Calories 15 (Calories from Fat 10); Fat 1g (Saturated 1g); Cholesterol 0mg; Sodium 90mg; Carbohydrate 2g (Dietary Fiber 1g); Protein 1g **% Daily Value:** Vitamin A 2%; Vitamin C 0%; Calcium 0%; Iron 0% **Diet Exchanges:** 1 Serving is free

Roasted–Yellow Split Pea Chutney, Steamed Basmati Rice (pages 202 and 203)

Raghavan Ki Baaten

☀ Dollop this chutney onto steamed rice and drizzle with Clarified Butter (Ghee) (page 40), and you will experience a natural state of euphoria! Or serve it with Spiced Puffed Breads (page 250) for a simple, satisfying lunch.

☀ This chutney, which will thicken considerably when it's stored, should have a pesto-like consistency. Stir in additional water if it becomes too thick.

Thuviyals are usually vegetable-based (cooked or raw) chutneys native to the southern states of India. Combining intense hot, nutty and sour flavors, thuviyals *pack a potent punch in even the smallest bite.*

Ridged-Squash Chutney

Peerkangai Thuviyal

ABOUT 2 1/4 CUPS CHUTNEY (36 SERVINGS)

1 tablespoon vegetable oil

2 tablespoons dried split and hulled black lentils (urad dal) or yellow split peas (chana dal), sorted

2 dried red Thai, serrano or cayenne chilies

2 large ridged squash (peerkangai), peeled, or 2 yellow summer squash (1/2 pound), cut into 1-inch cubes

1/2 cup water

2 tablespoons chopped fresh cilantro

1 teaspoon salt

1 teaspoon chopped dried tamarind pulp or 1/4 teaspoon tamarind concentrate paste or juice of 1 medium lime (2 tablespoons)

1 teaspoon black or yellow mustard seed

1. Heat oil in 6-inch skillet over medium-high heat. Add lentils and chilies; stir-fry 30 to 60 seconds or until chilies blacken and lentils are golden brown. Remove lentils and chilies with slotted spoon, leaving remaining oil in skillet; remove from heat.

2. Heat squash and water to boiling in 1 1/2-quart saucepan. Simmer uncovered 3 to 4 minutes or until squash is tender; reserve any remaining cooking liquid.

3. Place squash, reserved cooking liquid, lentil mixture, cilantro, salt and tamarind in blender. Cover and blend on medium speed until smooth. Transfer to small bowl; set aside.

4. Heat same oil and mustard seed in skillet over medium-high heat. Once seed begins to pop, cover skillet and wait until popping stops.

5. Pour hot oil mixture over chutney; mix well.

6. Tightly cover and store in refrigerator up to 2 weeks.

1 Tablespoon: Calories 5 (Calories from Fat 0); Fat 0g (Saturated 0g); Cholesterol 0mg; Sodium 65mg; Carbohydrate 1g (Dietary Fiber 0g); Protein 0g **% Daily Value:** Vitamin A 2%; Vitamin C 0%; Calcium 0%; Iron 0% **Diet Exchanges:** 1 Serving is free

Ridged-Squash Chutney

Raghavan Ki Baaten

☀ Ridged squash, called *peerkangai*, is wicely available in Asian and Indian grocery stores. This foot-long olive green squash has a tough ridged exterior, and tender flesh inside. The seeds in the flesh are normally not discarded, as they are soft and edible. The squash is usually peeled and cooked in a little water until tender and then pureed with spices and other ingredients. If unavailable, substitute peeled yellow summer squash.

☀ If split and hulled black lentils are unavailable, use dried yellow split peas for this recipe.

☀ To jazz up a cup of steamed rice, toss with 1 tablespoon chutney and drizzle with a teaspoon of Clarified Butter (Ghee), (page 40) or light-colored sesame oil.

Chutneys are not always fruit based or sweet. Most are spicy and sharp, and are meant to be eaten in small bites to enhance the flavors of a milder dish. Chutneys usually accompany appetizers, snacks and street foods. This simple mixture, the consistency of a thin pesto, is ubiquitous on the streets of all major cities in India's north and northwest.

Mint-Cilantro Chutney

ABOUT 1 2/3 CUPS CHUTNEY (16 SERVINGS)

1 cup chopped fresh cilantro

1 medium tomato, chopped (3/4 cup)

3/4 cup chopped fresh mint leaves

1 medium onion, chopped (1/2 cup)

1/4 cup water

Juice of 2 medium limes (1/4 cup)

1 teaspoon salt

2 medium cloves garlic

1 or 2 fresh Thai, serrano or cayenne chilies

1. Place all ingredients in blender. Cover and blend on medium speed until smooth.

2. Tightly cover and store in refrigerator up to 10 days.

1 Tablespoon: Calories 5 (Calories from Fat 0); Fat 0g (Saturated 0g); Cholesterol 0mg; Sodium 150mg; Carbohydrate 1g (Dietary Fiber 0g); Protein 0g **% Daily Value:** Vitamin A 2%; Vitamin C 6%; Calcium 0%; Iron 0% **Diet Exchanges:** 1 Serving is free

This chutney is synonymous with the cuisine of southeastern India. Every restaurant that specializes in this region's cuisine makes thénga chutney and often serves it with Stuffed Rice-Lentil Crepes (page 260) and steamed dumplings.

Coconut Chutney

Thénga Chutney

ABOUT 1 1/2 CUPS CHUTNEY (24 SERVINGS)

1 cup Shredded Fresh Coconut (page 45) or 1/2 cup dried unsweetened shredded coconut

3/4 cup water

1 tablespoon chopped fresh cilantro

1 teaspoon chopped dried tamarind pulp or 1/4 teaspoon tamarind concentrate paste or juice of 1 medium lime (2 tablespoons)

1/2 teaspoon salt

2 or 3 fresh Thai, serrano or cayenne chilies

1 tablespoon vegetable oil

1/2 teaspoon black or yellow mustard seed

1 tablespoon dried split and hulled black lentils (urad dal) or yellow split peas (chana dal), sorted

1. Place all ingredients except oil, mustard seed and lentils in blender. Cover and blend on medium speed until smooth. Transfer to small bowl; set aside. (Chutney will thicken as it stands; if it becomes too thick, stir in additional water until it reaches desired consistency.)

2. Heat oil and mustard seed in 6-inch skillet over medium-high heat. Once seed begins to pop, cover skillet and wait until popping stops. Add lentils; stir-fry about 30 seconds or until lentils are golden brown. Pour hot oil mixture over chutney; mix well.

3. Tightly cover and store in refrigerator up to 1 week.

1 Tablespoon: Calories 20 (Calories from Fat 20); Fat 2g (Saturated 1g); Cholesterol 0mg; Sodium 50mg; Carbohydrate 1g (Dietary Fiber 0g); Protein 0g **% Daily Value:** Vitamin A 0%; Vitamin C 0%; Calcium 0%; Iron 0% **Diet Exchanges:** 1/2 Fat

When you think of chutneys, the word dry never comes to mind—but this chutney will change all that. This potent condiment of roasted garlic, chilies and peanuts is a favorite in the western state of Maharashtra, home of Mumbai (Bombay).

Roasted-Garlic Chutney

Lasoon Thuviyal

ABOUT 1 2/3 CUPS CHUTNEY (26 SERVINGS)

1/4 cup raw blanched peanuts	2 tablespoons sesame seed
1 tablespoon cumin seed	12 medium cloves garlic, thinly sliced
5 or 6 dried red Thai, serrano or cayenne chilies	1 teaspoon salt

1. Heat 6-inch skillet over medium-high heat. Add peanuts, cumin seed and chilies. Roast 2 to 3 minutes, stirring constantly, until peanuts are brown, cumin seed crackles, chilies turn one shade darker and mixture has a nutty, sweet aroma. Transfer to a bowl; set aside.

2. Add sesame seed to same skillet. Roast 30 to 60 seconds, stirring constantly, until light golden brown. Add to peanut mixture.

3. Add garlic slices to same skillet. Roast 4 to 6 minutes, stirring constantly, until brown and dry. Add to peanut mixture. Let mixture stand 10 to 15 minutes or until cool.

4. Place about **1/3** of peanut mixture in spice grinder. Grind until finely ground, and transfer to a bowl. Repeat with remaining mixture. Stir in salt.

5. Tightly cover and store in refrigerator up to 3 days.

1 Tablespoon: Calories 15 (Calories from Fat 10); Fat 1g (Saturated 0g); Cholesterol 0mg; Sodium 90mg; Carbohydrate 1g (Dietary Fiber 0g); Protein 1g **% Daily Value:** Vitamin A 0%; Vitamin C 2%; Calcium 0%; Iron 2% **Diet Exchanges:** 1 Serving is free

Roasted-Garlic Chutney

Raghavan Ki Baaten

☼ Use this chutney as a spicy rub for any meat, fish or poultry prior to grilling or roasting. Or mix it with cream cheese for a great sandwich spread or dip.

☼ Tempted as you may be to roast all the ingredients at the same time, following the suggested roasting order ensures recipe success. Some of the spices have a tendency to burn faster when they are mixed with the slower-roasting garlic slices.

In this recipe, dates, brought to India from Central Asia by the Moghul rulers, are combined with India's native "date," the tamarind. This sinfully sweet-and-sour chutney is a popular accompaniment to many an appetizer and is often served with Pastry Shells with Spiced Potatoes (page 69).

Sweet-and-Sour Tamarind-Date Chutney

South

ABOUT 2 CUPS CHUTNEY (32 SERVINGS)

1 tablespoon tamarind concentrate paste

2 cups warm water

1 cup chopped dates

1/2 cup chopped jaggery (gur) or packed brown sugar

1/4 teaspoon ground red pepper (cayenne)

1. Mix tamarind paste and warm water in 1-quart saucepan until tamarind is dissolved.

2. Stir in remaining ingredients. Heat to boiling; reduce heat to medium. Simmer uncovered 15 to 20 minutes, stirring occasionally, to blend flavors.

3. Transfer sauce to blender. Cover and blend on medium speed until smooth.

4. Tightly cover and store in refrigerator up to 10 days.

Raghavan Ki Baaten

☀ Tamarind's sweet-sour flavor is essential to this recipe's success, so a substitute is not recommended. If fresh or dried pulp is more readily available than concentrate, soak a cup of pulp in 3 cups of hot water for 30 minutes. Strain the soaking liquid through a fine-mesh colander, squeezing pulp with the back of a spoon to extract as much of its potent flavor as possible. Discard the pulp, and use the strained liquid in place of concentrate mixed with warm water.

☀ Jaggery (*gur*), a raw form of cane sugar, is commonly available in stores that sell Indian food products. Packed brown sugar works well as an alternative.

☀ Do not use cast-iron cookware when making this chutney because the highly acidic tamarind will react with the metal and give the chutney an unpleasant metallic taste.

1 Tablespoon: Calories 30 (Calories from Fat 0); Fat 0g (Saturated 0g); Cholesterol 0mg; Sodium 0mg; Carbohydrate 7g (Dietary Fiber 0g); Protein 0g **% Daily Value:** Vitamin A 0%; Vitamin C 0%; Calcium 0%; Iron 0% **Diet Exchanges:** 1/2 Fruit

When pulikaachal *ends up in the lunch box of a southern Indian child, chances are high that lunch will be consumed in no time. Mothers also often mix this tart, nutty and hot chutney with steamed rice for an ideal picnic snack when the family embarks on a daylong journey.*

Tamarind Chutney with Cashews

Pulikaachal

ABOUT 3 CUPS CHUTNEY (48 SERVINGS)

3 cups warm water

1/2 cup tamarind concentrate paste

1 teaspoon salt

1/2 teaspoon asafetida (hing) or garlic powder

1/4 teaspoon ground turmeric

2 tablespoons vegetable oil

1 teaspoon black or yellow mustard seed

1/4 cup raw cashew pieces

1/4 cup dried yellow split peas (chana dal), sorted

2 tablespoons dried split and hulled black lentils (urad dal), sorted

6 dried red Thai, serrano or cayenne chilies

12 to 15 fresh karhi leaves or 2 dried bay leaves

1 tablespoon sesame seed

1/2 teaspoon fenugreek seed or crushed brown or yellow mustard seed

1. Mix warm water, tamarind paste, salt, asafetida and turmeric in 1-quart saucepan until tamarind is dissolved. Heat to boiling; reduce heat to medium. Simmer uncovered 15 to 20 minutes, stirring occasionally, to blend flavors.

2. While tamarind mixture is cooking, heat 1 tablespoon of the oil and mustard seed in 8-inch skillet over medium-high heat. Once seed begins to pop, cover skillet and wait until popping stops.

3. Add cashews, yellow split peas, lentils and 6 of the chilies to mustard seed; stir-fry 1 to 2 minutes or until cashews, peas and lentils are golden brown. Stir cashew mixture and karhi leaves into tamarind mixture.

4. Heat remaining 1 tablespoon oil in same skillet over medium heat. Add remaining 2 chilies, the sesame seed and fenugreek seed; stir-fry 30 to 60 seconds or until sesame seed is golden brown. Place mixture in spice grinder or mortar. Grind or crush with pestle until mixture looks like fine bread crumbs.

5. Stir ground mixture into tamarind mixture. Continue simmering tamarind mixture uncovered 10 to 15 minutes, stirring occasionally, to blend flavors.

6. Cool chutney 20 to 30 minutes. Tightly cover and store in refrigerator up to 10 days (If using bay leaves, discard before refrigerating).

Raghavan Ki Baaten

☀ **Tamarind is a crucial ingredient in this chutney, so there is no substitute. If split and hulled black lentils (urad dal) are not at hand, eliminate from recipe.**

1 Tablespoon: Calories 15 (Calories from Fat 10); Fat 1g (Saturated 0g); Cholesterol 0mg; Sodium 50mg; Carbohydrate 1g (Dietary Fiber 0g); Protein 1g **% Daily Value:** Vitamin A 2%; Vitamin C 0%; Calcium 0%; Iron 0% **Diet Exchanges:** 1 Serving is free

Chapter Nine

Desserts and Beverages

Clockwise from top: Cellophane Noodles with Rose Milk (page 311), Fresh Fruit with Cooling Spices (page 314), Cardamom-Scented Yogurt Cheese (page 310), Steamed Milk with Pistachio Nuts (page 315), Double-Chocolate Ice Cream (page 296)

Granted, rum is not native to India, but given the strong Indian influences in the islands of the West Indies and the Bahamas, it's only natural that this amber liquor is an ideal marriage partner to India's royalty among fruits, the mango.

Mango-Rum Sorbet

Bunfeelee Sherabi Aam

8 SERVINGS

3 cups canned mango pulp (pages 117 to 118)

1/2 cup dark rum

Juice of 1 medium lime (2 tablespoons)

1/4 cup chopped fresh mint leaves, if desired

1. Mix all ingredients in medium bowl. Cover and refrigerate 1 hour.

2. Transfer mixture to 1-quart ice-cream freezer and freeze according to manufacturer's directions.

1 Serving: Calories 70 (Calories from Fat 0); Fat 0g (Saturated 0g); Cholesterol 0mg; Sodium 0mg; Carbohydrate 11g (Dietary Fiber 0g); Protein 0g **% Daily Value:** Vitamin A 24%; Vitamin C 30%; Calcium 0%; Iron 0% **Diet Exchanges:** 1 Fruit

Mango-Rum Sorbet

Raghavan Ki Baaten

☀ This recipe uses canned mango pulp, which contairs some added sugar. If using fresh mango pulp, add 1/4 cup sugar to the sorbet mixture.

☀ For an attractive presentation, scoop out orange or lemon rinds and freeze sorbet in these "bowls."

When you think of Indian desserts, does ice cream ever come to mind? It should because kulfi, a frozen dessert, was already popular in the courts of the Moghuls hundreds of years ago, when few others in the world had learned to create this icy pleasure. Kulfi, made with the reduced milk that is the basis of many Indian desserts, is still enjoyed just as enthusiastically today.

Saffron–Pistachio Ice Cream

8 SERVINGS

4 cups whole milk

1/2 teaspoon saffron threads

1/4 cup fat-free cholesterol-free egg product*

3/4 cup sugar

1 cup whipping (heavy) cream

1 teaspoon vanilla

1/2 teaspoon cardamom seeds (removed from pods), ground

1/2 cup coarsely chopped unsalted pistachio nuts

Pasteurized fat-free cholesterol-free egg product is used in this recipe in place of fresh eggs to avoid any possibility of contamination with salmonella. Salmonella is destroyed by heat during cooking.

1. Heat milk to boiling in heavy 3-quart saucepan over medium-high heat, stirring constantly to prevent scorching; reduce heat to medium. Cook uncovered 40 to 45 minutes, stirring occasionally and scraping side of pan to release collected milk solids, until reduced to 1 1/4 cups.

2. Stir saffron threads into milk. Cover and refrigerate 1 hour.

3. Beat egg product and sugar in large bowl with electric mixer on medium speed, scraping bowl constantly, until smooth.

4. Add whipping cream, vanilla and ground cardamom to egg mixture. Beat 2 to 3 minutes or until slightly thickened. Beat in milk.

5. Transfer mixture and nuts to 1-quart ice-cream freezer and freeze according to manufacturer's directions.

1 Serving: Calories 290 (Calories from Fat 155); Fat 17g (Saturated 9g); Cholesterol 50mg; Sodium 80mg; Carbohydrate 28g (Dietary Fiber 1g); Protein 7g **% Daily Value:** Vitamin A 10%; Vitamin C 0%; Calcium 18%; Iron 4% **Diet Exchanges:** 1 Fruit, 1 Skim Milk, 3 Fat

Saffron-Pistachio Ice Cream

Raghavan Ki Baaten

☼ I like to use an electric ice-cream machine. It makes the process of freezing ice cream so much faster and easier than it used to be with the old-fashioned hand-cranked models. But this rich recipe will always be delicious, no matter what kind of machine you use.

☼ I often serve this ice cream on lettuce leaves. It's a familiar way to serve ice cream in India, so surprise your guests with this new serving twist sometime.

"Chocolate and Indian cooking?" you may ask. But for many of India's chocoholics, the English Cadbury company is synonymous with their delectable addiction. In the heart of Mumbai (Bombay), the oily steam that emanates from rich cocoa beans permeates the sultry oceanic air for a two-mile radius around the large Cadbury chocolate factory. Even the ice-cream boutiques in Mumbai rely on Cadbury for all their chocolate delights!

Double-Chocolate Ice Cream

Chocolate Ki Kulfi

10 SERVINGS

4 ounces unsweetened baking chocolate, coarsely chopped

1 cup half-and-half

1/4 cup fat-free cholesterol-free egg product*

1 cup sugar

2 cups whipping (heavy) cream

1 teaspoon vanilla

1 bar (5 ounces) milk chocolate, coarsely chopped

1/4 cup raw cashew pieces

1/4 cup golden raisins

*Pasteurized fat-free cholesterol-free egg product is used in this recipe in place of fresh eggs to avoid any possibility of contamination with salmonella. Salmonella is destroyed by heat during cooking.

Double-Chocolate Ice Cream is pictured on page 291.

1. Melt unsweetened chocolate in 1-quart saucepan over low heat, stirring frequently. Gradually add half-and-half, beating constantly with wire whisk, until smooth. (When half-and-half is first added to melted chocolate, the mixture will thicken or clump up. Once the mixture warms, it will become smooth.) Remove from heat. Cover and refrigerate 30 to 60 minutes or until completely chilled.

2. Beat egg product and sugar in large bowl with electric mixer on medium speed, scraping bowl constantly, until smooth.

3. Add whipping cream and vanilla. Beat 4 to 6 minutes or until slightly thickened. Stir in chilled chocolate mixture.

4. Transfer mixture to 1-quart ice-cream freezer and freeze according to manufacturer's directions. About halfway through freezing process, add milk chocolate, cashews and raisins.

1 Serving: Calories 430 (Calories from Fat 270); Fat 30g (Saturated 18g); Cholesterol 65mg; Sodium 50mg; Carbohydrate 38g (Dietary Fiber 3g); Protein 5g **% Daily Value:** Vitamin A 14%; Vitamin C 0%; Calcium 10%; Iron 6% **Diet Exchanges:** Not Recommended

Give a southern Indian soft, mushy bananas, day-old dark coffee (both consumed heavily in the South) and an ice-cream machine, come back in 30 minutes and voilà—indulge in a sinfully smooth ice cream.

Banana–Coffee Ice Cream

Kela Aur Coffee Ki Kulfi

10 SERVINGS

1/4 cup fat-free cholesterol-free egg product*

1 cup sugar

2 cups whipping (heavy) cream

1 cup cold strong coffee

2 large overripe bananas, mashed

1 teaspoon vanilla

1/2 cup chopped walnuts, if desired

*Pasteurized fat-free cholesterol-free egg product is used in this recipe in place of fresh eggs to avoid any possibility of contamination with salmonella. Salmonella is destroyed by heat during cooking.

1. Beat egg product and sugar in large bowl with electric mixer on medium speed, scraping bowl constantly, until smooth.

2. Add remaining ingredients. Beat 4 to 6 minutes or until slightly thickened.

3. Transfer mixture to 1-quart ice-cream freezer and freeze according to manufacturer's directions.

Raghavan Ki Baaten

☀ **Choose bananas that are very soft, almost to the point of being overripe. If you have a batch of bananas intended for making ice cream at a later date, freeze them whole, in their peels, for up to a month. When ready to use them, thaw, peel and mash until smooth.**

1 Serving: Calories 250 (Calories from Fat 135); Fat 15g (Saturated 9g); Cholesterol 55mg; Sodium 25mg; Carbohydrate 28g (Dietary Fiber 1g); Protein 2g **% Daily Value:** Vitamin A 12%; Vitamin C 2%; Calcium 4%; Iron 0% **Diet Exchanges:** 1 1/2 Fruit, 1/2 Skim Milk, 2 1/2 Fat

Mango-Pistachio Ice Cream

Aam Pista Kulfi

10 SERVINGS

1/4 cup fat-free cholesterol-free egg product*

1 cup sugar

2 cups whipping (heavy) cream

1 cup half-and-half

2 ripe mangoes (about 6 ounces each) or 1 cup canned mango pulp

1 teaspoon vanilla

1/2 cup coarsely chopped unsalted pistachio nuts

*Pasteurized fat-free cholesterol-free egg product is used in this recipe in place of fresh eggs to avoid any possibility of contamination with salmonella. Salmonella is destroyed by heat during cooking.

1. Peel mangoes; remove flesh from seeds. Place flesh in a blender. Cover and blend on medium speed until smooth (pulp may be fibrous). Measure 1 cup pulp; set aside.

2. Beat egg product and sugar in large bowl with electric mixer on medium speed, scraping bowl constantly, until smooth.

3. Add mango pulp and remaining ingredients except nuts. Beat 4 to 6 minutes or until slightly thickened.

4. Transfer mixture and nuts to 1-quart ice-cream freezer and freeze according to manufacturer's directions.

Raghavan Ki Baaten

☀ A mango is not always easy to cut because of the large, flat seed in the center. I have found an easy way to do it: Wash and dry the mango. Place the mango on a cutting surface with the thinner side facing up. With a sharp knife, cut down one side of the mango as close to the seed as possible. Repeat on the other side of the seed. Now you have two mango halves. On each half, score the flesh into squares without cutting through the skin. Push under the skin so the flesh pops up—like turning the mango half inside out. Cut the flesh from the skin. You can cut more flesh from the seed, but the flesh closest to the seed is fibrous, so you may not want to use it.

1 Serving: Calories 305 (Calories from Fat 190); Fat 21g (Saturated 11g); Cholesterol 60mg; Sodium 85mg; Carbohydrate 27g (Dietary Fiber 1g); Protein 3g **% Daily Value:** Vitamin A 20%; Vitamin C 8%; Calcium 6%; Iron 2% **Diet Exchanges:** Not Recommended

Here is an unusual dessert with only two ingredients: milk and sugar. As the term terrati *("stirred") suggests, whole milk is cooked down until all the water is evaporated, leaving behind thick, brown, hauntingly rich, heavy milk solids. The texture is not velvety smooth but rather, slightly grainy. Terrati Paal is often made during the festival of Diwali, ushering in the New Year for Hindus across the world. It is a celebration of the homecoming of Lord Rama, a reincarnation of Lord Vishnu after being exiled for fourteen years.*

Sweetened Reduced Milk

Terrati Paal

8 SERVINGS

1/2 gallon (8 cups) whole milk

1/2 cup coarsely chopped jaggery (gur) or 1 cup packed brown sugar

1. Heat milk to boiling in 6-quart Dutch oven or stockpot over medium-high heat, stirring constantly to prevent scorching; reduce heat to medium. Cook uncovered 1 1/2 to 2 hours, stirring occasionally and scraping side of pan to release collected milk solids, until water from milk has evaporated and milk solids are golden brown.

2. Stir in jaggery. Cook 1 to 2 minutes or until sugar is dissolved. Cool 15 to 20 minutes. Chill in refrigerator about 8 hours.

3. Serve at room temperature or chilled. Cover and refrigerate any remaining dessert up to 4 days or freeze up to 1 month.

Raghavan Ki Baaten

☀ Savor this dessert in small bites, as it is very rich. To balance its richness, I serve it with fresh fruit.

☀ Since jaggery is so intensely sweet and flavorful, a half cup is enough to sweeten this dessert.

1 Serving: Calories 255 (Calories from Fat 70); Fat 8g (Saturated 5g); Cholesterol 35mg; Sodium 130mg; Carbohydrate 38g (Dietary Fiber 0g); Protein 8g **% Daily Value:** Vitamin A 6%; Vitamin C 2%; Calcium 30%; Iron 4% **Diet Exchanges:** 1 1/2 Fruit, 1 Skim Milk, 1 1/2 Fat

Gulab means "rose" in Hindi, and jamuns *are "rounds." These delectable, rose syrup–soaked rounds are perfumed with cardamom and fittingly complete many an Indian meal.*

"Doughnut" Rounds in Rose Syrup

Gulab Jamuns

12 ROUNDS (6 SERVINGS)

Syrup:
1 1/2 cups water

1 cup sugar

1/2 teaspoon rose essence

Rounds:
1/2 cup nonfat dry milk

2 tablespoons all-purpose flour

1/4 teaspoon cardamom seeds (removed from pods), ground

1/8 teaspoon baking soda

1 tablespoon Clarified Butter (Ghee), melted, (page 40) or unsalted butter, melted

1 to 2 tablespoons plain yogurt (regular or fat-free)

Vegetable oil for deep-frying

MAKE SYRUP:

1. Heat water and sugar to boiling in 1-quart saucepan over medium-high heat; reduce heat to medium.

2. Cook uncovered 5 minutes, stirring occasionally; remove from heat. Stir in rose essence; set aside.

MAKE ROUNDS:

1. Mix nonfat dry milk, flour, ground cardamom and baking soda in medium bowl.

2. Add Clarified Butter. Rub mixture between palms of hands about 1 minute or until mixture is coarse.

3. Add yogurt, 1 teaspoon at a time, mixing by hand or spoon, until mixture starts to come together to form slightly sticky dough. Knead in bowl about 1 minute or until smooth.

4. Shape dough into 6-inch log. Divide into 12 equal pieces. Roll each piece into a ball; set aside.

5. Heat oil (2 to 3 inches deep) in wok or Dutch oven over medium heat until thermometer inserted in oil reads 325°.

6. Carefully place balls in hot oil and fry 1 to 2 minutes, turning occasionally, until golden brown. Remove with slotted spoon; place in serving bowl.

ASSEMBLE DESSERT:

1. Pour syrup over balls. Cover and let stand at room temperature at least 2 hours but no longer than 4 hours to blend flavors.

2. Cover and refrigerate any remaining dessert up to 5 days.

1 Serving: Calories 225 (Calories from Fat 65); Fat 7g (Saturated 2g); Cholesterol 5mg; Sodium 60mg; Carbohydrate 38g (Dietary Fiber 0g); Protein 2g **% Daily Value:** Vitamin A 6%; Vitamin C 0%; Calcium 8%; Iron 0% **Diet Exchanges:** 1 Starch, 1 1/2 Fruit, 1 Fat

"Doughnut" Rounds in Rose Syrup

Raghavan Ki Baaten

☼ A few drops of highly aromatic rose essence bring a smile to my face. Small vials of rose essence or less-strong rose water are available at Indian grocery stores and in some natural-food stores. It may also be called rose extract. Use 1 teaspoon of rose water for 1/2 teaspoon of rose essence. If neither is available, use 1/4 teaspoon vanilla instead (even though there will be no gulab in the jamuns).

Rich, creamy and dense, this pudding is India's response to America's carrot cake (or is it the other way around?). Here again, milk plays a crucial role, as is true of many Indian desserts. This pudding is devoid of eggs, thus keeping it within the boundaries of lacto-vegetarianism, a widely practiced dietary lifestyle among India's Hindus.

Carrot Pudding with Nuts

Gajar Halwah

8 SERVINGS

1/2 gallon (8 cups) whole milk

4 cups shredded carrots (6 medium)

1 teaspoon cardamom seeds (removed from pods), ground

1 can (14 ounces) sweetened condensed milk

2 tablespoons Clarified Butter (Ghee), (page 40) or unsalted butter

1/2 cup raw cashew pieces

1/2 cup whole unsalted pistachio nuts

1/2 cup golden raisins

1. Heat milk and carrots to boiling in heavy 4-quart Dutch oven or stockpot over medium-high heat, stirring occasionally to prevent scorching; reduce heat to medium. Cook uncovered 1 hour 45 minutes, stirring occasionally. Cook uncovered 15 minutes longer, stirring constantly to prevent scorching, until milk is almost evaporated.

2. Stir in ground cardamom and condensed milk. Cook 4 to 5 minutes, stirring constantly, to blend flavors.

3. Heat Clarified Butter in 8-inch skillet over medium heat. Stir in cashews, pistachios and raisins. Cook 2 to 3 minutes, stirring occasionally, until nuts are golden brown and raisins are plump.

4. Stir nut mixture into carrot mixture. Serve pudding warm or chilled. Cover and refrigerate any remaining pudding up to 2 days.

1 Serving: Calories 545 (Calories from Fat 225); Fat 25g (Saturated 12g); Cholesterol 65mg; Sodium 230mg; Carbohydrate 66g (Dietary Fiber 3g); Protein 17g **% Daily Value:** Vitamin A 98%; Vitamin C 8%; Calcium 52%; Iron 8% **Diet Exchanges:** Not Recommended

Carrot Pudding with Nuts

Raghavan Ki Baaten

☀ Unsalted pistachio nuts are commonly available in natural-food stores and in the health-food section of supermarkets. If unavailable, use salted pistachio nuts, but rinse them under cold water and dry on paper towels.

☀ This pudding is delicious when served warm, but during the long, hot summer months, serve it chilled with a scoop of your favorite premium vanilla ice cream for a sinful treat.

A popular wedding dessert in South India, this fairly thin milk pudding is served on banana leaves as the last course of an elaborate food fest. Milk and rice, often considered symbols of fertility and posterity, offer silent blessings to the newly married couple. "May you have eight sons" is a blessing an elder bestows upon the demure bride, while offering her extra helpings. (Nowadays, that blessing may prove impractical for the smaller nuclear families of modern India.)

Rice Pudding with Raisins

6 SERVINGS

1/2 gallon (8 cups) whole milk

1 can (14 ounces) sweetened condensed milk

1/4 cup uncooked basmati or regular long-grain rice

2 tablespoons Clarified Butter (Ghee), (page 40) or unsalted butter

1/4 raw cashew pieces

1/4 cup golden raisins

1/4 teaspoon cardamom seeds (removed from pods), crushed (page 31)

1. Heat whole milk to boiling in heavy Dutch oven over medium-high heat, stirring constantly to prevent scorching; reduce heat to medium. Cook 40 to 45 minutes, stirring occasionally and scraping side of pan to release collected milk solids, until reduced to about 4 cups.

2. Stir in condensed milk and rice. Cook 20 to 25 minutes, stirring occasionally, until rice is tender and milk is slightly thickened.

3. Meanwhile, heat Clarified Butter in 8-inch skillet over medium heat. Add cashews and raisins; stir-fry 2 to 3 minutes or until cashews are golden brown and raisins are plump.

4. Stir cashew mixture and crushed cardamom into rice mixture. Serve pudding warm or chilled. Cover and refrigerate any remaining pudding up to 2 days or freeze up to 1 month.

1 Serving: Calories 620 (Calories from Fat 235); Fat 26g (Saturated 15g); Cholesterol 85mg; Sodium 280mg; Carbohydrate 77g (Dietary Fiber 1g); Protein 20g **% Daily Value:** Vitamin A 18%; Vitamin C 4%; Calcium 65%; Iron 6% **Diet Exchanges:** Not Recommended

In the United States, this delicious dessert might be mistaken for a breakfast dish since hot wheat cereal is the prime ingredient. Whatever time of day it is consumed, the satisfaction of the person eating it will always be heartfelt. It's equally delicious hot or cold, and will keep in the refrigerator for up to 2 days.

Creamy Wheat Pudding with Bananas

Rava Kesar

6 SERVINGS

1 cup 2% milk

1 cup sugar

1/2 cup Clarified Butter (Ghee), (page 40) or unsalted butter

1/4 cup raw whole cashews

1/4 cup golden raisins

1 cup uncooked hot wheat cereal (not instant)

1 large overripe banana, mashed (1 cup)

1/4 teaspoon cardamom seeds (removed from pods), crushed (page 31)

1. Heat milk and sugar to boiling in 1-quart saucepan over medium-high heat, stirring constantly to prevent scorching; reduce heat to low. Keep warm.

2. Meanwhile, heat Clarified Butter in wok or deep 12-inch skillet over medium heat. Add cashews; stir-fry 30 to 60 seconds or until cashews are golden brown. Remove cashews with slotted spoon; drain on paper towels.

3. Add raisins to hot butter; stir-fry 15 to 30 seconds or until raisins plump up. Remove raisins with slotted spoon; add to cashews.

4. Reduce heat to low. Add uncooked hot wheat cereal to remaining hot butter. Toast 8 to 10 minutes, stirring constantly, until golden brown. Add milk-sugar mixture, 1/4 cup at a time, stirring constantly, until smooth.

5. Stir in banana and crushed cardamom. Simmer over low heat 3 to 5 minutes, stirring occasionally, to blend flavors. Serve garnished with roasted cashews and raisins.

Raghavan Ki Baaten

☀ Hot wheat cereal or farina (*sooji* or *rava* in Tamil) is widely available in supermarkets, but make sure you **do not** use the instant kind for this recipe.

☀ Choose bananas that are very soft, almost to the point of being overripe. If you have bananas ready to turn into pudding at a later date, freeze them, in their peels, for up to a month. When ready to use them, thaw, peel and puree in a food processor or mash with a potato masher until smooth.

☀ The flavor from Clarified Butter is crucial to this recipe's richness. This is not a low-fat dessert, but smaller portions still give you the same sinfully sweet pleasure that is so desirable after a meal.

1 Serving: Calories 485 (Calories from Fat 190); Fat 21g (Saturated 12g); Cholesterol 50mg; Sodium 280mg; Carbohydrate 70g Dietary Fiber 2g); Protein 6g **% Daily Value:** Vitamin A 16%; Vitamin C 2%; Calcium 10%; Iron 48% **Diet Exchanges:** Not Recommended

A tradition in many a Tamilian home, this nourishing, nurturing porridge of reduced milk and thin pasta (vermicelli) is accentuated with saffron, nuts and plump golden raisins. This dessert is often served interchangeably with Rice Pudding with Raisins (page 304) for weddings and religious occasions.

Saffron–Flavored Vermicelli

8 SERVINGS

1/2 gallon (8 cups) whole milk

1/4 cup Clarified Butter (Ghee), (page 40) or unsalted butter

1 cup 1-inch pieces uncooked vermicelli

1 cup sugar

1/2 teaspoon cardamom seeds (removed from pods), crushed (page 31)

1/2 teaspoon saffron threads

1/4 cup raw cashew pieces

1/4 cup unsalted pistachio nuts, coarsely chopped

1/4 cup golden raisins

1. Heat milk to boiling in heavy Dutch oven over medium-high heat, stirring constantly to prevent scorching; reduce heat to medium. Cook 40 to 45 minutes, stirring occasionally and scraping side of pan to release collected milk solids, until reduced to about 4 cups.

2. Meanwhile, heat 2 tablespoons of the Clarified Butter in wok or deep 12-inch skillet over medium heat. Add vermicelli. Cook 1 to 3 minutes, stirring constantly, until vermicelli is golden brown. Remove vermicelli with slotted spoon

3. Stir vermicelli, sugar, crushed cardamom and saffron threads into milk. Cook 8 to 10 minutes, stirring occasionally, until mixture is thickened.

4. Heat remaining butter in same wok over medium heat. Add cashews, pistachios and raisins; stir-fry 2 to 3 minutes or until nuts are golden brown and raisins are plump.

5. Stir nut mixture into milk mixture. Serve dessert warm or chilled.

1 Serving: Calories 410 (Calories from Fat 170); Fat 19g (Saturated 10g); Cholesterol 50mg; Sodium 120mg; Carbohydrate 50g (Dietary Fiber 1g); Protein 11g **% Daily Value:** Vitamin A 12%; Vitamin C 2%; Calcium 30%; Iron 6% **Diet Exchanges:** Not Recommended

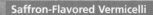

Saffron-Flavored Vermicelli

Raghavan Ki Baaten

☀ Vermicelli, often made with wheat flour, is widely available in Indian grocery stores. If unavailable, use thin spaghetti or capellini (angel hair pasta).

☀ Be extra careful when bringing milk to a boil. To prevent scorching, constant stirring is a must until the milk reaches the boiling point. Once the milk comes to a roaring boil, occasional stirring will suffice.

☀ For a richer flavor, I use 1 cup sweetened condensed milk instead of the sugar.

Originally from the eastern state of West Bengal, this richly sweetened delicacy, truly a labor of love, is rightfully crowned the Queen of India's dessert world—a definite crowd pleaser. You will bask in the accolades of a job well done after creating this masterpiece. The milk is curdled and the resultant cheese is kneaded and broken into rounds, soaked in rose-scented sugar syrup and drenched in a reduced cream sauce flavored with saffron and unsalted pistachio nuts.

Cheese Dumplings in Cream Sauce

Rasmalai

16 DUMPLINGS (16 SERVINGS)

Cheese Dumplings:
1/2 gallon (8 cups) whole milk

1/4 cup white vinegar

2 tablespoons nonfat dry milk

4 cups water

1/2 cup sugar

1/2 teaspoon rose essence or 1 teaspoon rose water

Cream Sauce:
3 cups half-and-half

1/3 cup sugar

1/2 teaspoon saffron threads

1/2 cup unsalted pistachio nuts, coarsely chopped

MAKE CHEESE DUMPLINGS:

1. Heat whole milk to boiling in heavy 6-quart Dutch oven or stockpot over medium-high heat, stirring constantly to prevent scorching.

2. Stir in vinegar; remove from heat. The milk will immediately separate into curds (solids) and whey (liquid).

3. Pour curds and whey mixture into colander placed in sink. Rinse with water 3 or 4 times to wash away the vinegar flavor. Drain in colander 10 to 15 minutes.

4. Combine cheese curds and nonfat dry milk in medium bowl. Knead in bowl 3 to 5 minutes or until a wet, soft dough forms. Divide into 16 equal pieces. Shape each piece tightly into a ball; place in single layer in wide-bottomed bowl or pan.

5. Heat water, 1/2 cup sugar and rose essence to boiling in 3-quart saucepan over medium-high heat; reduce heat. Simmer 3 to 5 minutes to blend flavors.

6. Pour syrup over cheese dumplings. Let stand 15 to 20 minutes or until dumplings fluff up and absorb some of the syrup. Remove dumplings with slotted spoon; place in single layer in separate shallow bowl. Discard remaining syrup.

MAKE CREAM SAUCE:

1. Heat half-and-half to boiling in heavy 2-quart saucepan over medium heat, stirring constantly to prevent scorching; reduce heat. Simmer uncovered 20 to 25 minutes, stirring occasionally and scraping side of pan to release collected milk solids, until reduced to 1 1/2 cups and slightly thickened.

2. Stir in remaining ingredients. Pour cream sauce over dumplings. Refrigerate at least 2 hours to blend flavors.

1 Serving: Calories 205 (Calories from Fat 100); Fat 11g (Saturated 6g); Cholesterol 35mg; Sodium 80mg; Carbohydrate 20g (Dietary Fiber 0g); Protein 6g **% Daily Value:** Vitamin A 8%; Vitamin C 0%; Calcium 20%; Iron 2% **Diet Exchanges:** 1/2 Fruit, 1 Skim Milk, 2 Fat

Cheese Dumplings in Cream Sauce

Raghavan Ki Baaten

☀ Use whole milk to make the cheese, as reduced-fat milk will not yield the same results.

☀ If rose essence is unavailable, substitute 1 teaspoon rose water or omit from recipe.

☀ Any leftovers (if you have any!) can be covered and refrigerated up to 1 week. Or freeze *rasmalai* up to 1 month. Make sure to thaw in the refrigerator for about 8 hours before serving.

A delicacy from the northwestern state of Gujarat, this sinfully rich cheese is often served with Puffy Whole Wheat Breads (page 248) at weddings, religious occasions and special family gatherings. The cooking skills of a new Gujarati bride are often judged by how good her shrikhand is. The dessert has the consistency of pudding and is very sweet.

Cardamom-Scented Yogurt Cheese

shrikhand

8 SERVINGS

2 cups regular or fat-free plain yogurt (1 pound),

1/4 teaspoon saffron threads

1 tablespoon hot milk

1 cup powdered sugar

1/4 cup chopped charoli nuts or 1/4 cup chopped unsalted pistachios plus 1/4 teaspoon freshly grated nutmeg

1/4 teaspoon cardamom seeds (removed from pods), ground

Cardamom-Scented Yogurt Cheese is pictured on page 291.

1. Line medium colander with cheesecloth or muslin. Place colander in large bowl. Place yogurt in lined colander; drain 1 hour.

2. Loosely cover colander and bowl and refrigerate 6 to 8 hours or until texture of yogurt cheese is smooth and silky.

3. Transfer yogurt cheese from cheesecloth to medium bowl; set aside. Discard whey (liquid) in bowl.

4. Stir saffron threads into hot milk. Let stand 1 to 2 minutes or until milk is a rich, golden yellow-orange color. Stir milk mixture and remaining ingredients into yogurt cheese.

5. Cover and refrigerate about 2 hours or until chilled. Cover and refrigerate any remaining dessert up to 1 week or freeze up to 1 month. Thaw in refrigerator about 8 hours.

Raghavan Ki Baaten

☀ Charoli is a small nut primarily used in Gujarati desserts. They are available in Indian grocery stores. Charoli nuts are dark brown with a shape similar to the French brown lentil. The nuts have a nutmeg-like flavor with a slight spiciness reminiscent of cloves. If unavailable, use shelled unsalted pistachio nuts along with 1/4 teaspoon grated nutmeg.

☀ Do not use yogurt that contains gelatin. Gelatin prevents the liquid from draining from the yogurt.

☀ I serve this rich cheese dessert with cut-up seasonal fresh fruits or berries for a simple summer dessert.

1 Serving: Calories 125 (Calories from Fat 25); Fat 3g (Saturated 1g); Cholesterol 5mg; Sodium 45mg; Carbohydrate 20g (Dietary Fiber 0g); Protein 4g **% Daily Value:** Vitamin A 0%; Vitamin C 0%; Calcium 12%; Iron 2% **Diet Exchanges:** 1/2 Fruit, 1 Milk

When you visit Mumbai (Bombay), be sure to see the Gateway of India, a majestic monument from India's colonial days, and then rush to the nearest restaurant that serves ice-cold falooda in tall frosted glasses. This dessert is oftentimes presented as a layered composition of yellow-colored cellophane noodles, sweetened rose syrup, chilled milk and a scoop of premium vanilla ice cream topped with soaked basil seeds. For a few extra rupees, you can request a side of sweetened cellophane noodles covered with crushed ice.

Cellophane Noodles with Rose Milk

Falooda

4 SERVINGS

1 package (1 3/4 ounces) yellow cellophane noodles (bean threads)

2 1/2 cups hot water

1 tablespoon basil seed (takmaria/sabja) or 1/4 cup chopped mint leaves

1/2 cup sweetened rose syrup

3 cups milk

1 pint (2 cups) vanilla ice cream

Cellophane Noodles with Rose Milk is pictured on page 291.

1. Place noodles in medium bowl. Pour 2 cups of the hot water over noodles. Soak 2 to 3 minutes or until softened; drain. Place noodles in ice-cold water 3 to 5 minutes; set aside.

2. Soak basil seed in remaining 1/2 cup hot water 4 minutes. Set aside.

3. To assemble dessert, drain noodles and divide among 4 tall glasses as bottom layer. Add 2 tablespoons rose syrup to each glass followed by 3/4 cup milk; mix well. Scoop 1/2 cup ice cream into each glass. Sprinkle with basil seed.

Raghavan Ki Baaten

☼ **Basil seed** (*takmaria/sabja*) comes from the holy basil plant, commonly known in Hindu households as *tulsi*. This plant is a must on the patios and verandas of every Hindu home, because of its affiliation with many a Hindu god. The tiny black seeds, when soaked in water, are mellow in flavor. They swell up and look similar to beluga caviar, with a comparable mouth-feel. Indian stores stock up on this seed, but if unavailable, eliminate from recipe. Use 1 tablespoon chopped fresh mint leaves per serving of *falooda* as a colorful alternative.

☼ **Yellow-colored cellophane noodles** are available in Indian grocery stores. If unavailable, substitute regular translucent cellophane noodles, available at supermarkets and Asian food stores.

☼ **Rose syrup** is available in Indian, Middle Eastern and specialty grocery stores. If unavailable, use any flavored syrup of your choice readily found in coffeehouses to flavor coffee.

1 Serving: Calories 325 (Calories from Fat 100); Fat 11g (Saturated 7g); Cholesterol 40mg; Sodium 140mg; Carbohydrate 48g (Dietary Fiber 1g); Protein 9g **% Daily Value:** Vitamin A 16%; Vitamin C 2%; Calcium 32%; Iron 4% **Diet Exchanges:** Not recommended

A Bombayite's version of bananas Foster, this recipe stirs in highly aromatic, menthol-like cardamom for that quintessential flavor associated with many an Indian dessert.

Red Bananas with Cardamom

4 SERVINGS

4 small red bananas

1/4 cup unsalted butter

1/4 cup jaggery, chopped, or 1/2 cup packed brown sugar

Juice of 1 medium lime (2 tablespoons)

1/2 teaspoon cardamom seeds (removed from pods), ground

1 quart vanilla ice cream

1. Peel bananas and cut lengthwise in half; set aside.

2. Melt butter in 12-inch skillet over medium heat. Cook brown sugar in butter, stirring gently, until sugar is dissolved.

3. Stir in bananas, lime juice and ground cardamom; reduce heat. Cover and simmer 3 to 5 minutes, stirring occasionally, until bananas are tender.

4. Scoop ice cream into 4 bowls. Spoon bananas with sauce over ice cream.

1 Serving: Calories 585 (Calories from Fat 245); Fat 27g (Saturated 16g); Cholesterol 90mg; Sodium 120mg; Carbohydrate 82g (Dietary Fiber 2g); Protein 6g **% Daily Value:** Vitamin A 20%; Vitamin C 10%; Calcium 20%; Iron 4% **Diet Exchanges:** Not Recommended

Red Bananas with Cardamom

Raghavan Ki Baaten

☀ Red bananas are available in some large supermarkets. Choose ripe firm ones that are unblemished. If unavailable, use unripened yellow bananas with green skins. Cut each banana crosswise in half, then lengthwise in half.

Step off any bus or train in Mumbai (Bombay), and chances are you'll run into a vendor displaying mango, papaya, watermelon and pineapple slices on blocks of ice. During the hot days of summer, this is a welcoming sight, offering much needed relief from the oppressive heat and humidity. Sprinkled over the fruit is a combination of spices that brings together tart (mango powder), hot (black pepper), salty (black salt) and nutty (roasted ground cumin) flavors. It is known to have a cooling effect on the body's internal temperature.

Fresh Fruit with Cooling Spices

8 SERVINGS

2 cups seeded diced watermelon

1 medium papaya, peeled, seeded and diced (1 1/2 cups)

1/2 medium pineapple (1 1/2 pounds), peeled and cubed (1 1/2 cups)

1 medium ripe mango, peeled, pitted and diced (page 298) (1 cup)

2 medium apricots, pitted and diced (1 cup)

1 tablespoon mango powder (amchur) or juice of 1 medium lime (2 tablespoons)

1 teaspoon roasted cumin seed (page 31), ground

1/2 teaspoon black peppercorns, crushed

1/2 teaspoon black salt or regular salt

1. Mix all ingredients in large bowl. Refrigerate 1 to 2 hours or until chilled.

2. Cover and refrigerate any remaining fruit up to 3 days. Do not freeze.

Fresh Fruit with Cooling Spices is pictured on page 291.

☀ Use any combination of fruit desired, choosing ones that are seasonal and ripe. If using fruits that turn brown after cutting, such as apples and bananas, make sure you combine them with pineapples or lemon or lime juice. The acidity in the fruits' juices will help to prevent oxidation (browning).

1 Serving: Calories 70 (Calories from Fat 10); Fat 1g (Saturated 0g); Cholesterol 0mg; Sodium 5mg; Carbohydrate 10g (Dietary Fiber 2g); Protein 1g **% Daily Value:** Vitamin A 14%; Vitamin C 68%; Calcium 2%; Iron 2% **Diet Exchanges:** 1 Fruit

On many street corners in Mumbai (Bombay), you'll see a dairy vendor balancing a gargantuan wok filled with whole milk on a kerosene burner, gently stirring to release the nutty aroma that attracts passers-by. Ask for a glass, and the vendor takes two brass containers, like vases, filling one with steamed milk and topping it with sugar, pistachio nuts, cardamom seeds and (for a few extra rupees) saffron. He pours it into the other container, then repeats pouring back and forth without spilling a drop, to create a frothy beverage sans blender.

Steamed Milk with Pistachio Nuts

Masaala Doodh

4 SERVINGS

6 cups whole milk

1/4 cup coarsely chopped unsalted pistachio nuts

3 tablespoons sugar

1/2 teaspoon saffron threads

1/4 teaspoon cardamom seeds (removed from pods), crushed (page 31)

Steamed Milk with Pistachio Nuts is pictured on page 291.

1. Heat milk to boiling in heavy 3-quart saucepan over medium-high heat, stirring constantly to prevent scorching; reduce heat to medium. Cook uncovered 20 to 25 minutes, stirring occasionally and scraping side of pan to release collected milk solids, until reduced to about 4 cups.

2. Stir in remaining ingredients. Pour milk into 4 coffee mugs. Serve warm.

Raghavan Ki Baaten

☼ In the United States, green cardamom pods are available in supermarkets with their skin sun-bleached to white. Use seed from either green or white cardamom pods for this recipe. To get at the seed, gently pry open a pod. Remove the seed and discard the skin and small vein that holds them together.

☼ For a richer, creamier flavor, try 1/4 cup sweetened condensed milk instead of the sugar. For a more wicked indulgence, top off each serving with a dollop of freshly whipped cream.

1 Serving: Calories 310 (Calories from Fat 145); Fat 16g (Saturated 8g); Cholesterol 50mg; Sodium 180mg; Carbohydrate 29g (Dietary Fiber 1g); Protein 14g **% Daily Value:** Vitamin A 10%; Vitamin C 2%; Calcium 44%; Iron 4% **Diet Exchanges:** 2 Skim Milk, 3 Fat

There is no escaping this ubiquitous beverage that forms the basis of every social gathering in India. Chai is Hindi for "tea," so adding the word tea after chai, as is so often seen in coffee- and tea houses in this country, is redundant. Chai is always brewed in milk, giving it that rich creamy flavor. Oftentimes, chai is sweetened with cane sugar or jaggery, a raw form of sugar, making it an ideal marriage partner for many an Indian dessert.

Darjeeling Tea with Cardamom

4 SERVINGS

2 cups water

1/4 cup loose Darjeeling tea leaves or 5 tea bags black tea

2 cups whole or 2% milk

1/8 teaspoon ground cardamom

2 whole cloves, crushed

2 to 4 black pepper- corns, crushed

Pinch of ground cinnamon

1/4 cup sweetened condensed milk or 4 teaspoons sugar

1. Heat water to a rapid boil in 2-quart saucepan over medium-high heat; reduce heat to low. Add tea leaves; simmer 2 to 4 minutes to blend flavors. (If using tea bags, remove and discard.)

2. Stir in remaining ingredients except sweetened condensed milk. Heat to boiling, taking care not to let milk boil over.

3. Stir in condensed milk. Strain tea into cups.

1 Serving: Calories 130 (Calories from Fat 35); Fat 4g (Saturated 3g); Cholesterol 15mg; Sodium 90mg; Carbohydrate 17g (Dietary Fiber 0g); Protein 6g **% Daily Value:** Vitamin A 8%; Vitamin C 2%; Calcium 20%; Iron 0% **Diet Exchanges:** 1 Skim Milk, 1 Fat

Darjeeling Tea with Cardamom

Raghavan Ki Baaten

☀ *Chai* is never served during a meal, but this spicy brewed beverage is
served afterward to aid digestion. When served with spicy savories,
such as appetizers, *chai* offers soothing relief.

In Punjab, the wheat-growing capital of India, the burly, turbaned men who till the rich soil take breaks from the intense heat to pour large tumblers of a cooled yogurt beverage from earthen pots. Sometimes sweetened with sugar (meetha), oftentimes laced with salt (namkeen), lassi provides soothing relief for any ailment.

Sweetened Yogurt with Sparkling Water

meetha Lassi

4 SERVINGS

2 cups ice cubes

2 cups plain yogurt (regular or fat-free)

1 cup unflavored sparkling water

1/4 cup sugar

1/4 teaspoon rose essence or 1/2 teaspoon rose water

1. Place all ingredients in blender. Cover and blend on medium speed until well blended and slightly frothy.

2. Pour into glasses; serve immediately.

Raghavan Ki Baaten

☀ **If you would like to try salted *lassi*, replace the sugar with 1/2 teaspoon salt and eliminate the rose essence.**

1 Serving: Calories 125 (Calories from Fat 20); Fat 2g (Saturated 1g); Cholesterol 5mg; Sodium 85mg; Carbohydrate 21g (Dietary Fiber 0g); Protein 6g **% Daily Value:** Vitamin A 2%; Vitamin C 2%; Calcium 22%; Iron 0% **Diet Exchanges:** 1/2 Fruit, 1 Skim Milk

True buttermilk is the residual whey (liquid) left after churning fresh butter. Watery-thin and sweet, it is very different from the commercial buttermilk widely available in the United States. Stories of the Hindu god Lord Krishna, raised by cowherds, abound with accounts of his passion for freshly churned butter during his playful youth. Innumerable South Indians consider buttermilk a powerful digestive, and rarely does a meal go by without a tall glass, plain or spiced, being consumed.

Spiced Buttermilk

4 SERVINGS

3 cups buttermilk

1 cup cold water

1 teaspoon vegetable oil

1 teaspoon black or yellow mustard seed

2 tablespoons julienne strips gingerroot

1/2 teaspoon salt

1/2 teaspoon coarsely cracked black peppercorns

10 to 12 fresh karhi leaves

1. Beat buttermilk and cold water in medium bowl, using wire whisk, until well blended; set aside.

2. Heat oil and mustard seed in 6-inch skillet over medium-high heat. Once seed begins to pop, cover skillet and wait until popping stops. Stir hot oil mixture and remaining ingredients into buttermilk-water blend.

3. Serve at room temperature or chilled. Cover and refrigerate any remaining Spiced Buttermilk up to 1 week.

Raghavan Ki Baat

☼ **Fresh karhi leaves impart a perfumed sweetness to this** unavailable, use 1 tablespoon chopped fresh cilantro

Indian Menus

The following menus, suggested for various occasions, are mere starting points that are designed to provide you a combination of flavors, textures and color. Eat them as individual courses to prolong your dining experience, or enjoy them buffet style. Pass them among your friends and family in platters and bowls, or relish them on one large communal platter, as is done in some Indian communities.

"Getting Started"

Creamy Grilled Chicken on Skewers *(Malai Kabobs)*, page 67 with
Mint-Cilantro Chutney *(Pudhina Chutney)*, page 284
Yellow Split Peas with Caramelized Onions *(Lucknowi Chana Dal)*, page 193
Steamed Basmati Rice *(Saada Chaawal)*, pages 202 and 203
Cauliflower with Peppers *(Phool Gobhi Chi Bhaaji)*, page 124
Rice Pudding with Raisins *(Pal Paysam)*, page 304

Northern Regional

Garlic-Potato Croquettes *(Aloo Ki Tikkis)*, page 58, with Mint-Cilantro Chutney *(Pudhina Chutney)*, page 284
Marinated Grilled Chicken *(Tandoori Murghi)*, page 108
Stuffed Bell Peppers *(Bharee Simla Mirch)*, page 120
Creamed Black Lentils *(Makhani Dal)*, page 169
Basmati Rice with Green Peas *(Mutter Pulao)*, page 204
Tandoori Breads *(Naan)*, page 252
Carrot Pudding with Nuts *(Gajar Halwah)*, page 302

Southern Regional

Lime-Flavored Potato Croquettes *(Bondas)*, page 50, with Ridged-Squash Chutney *(Peerkangai Thuviyal)*, page 282
Fish Poached with Coconut Milk *(Meen Curry)*, page 81
Eggplant with Shallots *(Katarikai Goshtu)*, page 135
Squash-Coconut Stew *(Shorakai Kootu)*, page 196
Rice Noodles with Pepper *(Podi Sevai)*, page 229
Wheat Crepes *(Rava Dosas)*, page 259, with Raw Mango Pickle *(Maangai Urughai)*, page 274
Banana-Coffee Ice Cream *(Kéla Aur Coffee Ki Kulfi)*, page 297

Western Regional

Tapioca Pearl Fritters *(Sabudana Vadaas)*, page 55, with Roasted-Garlic Chutney *(Lasoon Chutney)*, page 286
Pork in Cashew-Pepper Curry *(Sorpotel)*, page 92
Fresh Okra with Peanuts *(Bhindi Nu Shaak)*, page 140
Lima Beans with Raisins and Onions *(Vaal Nu Dal)*, page 178
Spiced Basmati Rice with Peanuts *(Masaala Bhat)*, page 209
Spiced Puffed Breads *(Masaala Pooris)*, page 250
Fresh Fruit with Cooling Spices *(Namkeen Phul)*, page 314

Eastern Regional

Spiced Lentil Wafers
(Masaala Pappadums), page 72

Fish Steamed with Mustard-Fennel Paste
(Sorshe Bata Diyea Maach), page 79

Sweet-and-Sour Eggplant
(Mithu-Tauk Begun), page 131

Red Lentils with Ginger
(Masoor Dal), page 177

Steamed Basmati Rice
(Saada Chaawal), pages 202 and 203

Whole Wheat Unleavened Breads
(Rotts), page 236

Cheese Dumplings in Cream Sauce
(Rasmalai), page 308

Multi-Regional Vegetarian

Griddle Rice Croquettes
(Chaawal Nu Theplas), page 59,
with **Sweet-and-Hot Mango Pickle**
(Maangai Pachadi), page 273

Banana Fritters *(Vazhaipazham Pakodas)*, page
56, with **Red Onion Chutney** *(Vengayam
Thuviyal)*, page 277

Gujarati-Style Mixed-Vegetable Curry
(Undhiyu), page 186

Squash Croquettes in Cream Sauce
(Malai Koftas), page 152

New Potatoes with Red Onions
(Aloo Do Piaza), page 144

Coconut Rice Pilaf
(Thenga Shaadum), page 213

Griddle Breads with Clarified Butter
(Paranthas), page 238

Red Bananas with Cardamom
(Elaichi Kéla), page 312

Multi-Regional Nonvegetarian

Grilled Tandoori-Style Lamb Kabobs
(Mutton Kabobs), page 66,
with **Mint-Cilantro Chutney**
(Pudhina Chutney), page 284

Pigeon Pea Fritters *(Aamai Vadaas)*,
page 48, with **Yogurt with
Stewed Tomatoes** *(Pachadi)*, page 270

Fish Steamed in Greens
(Patra Ni Muchee), page 82

Spiced Eggplant with Peanuts
(Maratha Vanghee), page 134

Sweet Potato Curry
(Shakarai Urulikazhangu Curry), page 150

Coconut Rice Noodles
(Thénga Sevai), page 228

Sorghum Griddle Bread
(Bhaakra), page 243, with **Yogurt with Apples**
(Sev Raita), page 263

Mango-Pistachio Ice Cream *(Aam Pista Kulfi)*,
page 298

Indian Brunch

Spiced Homemade Cheese
(Masaala Paneer), page 74

Chopped Tomato Salad
(Tamatar Nu Salade), page 266

Persian-Influenced Scrambled Eggs *(Akuri)*,
page 156

Spicy Potato Fry
(Batata Nu Shaak), page 142

Greens with Garlic and Raisins
(Saag), page 136

**Warm Garbanzo Bean Salad with Roasted
Chilies** *(Shundal)*, page 184

Spiced Creamy Wheat with Cashews
(Uppamma), page 230

Puffy Whole Wheat Breads
(Pooris), page 248

Cardamom-Scented Yogurt Cheese
(Shrikhand), page 310

Indian High Tea

Stuffed Vegetable Cutlets
(Angrezi Kabobs), page 61

Grilled Ground Lamb on Skewers
(Seekh Kabobs), page 64, with **Mint-Cilantro Chutney** *(Pudhina Chutney)*, page 284

Pastry Shells with Spiced Potatoes
(Punjabi Samosas), page 69, with
Sweet-and-Sour Tamarind-Date Chutney
(Sonth), page 288

Fresh-Roasted Spiced Peanuts
(Mungphalli Masaala), page 71

Darjeeling Tea with Cardamom
(Chai), page 316

Indian Picnic

Grilled Rock Cornish Hens
(Kozhi), page 111

Gujarati Cabbage Slaw
(Bund Gobhi Nu Shaak), page 122

Raw Beet Salad
(Kaccha Chukandar Salade), page 119

Haryana-Style Garbanzo Beans
(Pindi Channa), page 182

Lime-Flavored Rice Noodles with Cashews
(Limboo Sevai), page 226

Potato-Filled Whole Wheat Breads
(Aloo Paranthas), page 245

Grated Mango Pickle
(Maangai Tokku), page 276

"Doughnut" Rounds in Rose Syrup
(Gulab Jamuns), page 300

New Year's Nonvegetarian

Vegetable Fritters *(Subzi Pakoras)*,
page 49, with **Yogurt with Fresh Mint**
(Pudhina Raita), page 271

Pan-Seared Coconut Shrimp
(Keralite Jhinga), page 84

**Chicken Breast Stuffed with Cheese
and Raisins** *(Sultani Murghi)*, page 106

Homemade Cheese with Peas
(Mutter Paneer), page 160

Lentil Dumplings in Tamarind Sauce
(Paruppu Undhai Sambhar), page 190

Basmati Rice with Saffron
(Zaffrani Pulao), page 210

Griddle Breads with Daikon
(Mooli Paranthas), page 242

Double-Chocolate Ice Cream
(Chocolate Ki Kulfi), page 296

New Year's Vegetarian

"Doughnut" Fritters
(Medu Vadaas), page 52,
with **Coconut Chutney**
(Thénga Chutney), page 285

Pigeon Pea Stew *(Sambhar)*, page 188

Layered Rice-Potato Pilaf
(Aloo Biryani), page 219

Grilled Eggplant Pâté
(Baingan Bhurta), page 132

Homemade Cheese with Spinach
(Saag Paneer), page 159

Stuffed Rice-Lentil Crepes
(Masaala Dosai), page 260

Saffron-Pistachio Ice Cream
(Kulfi), page 294

Helpful Nutrition
and Cooking Information

Nutrition Guidelines

We provide nutrition information for each recipe
that includes calories, fat, cholesterol, sodium,
carbohydrate, fiber and protein. Individual food
choices can be based on this information.
Recommended intake for a daily diet of 2,000
calories as set by the Food and Drug
Administration.

Total Fat	Less than 65g
Saturated Fat	Less than 20g
Cholesterol	Less than 300mg
Sodium	Less than 2,400mg
Total Carbohydrate	300g
Dietary Fiber	25g

Criteria Used for Calculating Nutrition Information

☼ The first ingredient was used wherever a choice is given (such as 1/3 cup sour cream or
plain yogurt).

☼ The first ingredient amount was used wherever a range is given (such as 3- to 3-1/2–pound
cut-up broiler-fryer chicken).

☼ The first serving number was used wherever a range is given (such as 4 to 6 servings).

☼ "If desired" ingredients were not included (such as sprinkle with brown sugar, if desired).

☼ Only the amount of a marinade or frying oil that is estimated to be absorbed by the
food during preparation or cooking was calculated.

Ingredients Used in Recipe Testing and Nutrition Calculations

☼ Large eggs and 2% milk were used for testing, unless otherwise indicated.

☼ Fat-free, low-fat or low-sodium products were not used, unless otherwise indicated.

☼ Nonstick cooking spray was used to grease pans, unless otherwise indicated.

Equipment Used in Recipe Testing

We use equipment for testing that the majority of consumers use in their homes. If a specific
piece of equipment (such as a wire whisk) is necessary for recipe success, it is listed in the recipe.

☼ Cookware and bakeware without nonstick coatings were used, unless otherwise indicated.

☼ No dark-colored, black or insulated bakeware was used.

☼ When a pan is specified in a recipe, a metal pan was used; a baking dish or pie plate means
ovenproof glass was used.

☼ An electric hand mixer was used for mixing only when mixer speeds are specified in the
recipe directions. When a mixer speed is not given, a spoon or fork was used.

Metric Conversion Guide

Volume

U.S. Units	Canadian Metric	Australian Metric
1/4 teaspoon	1 mL	1 ml
1/2 teaspoon	2 mL	2 ml
1 teaspoon	5 mL	5 ml
1 tablespoon	15 mL	20 ml
1/4 cup	50 mL	60 ml
1/3 cup	75 mL	80 ml
1/2 cup	125 mL	125 ml
2/3 cup	150 mL	170 ml
3/4 cup	175 mL	190 ml
1 cup	250 mL	250 ml
1 quart	1 liter	1 liter
1 1/2 quarts	1.5 liters	1.5 liters
2 quarts	2 liters	2 liters
2 1/2 quarts	2.5 liters	2.5 liters
3 quarts	3 liters	3 liters
4 quarts	4 liters	4 liters

Weight

U.S. Units	Canadian Metric	Australian Metric
1 ounce	30 grams	30 grams
2 ounces	55 grams	60 grams
3 ounces	85 grams	90 grams
4 ounces (1/4 pound)	115 grams	125 grams
8 ounces (1/2 pound)	225 grams	225 grams
16 ounces (1 pound)	455 grams	500 grams
1 pound	455 grams	1/2 kilogram

Measurements

Inches	Centimeters
1	2.5
2	5.0
3	7.5
4	10.0
5	12.5
6	15.0
7	17.5
8	20.5
9	23.0
10	25.5
11	28.0
12	30.5
13	33.0

Temperatures

Fahrenheit	Celsius
32°	0°
212°	100°
250°	120°
275°	140°
300°	150°
325°	160°
350°	180°
375°	190°
400°	200°
425°	220°
450°	230°
475°	240°
500°	260°

Note: The recipes in this cookbook have not been developed or tested using metric measures. When converting recipes to metric, some variations in quality may be noted.

Index

Note: *Italicized* page references indicate photographs.